*Death and Dying
in the Working Class,
1865–1920*

THE WORKING CLASS IN AMERICAN HISTORY

Editorial Advisors
James R. Barrett, Julie Greene, William P. Jones, Alice Kessler-Harris, and Nelson Lichtenstein

A list of books in the series appears at the end of this book.

Death and Dying in the Working Class, 1865–1920

MICHAEL K. ROSENOW

University of Illinois Press
URBANA, CHICAGO, AND SPRINGFIELD

© 2015 by the Board of Trustees
of the University of Illinois
All rights reserved
Manufactured in the United States of America
1 2 3 4 5 C P 5 4 3 2 1
♾ This book is printed on acid-free paper.

ISBN 978-0-252-03913-3 (hardcover)
ISBN 978-0-252-08071-5 (pbk.)
ISBN 978-0-252-09711-9 (e-book)
Library of Congress Control Number: 2015932947

For Trisha, Bryant, and Brady

Contents

List of Illustrations   ix

Acknowledgments   xi

Introduction: In Search of John Henry's Body   1

1. The Marks of Capital: The Accident Crisis and Cultures of Industrialization, 1865–1919   7

2. The Power of the Dead's Place: Chicago's Cemeteries, Social Conflict, and Cultural Construction, 1873–1913   42

3. Every New Grave Brought a Thousand Members: The Politics of Death in Illinois Coal Communities, 1883–1910   68

4. As Close to Hell as They Hoped to Get: Steel, Death, and Community in Western Pennsylvania, 1892–1919   98

Conclusion: (Un)Freedom of the Grave   141

Notes   157

Bibliography   185

Index   219

Illustrations

Map
Chicago-Area Cemeteries   45

Tables
1. Percentage of foreign-born employees reported from each country of birth   111
2. Men killed in the Allegheny County steel industry, July 1, 1906–June 30, 1907   115

Figures
1. Drawings of newsworthy events from the April 7, 1883, issue of *Frank Leslie's Illustrated Newspaper*   77
2. Fraternal organizations on parade   126
3. Steve Horvath's funeral procession   132

Acknowledgments

Writing a book on death and dying has required a vibrant, and lively, network of support. The project first took shape during my graduate studies at the University of Illinois. A spirit of camaraderie and shared intellectual endeavor made Urbana-Champaign a wonderful place to study. Faculty and graduate students made the seminar rooms places of lively debate and reasoned reflection. Members of the Working-Class Reading Group endured reading chapter drafts and provided key insights for improving the project. For their help and encouragement in these venues and beyond, I would like to thank Professors Sundiata Cha-Jua, Clare Crowston, Max Edelson, Kristin Hoganson, Fred Hoxie, Diane Koenker, Craig Koslofsky, Mark Leff, and John Marsh. Thanks also to graduate students Jen Guiliano, Dave Hageman, Brian Hoffman, Kwame Holmes, Brian Ingrassia, Danielle Kinsey, Michelle Kleehammer, Julilly Kohler-Hausmann, Bryan Nicholson, Karen Phoenix, Karen Rodriguez, and Anthony Sigismondi. Others provided valuable help from afar. I greatly appreciated the advice and friendships of Ken Fones-Wolf, Toby Higbie, Lou Martin, Sarah Rose, Tsuguyoshi "Yoshi" Ueno, and Greg Wood.

Some friends and colleagues were especially important during the project's early stages and helped nurture it along. Will Cooley's astute observations and frequent suggestions for sources proved both welcome and invaluable. Tom Mackaman provided keen insights, and I treasured our conversations about the worlds of life and labor during the first decades of the twentieth century. Melissa Rohde shared her unique gift for probing the limits of historical categories and pushed me to more fully engage assumptions in my work and in the field of labor history. Jason Kozlowski offered incisive suggestions and listened patiently as I rambled about research and writing during weekly meetings over coffee.

Kathryn Oberdeck, Elizabeth Pleck, and David Roediger all challenged me to become a better historian during my research and provided excellent suggestions. Few words can express the appreciation I have for my mentor and friend Jim Barrett. His passion for the past first infected me as an undergraduate student sitting in a crowded lecture hall. As I worked to become a historian, he taught me the multifaceted responsibilities of being a historian, from nurturing students' intellectual development to maintaining civic engagement outside the walls of the academy.

My colleagues at the University of Central Arkansas provided encouragement, advice, and support. Thank you to Ken Barnes, Jim Brodman, Wendy Castro, Chris Craun, Lorien Foote, Sondra Gordy, Joe Green, Matt Harper, Don Jones, Story Matkin-Rawn, Dave Neilson, David O'Hara, Roger Pauly, and David Welky.

My research benefited from generous funding from the Illinois Program for Research in the Humanities, the Center on Democracy in a Multiracial Society, the Illinois State Historical Society, the Departments of History at the University of Illinois and University of Central Arkansas, and the University of Central Arkansas University Research Council.

Finally, and most of all, I want to thank my family. My mom, Pat Rosenow, inculcated in me her beliefs of the power of education and the virtue of hard work. Cris and Lon Hicks welcomed me into their family and have exhibited patience and generosity that have often left me in awe. Trisha, my cherished partner, has provided unwavering support. She endured the self-imposed poverty of graduate school with grace and firmly, but lovingly, motivated me to finish in a timely manner and "get a real job." My two sons, Bryant and Brady, made this journey both enjoyable and worthwhile. They cheerfully embraced "vacations" to archives and libraries; they offered welcome respite from the rigors of research and writing through play. My family's unconditional love and support reminded me daily about the joys of living even while I studied the dead.

*Death and Dying
in the Working Class,
1865–1920*

Introduction

In Search of John Henry's Body

John Henry was a steel-driving man. Forged from the shackles of slavery, Henry's hammer built railroads that propelled the United States' economy. He was also one of the most famous men murdered by industrialization. In an act of principled bravado, Henry took a stand and agreed to race a machine that threatened to mechanize railroad construction. Whichever won, man or machine, could claim the glory. Henry prevailed, but he paid a price—his life. The John Henry legend, which continues to be told and retold, has longevity for good reason. It depicts a nation coming to grips with industrialization, celebrates black masculinity and the fortitude of human labor, and recognizes that the stakes of the economic and social transformations of the late nineteenth century could not have been higher.

But what happened to John Henry's body? Some versions of the legend bury Henry near a nondescript white house. Others do not bury him at all. His death punctuates the story as the peak of drama, the most piercing spike through the heart of a mechanizing country devoid of moral reckoning. Yet the dramas that unfolded after Henry's fatal collapse are just as important, just as gendered, just as crucial to understanding his climactic race with the steam drill and his untimely demise. If Henry was a free laborer, his death would have initiated a series of rituals—transporting the body, holding a wake or memorial, performing burial rites. If Henry was a convict laborer during the 1870s, as historian Scott Reynolds Nelson suggests, his body would have been simply tossed aside to be "buried in the sand" along the track, "and no one was the wiser."[1] Henry's living body carried the hopes of dignity in the face of degradation, and his story lived on through song and legend. His dead body disappeared.

Another railroad man of the 1870s did not have to worry that his body would be unceremoniously cast aside upon his death. Cornelius "Commodore" Vanderbilt stood at the center of the transportation revolution that reshaped the American economy during the nineteenth century. He created a steamboat empire and then, around midcentury, shifted his attention to railroads. When newsboys began crying the news of Vanderbilt's declining health in the mid-1870s, he had become the wealthiest man in the United States, "the one person whose private resources could break the market and throw a large part of the American economy in turmoil."[2]

Vanderbilt's wealth and power commanded attention as he slid toward death. Newspaper reporters watched the residence at 10 Washington Place in New York City day and night and devoted columns to update the public on the Commodore's health, what he had eaten, and how he had slept. On January 4, 1877, Vanderbilt died at the age of eighty-three. His funeral on January 7 attracted "the great and powerful, past and present" who wanted to pay respects to the tycoon. After a viewing of the body and a service at the Church of Strangers, Vanderbilt was laid to rest in the family tomb.[3] The tomb was only one monument to the Commodore. He left others. Railroads, Grand Central Depot in New York City, and Vanderbilt University were all tangible reminders of the life of one of the wealthiest Americans to have ever lived.

The fate of the two bodies—John Henry's and Cornelius Vanderbilt's—reveals the dramatic tensions that characterized the United States after the Civil War through the era of World War I. Hundreds of thousands of workers died in service to industrialization. They gave their lives to fuel the United States' economic engines and propel it to technological, economic, and political preeminence. Leading businessmen like Vanderbilt organized capital, profited handsomely, and wielded unprecedented influence. If workers were casualties in the United States' industrial army, the corporate titans were the victors left standing to enjoy the spoils of war. These changes to the American economy and the relationships they produced forced Americans to reassess the meaning of life and death. The rituals of dying and the politics of death provided a running commentary on how Americans struggled to understand the broader forces transforming their world. The ways social class shaped Americans' attitudes toward death have largely been buried in the past, unexhumed and unexamined.

The central purpose of this book is to explore how wageworkers and their families experienced death in the United States between the Civil War and the end of World War I. *Experience* for historians is a complicated word. It gestures toward the nature of what happened and when. But the events themselves, though important, are not enough. Studying experience must also address the thoughts, attitudes, and beliefs that historical actors used to give events meaning.[4] This is particularly the case when studying death. Everyone may die, but, as historian Drew Gilpin Faust notes, "men and women approach death in ways shaped by history, by culture, by conditions that vary over time and space."[5] The Civil War marked a turning point in American history. Americans embarked on a mission to give meaning to the estimated 620,000 Civil War dead. They also had to redefine boundaries of citizenship and make sense of a rapidly changing country. Just as it had during the Civil War, the work of death became a crucial way to reflect on life between 1865 and 1920. Wageworkers, in particular, developed specific rituals and attitudes that crystallized by World War I, although the meanings they attached to those deaths exhibited remarkable diversity over space and time.

Death provided moments of reflection that were pregnant with possibility. Dying destroyed a life, but it also produced an absence in which the living reflected on what a life meant during the industrial era. The living solidified or refashioned identities along the lines of class, race, gender, and religion. Rituals could reflect, solidify, or challenge prevailing sentiments and social order. The "history of death," historian Craig Koslofsky astutely observes, "is never the history of death alone."[6] Dead bodies may have been the focus of attention, but the rituals surrounding them reflected the conditions of life and the attitudes of the living.

Historians of death and dying in the United States have demonstrated this point in studies ranging from the colonial period to the twentieth century. Americans' attitudes and practices shifted remarkably over the course of the nineteenth century. The middle and upper classes transformed the minimalist practices of the colonial and early republic periods into lavish displays brimming with Victorian-era sentimentalism.[7] Funerals became a domestic occasion to relieve the stress and soothe the anxieties caused by "the transformation of an agrarian society into an urban and commercial one," as historian Elizabeth Pleck suggests.[8] Influenced by prevailing Victorian-era customs, Americans spent lavishly on flowers and caskets. They jockeyed for social status by erecting stately monuments in desirable cemeteries. Rituals of death and dying became a central feature of middle-class culture during the nineteenth century.[9]

Most scholars agree that the carnage of the Civil War caused a turning point in American attitudes and practices of remembering the dead. The unprecedented slaughter shattered romanticized antebellum views about death.[10] Battlefields strewn with bodies caused doubt to creep into American minds about the nature of the human soul and the existence of a benevolent deity. "Death without dignity, without decency, without identity imperiled the meaning of the life that preceded it," Faust concludes. "Americans had not just lost the dead; they had lost their own lives as they had understood them before the war." The war did more than challenge attitudes about death. It created new technologies, such as embalming, to transform the rituals of dying.[11]

As a result of the Civil War, Americans gradually retreated from the lavish Victorian-era celebrations. They began to remove the haunting specter of death from their lives as much as possible. As the twentieth century advanced, the last stages of life became the provenance of hospitals. Dead bodies became the responsibility of undertakers and funeral directors. The effect was that death became sequestered from public view. It became less familiar to Americans' daily lives and their concerns. Such changes produced "the dying of death" in American culture, according to historians.[12] By the middle of the twentieth century, death had become a taboo topic. Americans successfully made dying a private, professional experience that only briefly intruded on their daily lives.[13] Death was no longer so much to be feared, as in the colonial era, or celebrated, as in the Victorian period. It was to be forgotten. By the middle of the twentieth century, Americans had created a culture that denied death.[14]

These studies provide remarkable insights into broad changes in the ways Americans thought about death and transformed their rituals over time. However, most of the literature focuses almost exclusively on the middle classes. The narrative of historical development suggests that working people passively absorbed the evolving attitudes as they filtered down from above. It implies that the middle classes created the rituals that defined the American way of death and that working people sought to emulate their social betters.

Working-class historians studying an array of topics have challenged the primacy of the middle class in establishing cultural norms by suggesting that working people invested their practices—whether resisting work discipline, attending nickelodeons, or reading dime novels—with meanings related to their specific social positions.[15] Few historians have extended this approach to examining working people's relationships with dying or how they sought to understand death during the industrial era.[16] Studying working-class experiences with death contributes to this discussion by more carefully considering the complexity and diversity of American beliefs during the social and economic transformations that followed the Civil War.

Such a focus forces a reexamination of the old cliché that death is the great equalizer. Death during the Gilded Age and Progressive Era may have been the great equalizer in the sense that every person died, but not all

Americans experienced it in the same way. There may have been equality of opportunity, but there was no equality of condition. This was particularly the case for wageworkers and their families. Workers in key sectors of the growing industrial economy oftentimes died in different ways than middle- and upper-class Americans, as is vividly demonstrated in the comparison between John Henry and Cornelius Vanderbilt. Investigating wageworkers' experiences with death entails understanding some of the historical conditions and relationships that produced their end. It also requires investigating how families, coworkers, employers, and broader swaths of the country interpreted the deaths.

To exhume working communities' relationships with death, the book proceeds thematically in a series of interpretive essays that provide particular snapshots of experiences with death and dying. This approach has the advantage of isolating specific communities and lived experiences—especially industrial workers, on-the-job accidents, and strike-related violence—that emphasize the politics of death and reflect some of the broader relationships that structured the industrial era. Such focal points are meant to be suggestive rather than exhaustive; they suggest ways in which historians might further explore workers' beliefs, customs, and debates about death that are treated in these pages only peripherally or not at all.

Chapter 1 frames the study by investigating the politics of death regarding industrial accidents in the United States. It establishes the broader social and cultural contexts that shaped interpretations of workers' deaths that resulted from work accidents. Identifying the evolving views about the role wageworkers played in the expanding industrial economy suggests workers' experiences with death were intimately intertwined with broader economic and social changes.

Chapters 2, 3, and 4 use case studies to investigate how workers used the rituals of death to interpret, accommodate, and resist their living and working conditions. Chapter 2 explores Chicago's cemeteries as social and cultural spaces on the city's landscape. Cemeteries, like other aspects of death and dying, reflected the concerns of the living and mirrored the fissures that divided society. Just as the city had discernible ethnic and racial neighborhoods, the cemeteries catered to specific ethnic groups and produced segregated cities of the dead. More than simply mirroring the social space of the living, however, cemeteries served as spaces that promoted ethnic nationalism, racial hostility, and class solidarity. Upon death, workers negotiated the politics of burial spaces. Chapter 3 examines how Illinois coal miners and their families experienced death in one of the most dangerous occupations in the country. Catastrophic disasters and more common everyday accidents revealed dynamics of power between corporations, local government, and workers. Illinois served as a key incubator for the union that grew into the United Mine Workers of America (UMWA), one of the strongest unions in the country at the turn of the century. Chapter 4 moves from the Illinois prairie to Pennsylvania's Monongahela Valley. Workers' experiences in the mills contrasted with the freedom miners exercised underground. Open-shop drives attacked unions, work reorganization transplanted control from workers to foremen, and an influx of immigrant workers created tensions on the shop floor and in the community. These conditions influenced how common people practiced rituals of death in the shadow of one of the most important industries in the U.S. economy.

Taken together, these chapters reveal some of the ways workers experienced death and reflected on life from 1865 to 1920. Rituals of death reflected how working communities articulated beliefs about family, community, and class and negotiated social relationships—how common people interpreted their roles in the industrial republic. These processes fueled reform movements of the period, as workers asserted their human worth and struggled to remain respected members of society.

These venues also demonstrate that John Henry's death persisted in the American cultural lexicon because it captured a fundamental relationship of nineteenth-century America. Men and machines—sometimes in competition, sometimes in concerted effort—built the United States. Henry's tale reveals anxiety about the machine age and implies concern about human agency in the future of work. Had accounts of his burial survived, they would have likely illustrated these concerns in the poignant reflection of the rituals of death. No such texts exist. Yet the industrial working classes that followed on Henry's heels reveal what his burial services might have looked like. When we go looking for John Henry's body, we find people who struggled to understand the broad changes sweeping through the United States.

1 The Marks of Capital

The Accident Crisis and Cultures of Industrialization, 1865–1919

At the turn of the twentieth century, Big Bill Haywood, hard-rock miner turned union leader and Industrial Workers of the World (IWW) spokesman, used to say, "I've never read Marx's *Capital,* but I have the marks of Capital all over me." He began to acquire his scars early in his life. At the age of nine, his stepfather took him to work in a western mine. Later, his mother bound him to a farmer for a term of six months, where Haywood learned labor discipline by way of a whip. Upon leaving home at the age of fifteen, he once again entered the mines to earn a living. In the 1890s, he fell victim to one of the many hazards of the occupation and was injured. The time he spent recuperating allowed him to learn about a new union in the West—the Western Federation of Miners. Even before he embarked on a career as IWW organizer, Haywood could point to the marks of capital on his body.[1]

Although Haywood's life and career as an agitator were extraordinary, his work experiences were far more common among workers toiling in the United States' evolving industrial economy between the Civil War and World War I. The changing techniques of production, the reorganization of labor, and the growing intensity of class conflict created the conditions in which hundreds of thousands of American workers were, like Haywood, marked by capital. The marks were both physical and emotional. Workers' bodies bore the brunt of workplace accidents and occupational diseases. Their emotions suffered the disorienting cultural transformations of an age that slowly strangled the nineteenth-century notions of republican independence. Changing ideas about work and citizenship threatened to marginalize the nation's producers. One way to grasp the extent, and the effects, of these changes is to focus on the marks that industrial capitalism left on workers' bodies.

Statistical estimates of industrial fatalities across the United States during the period ranged between 25,000 to 80,000 per year, while between 300,000 and 1.6 million workers sustained serious injuries.[2] In the first decade of the twentieth century, newspapers reported that working in America's industries was more dangerous than being a soldier in the mid- to late nineteenth century. The *Chicago Tribune* wrote that industry killed 80,000 more in four years than the two armies of the Civil War.[3] Railroads alone produced a "yearly Gettysburg," causing 40,000 casualties per annum.[4] Such dramatic numbers demonstrated that dangerous workplaces were a central component of the United States' industrial ascent. They also, to a certain degree, set the country apart from its economic rivals in Europe. In 1908 the British *Colliery Guardian* bluntly proclaimed, "There is one record to which our transatlantic cousins may lay claim without fear of emulation; for in the matter of safeguarding its workmen, the United States enjoys the unenviable reputation of being the most backward of the civilized nations." Economic, social, cultural, and political changes facilitated what historian John Fabian Witt has termed the "industrial accident crisis."[5]

Why did the United States lead the world in workplace casualties between the Civil War and World War I? How did ideas about the body—and the classed, raced, and gendered meanings mapped to it—facilitate the industrial accident crisis and impact workers' experiences with death? The industrial accident crisis was one aspect of the transformations that occurred in the United States between the Civil War and World War I. Exploring its causes and consequences reveals how Americans developed cultures of industrialization to give meaning to industrial work and position the people who performed it in the larger social body.

Using "the body" as a category of analysis provides the fullest exploration of how workers and observers interpreted and, in some cases, justified the human cost of industrialization. When invoking "the body," scholars conjure a variety of interrelated meanings. First, studying "the body" necessarily involves recognizing the corporeality of human subjectivities. In other words, historical actors experienced their lives through their material presence as a body, as owners of arms and legs, fingers and toes. They felt pleasure and pain; they bled and healed; they worked and loafed; they ate and starved. Second, studying "the body" recognizes it as a site of regulation and discipline. Third, "the body" as a category of analysis reveals that representations of bodies and the discourses mapped to them had profound effects on human experiences.[6] Fully understanding the industrial accident crisis requires an acknowledgment of each of these three elements. As sociologist Pierre Bourdieu notes in his theory of habitus, historical changes are mapped to the body, "so that the body reveals the effects of social power."[7] The body also reveals the effects of economic power. A key to understanding the industrial accident crisis and workers' experiences with death and dying is to look at how workers' bodies were sites of regulation and representation.

This chapter primarily focuses on how others—principally those Americans who mainly observed, rather than participated in, wage work—reinterpreted work and viewed workers. To understand how workers experienced death, it is necessary to understand some of the broader forces that shaped their lives. Cultures of industrialization developed that focused on disciplining bodies, celebrating progress, imagining industrial work, and representing workers. A worker's death thus interacted with layers of meanings that came to define the industrial era, which in turn produced a fifth culture of industrialization: protest. Beliefs associated with each of these offered particular interpretations of workers' lives and deaths.

Cultures of Order: Corporeality and the Industrial Imperative

Experiences of work and what it meant to be a worker changed over the course of the nineteenth century. New England textile factories epitomized early industrial development. From there, innovations in production crawled across the northeastern landscape. Transportation improvements—first roads and canals, then steamboats and railroads—quickened the pace. Americans witnessed veritable explosions of economic growth in the decades following the Civil War. Shops, mills, and factories hummed, as workers sweated over their tools and innovative machines made mass production in fields and cities part of the American system. Manufacturers recorded on average a fivefold increase in production between 1860 and 1900. The gross national product surged as well, witnessing a sixfold increase over the last three decades of the century, despite two severe depressions from 1873 to 1877 and from 1893 to 1897. This industrial expansion catapulted the United States to a position of economic power on the world stage. In 1860 the United States had trailed Great Britain, France, and Germany in industrial output. By 1900 the United States produced more than its three closest economic rivals combined.[8]

Historians refer to these broad changes as the Industrial Revolution for good reason. Americans' everyday lives were transformed. They increasingly moved from farms to factories, as industrialization restructured the labor market. In 1820 more than 90 percent of Americans worked in agriculture. By 1870 the figure had shrunk to just over 50 percent, and by 1890, for the first time in U.S. history, a majority of Americans worked in nonagricultural pursuits.[9] These population movements were not enough to satisfy the demand for labor that bustling enterprises required. Immigrants landed on American shores with dreams of economic opportunity. In most cases, they joined the industrial workforce in growing cities like New York, Pittsburgh, and Chicago. Between 1860 and 1900, the industrial workforce quadrupled from 1.5 to 6 million. Among the many other changes to daily life wrought by industrialization, the United States was becoming a nation of wage earners.

The second half of the nineteenth century became a struggle to come to terms with these vast changes. Industrialization did not merely change how people traveled or communicated, the goods they purchased, or where they worked or lived. The economic and social changes forced Americans to grapple with the meanings of work and the beliefs associated with wage labor. Ideas of freedom and independence had a long history of being envisioned through representations of work and bodily experiences.

During the first half of the nineteenth century, when a majority of Americans worked the land or sought the independence associated with artisanal labor, Jeffersonians and Jacksonians alike associated liberty and the fulfillment of the republican promise with the ability to control one's own labor. When Jefferson extolled the virtues of the yeoman farmer and skilled artisan, he mapped the meanings of independence and freedom to white, usually male, bodies. This embodied representation of freedom helps explain much about the early nineteenth century. Nonwhites—a category that at various times encompassed American Indians, African slaves, or Irish immigrants—became the "others" against which freedom and the advance of civilization could be measured. Americans justified expropriating American Indian lands and tightening the chains of slavery as necessary to maximizing the opportunities available to whites. Inspired by a sense of manifest destiny, whites pushed westward. They warred with Mexico. They defended slavery and the patriarchal relationships between men and women. Toward midcentury Abraham Lincoln and other Republicans came to criticize the institution of slavery through the rhetoric of free labor, further cementing the connection between the body and its control, on one hand, with liberty and the realization of the American dream, on the other. These ideas and movements were never beyond reproach, whether from antiwar Whigs, from the rising movement for women's equality, or from abolitionists. But the idea of free labor provided a powerful trope that attracted believers in the white republic.[10]

The economic boom that followed the quieting of the guns of the Civil War forced Americans to reevaluate traditional cultural symbols. Farmers bore the full brunt of the economic changes. Squeezed by higher operating costs and diminishing crop prices, many were forced away from the land. In Kansas, one of the areas hardest hit, creditors foreclosed on more than eleven thousand mortgages between 1889 and 1893.[11] As the number of farm mortgages and foreclosures testified, fewer Americans could aspire to the ideal of the Jeffersonian independent farmer. The number of Americans who owned property declined precipitously in the last decades of the century. In 1870 between 50 and 56 percent of household heads claimed property holdings. In 1901 only 19 percent of U.S. families owned their own homes.[12] The pedestal on which Americans had placed the agricultural producer as a symbol of freedom and independence was being whittled away. The symbol tottered on the brink of the unattainable.

To replace the smallholding farmer, Americans had to think about new symbols better fit for the industrial era: the inventor, the industrialist, the capitalist, the wageworker.[13] Like the streets of growing urban areas, these were messy and contested categories. Which of these could perform the cultural work of Jefferson's farmer or Jackson's frontiersman? Which could represent the unbounded optimism of success, social mobility, and strength of American character? Was America's future after 1865 to be determined by the elite ranks of the Vanderbilts, Fisks, Goulds, Rockefellers, Carnegies, and Morgans? Or would the producing classes of workers and farmers continue to be held aloft as the pride of the country and revered as the source of liberty and prosperity?

It is necessary to consider these questions alongside the changes in the workplace to understand and explain the industrial accident crisis and the changing environments of workers' deaths. As manufacturers reorganized work processes and sought to maximize efficiency to better compete in the marketplace, they also fostered interpretations about what the changes meant. Workers offered their own interpretations—sometimes in agreement with employers and sometimes in staunch opposition. Americans created cultures of industrialization that helped them come to terms with the changes swirling around them. These evolving, and sometimes contradictory, beliefs and attitudes about work and workers' bodies help explain the industrial accident crisis.

One culture of industrialization, the desire to impose order on the workplace and discipline the workforce, developed as a means to rationalize production and maximize efficiency. Americans in the industrial era seemed caught in cycles of innovation. Efficiency, speed, and order became central tenets of the manufacturing classes. Manufacturers sought success by reorganizing production and fundamentally changing the rhythms and relationships of work. This happened in numerous ways across different industries.

The factory system spread where practicable, replacing home production and the small shop. Machines made hand tools obsolete and, along with the division of labor, created massive ranks of semi- and unskilled wage earners.

Manufacturers, business leaders, and bankers all sought to carve some sort of order out of the chaos of the rapid industrial expansion. They confronted the challenges of intense competition, and the workplace became a battlefield. It pitted the disciples of discipline against the perceived purveyors of disorder, which could assume the form of inefficient production methods, slow distribution networks, or the workers themselves. The culture of industrialization that emerged from this battle for control of the workplace placed great value on individualism and the authority of capital to dictate the terms of labor. Although workers mounted challenges at nearly every turn, manufacturers sought to regulate and discipline workers' bodies to better control the workplace. The quest to rationalize production and construct stricter regimes of discipline around workers' bodies provided a key factor in explaining why the United States led the world in workplace casualties.

After the Civil War, manufacturers refined the factory system and fundamentally changed the environment of work. Factories featured power-driven machinery, the integration of different production processes at a single site, an elaborate division of labor, and new methods of administration based on overseers and foremen. Machines did more than replace manual labor. They increased production to dizzying figures in some cases. Before James Bonsack patented a cigarette-making machine in 1881, the most highly skilled handworkers produced 3,000 a day. One of Bonsack's machines produced more than 70,000 in a ten-hour day. By the late 1880s, one cigarette machine could make 120,000 per day. "Fifteen such machines could fill the total demand for cigarettes in the United States in 1880," historian Alfred Chandler notes, "and thirty could have saturated the 1885 market."[14] The invention of comparable machines in other industries transformed manufacturing. Factory owners planned their workspaces carefully to facilitate the most expeditious flow of materials through the plant. Increased efficiency meant increased production.

Industrialists hoped this formula would lead to profits and therefore adopted the factory system in increasing numbers. Until the 1840s, the factory system had been primarily limited to the textile industry. By 1880 Carroll D. Wright estimated in the introduction to the census of manufactures, "Of the nearly three millions of people employed in mechanical industries of this country at least four-fifths of them are working under the factory system."[15] As more Americans worked in factories, the size of the workplaces grew as well. As early as the 1870s, large factories dotted the North. The Cambria Iron Works in Johnstown, Pennsylvania, employed six thousand workers. Both the Standard Oil Works in Cleveland and the Baldwin Locomotive Works in Philadelphia employed more than twenty-five hundred people.[16] By 1900 443 factories employed more than one thousand wage earners, and over 1,000 factories employed between five hundred and one thousand workers. Historian Daniel Nelson estimates that "the 'average' plant in 11 of 16 industries more than doubled in size" during the last third of the nineteenth century.[17]

Concentration of production helped manufacturers capitalize on economies of scale; it also began a process of transferring the power of production from workers, especially artisans, to employers. Before mechanization, or in industries such as iron and steel where mechanization was more difficult, skilled workers could better dictate the terms and pace of their work. Employers combated workers' control in a number of ways. Where possible, they emphasized the transition to machinery and increased reliance on technology, which boosted efficiency but also eroded workers' influence.[18] Cyrus McCormick Jr. used such tactics during a heated labor dispute at the Chicago reaper works in 1885 and 1886. He dismissed an entire group of unionized molders and replaced them with molding machines and unskilled laborers to tend them.[19] Workers were reduced to machine tenders rather than knowledgeable craftsmen plying a trade. Employers like McCormick reasoned that machines did not ask for higher wages or shorter hours.

Where technology could not effectively replace skilled workers, industrialists relied on minute divisions of labor to effect similar ends. Economists David M. Gordon, Richard Edwards, and Michael Reich argue that the late nineteenth and early twentieth centuries represented a homogenization of labor, where "more and more work tasks had been reduced to detailed, atomized, semiskilled operations. This new system enhanced employers' control over production and consequently enabled expanded extraction of labor from their workers."[20] Chicago's meatpacking industry became a model of this process. Beginning in the 1870s and 1880s, meat processors initiated the precursor to the assembly line. Using a moving pulley system, animals passed by semiskilled workers who repeated the same cut for an entire shift. The system allowed supervisors greater control over the pace of work, while the economies of scale and the concentration of production meant that the individual skilled butcher toiling in his own shop seemed a relic of a preindustrial past.[21]

Deskilling facilitated the transfer of the knowledge from workers to foremen and managers. Before the erosion of skilled work, craft workers exercised a good deal of power at work. Skilled ironworkers, for example, normally had the ability to hire and fire members of their work gangs, could determine the definition of a fair day's work, and had bargaining power with the mill owner over wages. Instead of a top-down management structure, factories resembled "congeries of workshops," where the manager's brain was under the workman's cap.[22] The process of deskilling and the emergence of larger firms and bureaucratically organized corporations altered the social relations of production and created new occupations—foremen and managers. The number of foremen in manufacturing increased during the late nineteenth century and exploded during the first decades of the twentieth century, growing by 300 percent from 1900 to 1920.[23] Instead of "congeries of workshops" where skilled workers exercised a great deal of autonomy, work became lorded over by the "foreman's empire."[24] Foremen took control over many of the day-to-day operations. They hired, fired, and promoted in ways that often seemed arbitrary, vindictive, or criminal to workers. Work in steel became, in the words of steelmaker John Fritz, "small principalities, each of them governed by a despotic foreman." Practitioners of Frederick W. Taylor's scientific management added additional layers of managerial control over the work process. With stopwatch in hand, they observed workers' movements throughout the day and used their managerial prerogative to modify behavior as they saw fit.[25]

The appropriation of workers' knowledge played an important role in disciplining the workforce while redefining the industrial worker as ancillary to producing the nation's goods and wealth. This organization of work facilitated the industrial accident crisis. Employers could train workers quickly and cheaply; if a worker met death or sustained a serious injury in the plant, his or her lack of skill meant that another worker could easily step in to fill the gap in the line. In 1887 economist David Wells—friend and adviser to presidents, a railroad trustee, and outspoken advocate of free trade—summed up the broader implications:

> The individual no longer works as independently as formerly, but as a private in the ranks, obeying orders, keeping step, as it were, to the tap of the drum, and having nothing to say as to the plan of his work, of its final completion, or of its ultimate use and distribution. In short, the people who work in the modern factory are, as a rule, taught to do one thing—to perform one and generally a simple operation. . . . The result has been that the individualism or independence of the producer in manufacturing has been in a great degree destroyed.[26]

Wells's description poignantly summarized the tendencies in the late-nineteenth-century workplace. Employers sought to supplant workers' control by increasing reliance on technology and the concomitant deskilling of the industrial worker. Such rationalization schemes aided manufacturers in improving the stability of production and, in many cases, padding profit margins. Devising a system where workers' bodies were objects of regulation and discipline fundamentally harked back to regimes of slave labor and altered traditional notions of producers as the revered classes of the independent yeoman farmer or artisanal craftsman. Unskilled and semiskilled workers became interchangeable parts within the economic engines that propelled the American economy. Production could continue with minimal disruption even as injuries soared and the death toll increased.

The broader changes in the economy and restructuring of work directly impacted the relationships between workers and bosses. "Well, I remember that fourteen years ago the workmen and the foremen and the boss were all as one family; it was just as easy and as free to speak to the boss as any one else," Joseph T. Finnerty testified in 1883 to the Senate committee investigating relations between capital and labor. These intimate work relationships were changing, however. A seemingly insuperable chasm began to divide workers from foremen and bosses. The men "would not think of looking the foremen in the face now any more than we would the boss," Finnerty claimed. "The average hand growing up in the shop now would not think of speaking to the boss, would not presume to recognize him, nor the boss would not recognize him either."[27] Workers across the country would have nodded in recognition of the scenes Finnerty described. They questioned if long-held notions of equality could withstand the onslaught of industrialization.

The hierarchical relationship between workers and bosses contributed to the accident crisis and shaped the meanings attached to workers' dead bodies. Workers were merely cogs in the great industrial machine to some manufacturers. Employees were "simply so much producing power," according to one iron maker. "I've no time to even remember their faces, much less their names."[28] Theories of contract and trends in corporate accounting encouraged employers to consider workers as labor power that was distinct from the person who performed the work. This was one result of the Civil War and the triumph of "freedom of contract." Humans could no longer be bought and sold, but labor power—which was abstracted from physical bodies—could be.[29] Workers felt this commodified their bodies, which they did not divorce from their labor power. Labor reformer and leader of the shorter-hours movement Ira Steward proclaimed, "The employer is the master, and the employee is the slave."[30] William McLelland, an engineer and member of the Amalgamated Society of Engineers, captured this dynamic. "The employer has pretty much the same feeling towards men that he has towards his machinery. He wants to get as much as he can out of his men at the cheapest rate," he told a Senate committee.[31] Workers felt the effects of these attitudes directly.

Once a man, woman, or child agreed to work for a wage, they could be ordered to speed up, toil for longer hours, and jeopardize life and limb to maximize their utility in production. The wage relationship made it easier for employers to discount the perils of industrial work. The sheer numbers of accidents suggest that labor power occupied a line in corporate ledgers near raw materials. Critics of industrial development such as journalist Helen Campbell certainly thought so. Campbell documented sensational examples of callous indifference to workers' well-being in her book *Prisoners of Poverty*. She claims one railroad superintendent justified his refusal to repair a hole in the roof of a railroad car by bluntly proclaiming, "Men are cheaper than shingles. There's a dozen waiting to fill the place of one that drops out."[32] While Campbell may have embellished this quote to maximize its impact, the sheer numbers of accidents and dangerous workplaces imply such sentiments existed. When a machine stopped working, you replaced it. When a man wore out or died, you replaced him too. In both instances, work continued. An owner might have regretted the loss of a machine, but to mourn it would have been ridiculous even during the sentimentalist Victorian era. It seemed that a similar logic applied to workers. Their deaths might have been regretted, but few employers in the largest and most dangerous trades mourned them enough to bring meaningful safety reform to deadly workplaces before 1906.

Cultures of Progress: The Triumph of the Machine and of Individualism

While the reorganization of work threatened to marginalize working people, the eye-popping successes of America's surging industrial economy created a culture of progress that privileged the benefits of the changing economy while discounting its costs, especially when those costs were calculated in the number of dead workers. Americans watched the economy transform before their eyes. They witnessed the greatest industrial growth the country had seen. Newspapers ticked off the increasing miles of railroad, the growing piles of coal extracted from the earth, and the soaring tons of steel rolling out of American mills. Fairgoers marveled at the seeming endless spate of technological innovations. All Americans could agree that they lived during decades of great change. They "became conscious of living in an *industrial* economy," as economist Peter Temin suggests.[33] But Americans could not agree on what the changes meant.[34] Should mechanization, the division of labor, and all of the other facets of industrialization be embraced or resisted? Such questions had emerged with the first textile factories in the early nineteenth century. They became more important as the pace and geographical scope of industrialization increased after 1865. Fierce debates erupted over the "labor question." Who should accrue the benefits of industrial production—the workers who made the goods or the employers who controlled the capital necessary for the work? Should the people who made the country's products benefit from the wealth they generated, or should those riches belong to the owners of the shops, mills, and factories? What was the proper relationship between employer and employee? These questions plagued Americans, especially after class conflict became a pronounced feature of American life after the railroad strike of 1877. Americans wondered if any semblance of equality or democracy should be allowed into the workplace. They thought about the consequences of becoming a nation of machine tenders. These broader debates produced knowledge about what industrialization meant to the United States. The perspectives informed how Americans viewed working conditions, urban living conditions, and wage earners' deaths.

Many Americans celebrated the machine age with few reservations. They embraced mechanical innovations as symbols of progress. Machines became the center of a popular social theory, historian Allen Trachtenberg explains, as Americans imagined machines as a "human benefactor," a "great emancipator of man from the bondage of labor."[35] Popular reverence for the mechanical was on clear display in 1876. Visitors to the American Centennial Celebration in Philadelphia made Machinery Hall the most popular attraction. Thousands jostled for a view of the centerpiece exhibit, the Corliss steam engine. Standing at forty feet and weighing seven hundred tons, the engine was a hulking mass of pure power. Onlookers marveled as the engine churned out 1,400 horsepower and powered the eight thousand presses, pumps, gins, mills, and lathes on display.[36] Essayist and novelist William Dean Howells wrote with awe of the display for readers of the *Atlantic Monthly*. "It is in these things of iron and steel that the national genius most freely speaks," he rhapsodized.[37] Howells represented a growing chorus of voices that equated machines with "the glorious triumphs of [American] skill and invention."[38] Machinery Hall, as historian Bruce Laurie astutely observes, underscored the transition from the labor-intensive methods of domestic production and the sweating system to the capital-intensive, machine-paced processes of the factory.[39]

Beyond the walls of Machinery Hall, Americans extolled the virtues of machine production and factory work. In 1882 Carroll D. Wright, then chief of the Massachusetts Bureau of Statistics of Labor, described the factory system as a "civilizing force" that eradicated superstition, poverty, and ignorance.

"Better morals, better sanitary conditions, better health, better wages," Wright wrote, "these are the practical results of the factory system, as compared with what preceded it, and the results of all these have been a keener intelligence." He suggested that the order and discipline of the factory system replaced the inefficient domestic system of production. This shift was a step of progress in the march toward an industrial future.[40]

Manufacturers echoed Wright's assessment. The *Iron Age*, the trade journal for the iron and steel industry, praised the late-nineteenth-century organization of labor as replacing chaos with order. The workman was the ultimate benefactor, as the changes in production "lifted the workmen to a higher plane and has given them a greater capacity for the enjoyment of life."[41] Inventors and business owners continually compared machine work to handwork. They argued that modern technology produced "labor saving" machinery that not only increased production but also improved working conditions. Charles R. Flint, a businessman nicknamed "father of trusts" because of his role in merging companies in areas as diverse as rubber, chewing gum, and business machines, told a meeting of the National Civic Federation in 1901 that mechanization and factory work had benefited American workingmen directly. "The American wage earner is raised to the dignity of an overseer, not over degraded humanity, but over a more reliable and effective slave—machinery."[42] Flint perpetuated the rhetoric of masters and slaves to emphasize his view that American factory workers had improved their status as a result of industrialization. Other businessmen extended the benefits of the machine age beyond the shop floor. B. F. Eshelman, Confederate veteran and owner of the hardware firm Stauffer, Eshelman & Co., argued, "American inventive genius has contributed more to the advancement of civilization during the century just past than the whole world in many hundreds of years, if we except the invention of printing."[43] From perspectives like Wright's, Flint's, and Eshelman's, factories, machines, and the broader restructuring of the economy promised to benefit workers and consumers. Americans' "inventive genius" meant that the United States could serve as a country atop the manufacturing hill for others to emulate.

Many industrialists also welcomed the changing structures of labor organization on the shop floor. A disciplined workforce—which arrived on time, abstained from alcohol, and obeyed orders—was a productive workforce. Stratified organizational structures and the attendant rank inequality between employers and workers were interpreted as signs of progress akin to the technological advances of the nineteenth century. "It is one of the wildest chimeras to imagine that there can be a perfect equality of possession and position," one anonymous author wrote in the wake of the 1877 railroad strikes. "The constitution of society requires that there be masters and servants."[44]

Steel magnate Andrew Carnegie echoed this sentiment in his influential writings on wealth. He championed the economic changes in U.S. society, writing, "We accept and welcome, therefore, as conditions to which we must accommodate ourselves, great inequality of environment, the concentration of business, industrial and commercial, in the hands of a few, and the law of competition between these, as being not only beneficial, but essential for the future progress of the race."[45] Carnegie's ode to individualism outlined a clear social order that put the wealthy at the top and established economic inequality as the barometer of progress. It also adapted a Darwinian survival of the fittest to the U.S. economy. Carnegie trod a similar path as Herbert Spencer and William Graham Sumner, who argued that the poor were the least valuable members of society and candidates for elimination in the great struggle for survival.[46]

Social Darwinists' arguments had implications for the industrial accident crisis and interpretations of workers' deaths. When applied to a workplace fatality, the logic would suggest that a fit individual would not be occupying such a job in the first place or that a better person would have avoided the accident. A death resulting from industrial accidents could be ascribed to a process of "natural selection" and "survival of the fittest" rather than an economic system that had increasingly placed an emphasis on profit rather than the well-being of people. Metallurgist H. W. Howe made this point. "As humanitarians, we might regret" industrial work's harmful impact on workers' bodies, but as "managers . . . we would not be justified in diminishing our employers' profits."[47] This was the necessary consequence for the future success of the country, according to one current of the culture of progress. When combined with the celebration of the machine age, it meant that workers' deaths were either obscured from view or interpreted as a just result of the natural order of things.

Cultures of Work: Representations of Work and Workers

Manufacturers' desire to regulate and discipline workers' bodies and the culture of progress that accompanied industrialization help account for the industrial accident crisis, but they reveal only part of the explanation. Representations of workers' bodies provide another crucial component. To put it simply, Americans saw vastly different things when they visited or imagined American workplaces. They envisioned different scenes when they read about work in the popular press or watched a Labor Day parade. The meanings that Americans created about work and mapped to workers' bodies were conditioned by ideas about class, gender, race, and religion. Some of these ideas clearly perpetuated the dangerous working conditions. Others, which fully emerged during the Progressive Era, mobilized ideas about the body to lead the charge for safety reform, factory inspection, and workmen's compensation.

Representations of workers' bodies and conversations about dangerous workplaces were part of a national discussion about modernity and advancing civilization. Historians have characterized the late nineteenth century as a period in which middle-class men felt their manhood was under attack. Politicians openly fretted about challenges to the male prerogative to declare and wage war that came from arbitrationists—a group often led by women and nearly always characterized as feminine.[48] Other middle-class figures worried that urbanization and modern civilization threatened men's virility and the rugged individualism that characterized the westward expansion across the frontier.[49]

Theodore Roosevelt became a key spokesperson for preserving American manhood. He advocated a return to nature and encouraged American men to lead a "strenuous life." In the early 1890s, he argued that football's ability to enhance manhood was worth an occasional death on the gridiron.[50] He publicly denounced men who had been softened by modern life to a Harvard audience in 1907. Colleges would provide a disservice to the country, he reasoned, if they turned out "mollycoddles instead of vigorous men."[51] *Mollycoddle* became a term of derision applied to men who lacked manly fortitude and virility. It became part of a pantheon of other epithets, such as *dude*, *sissy*, and *pussyfoot*, that criticized men who might behave or speak in a way characterized as feminine.[52]

These middle-class fears about waning manhood had a direct impact on representations of work and workers. Many middle-class men romanticized physical labor and the hard work that propelled the economy. Industrial and manual labor became an effective antidote to the feminizing tendencies threatening their manhood. Philosopher William James envied men's dangerous work as proving grounds for manliness. He argued in a lecture to students that the "demand for courage is incessant. . . . [W]herever a scythe, an axe, a pick, or a shovel is wielded, you have [human nature] sweating and aching and with its powers of patient endurance racked to the utmost under the length of hours of the strain."[53] Glorifying manual work, James suggested society needed the danger and courage of perilous work to protect it from the enervating effects of middle-class culture. Doctors, in some cases, prescribed manual labor as a restorative cure. Frederick W. Taylor, on his way to becoming a key proponent of scientific management, once took his medicine as a machine tender.[54] Other middle-class authors donned overalls and transgressed class boundaries in an urban equivalent of "going native" to level commentaries about the dangers of middle-class comfort as well as working-class debauchery.[55] In this way, observers rationalized unsafe workplaces for men as a positive by-product of industrialization that preserved masculinity.[56] Such glorification had a tendency to romanticize industrial labor. Characterizations of work became a location (both real and imagined), like the wilderness and warfare, where men could prove themselves. The workplace was a Roman Colosseum where heroes could be made and tested. Removing danger from the industrial workplace would be like putting toothless lions in the Colosseum. It would diminish the test of manly fortitude.

Elements of nineteenth-century law contributed to the romantic notion of industrial labor and added an element of nostalgia for simpler, perhaps preindustrial, eras of artisanal production. A triumvirate of tort law rooted in the 1840s—the assumption of risk, contributory negligence, and fellow servant—centered on the freedom of contract as the guiding principle of all labor relations. When confronted with mangled bodies of workers or widows who grieved over the dead bodies of husbands, judges harked back to ideas of free labor and conjured images of simple workshops. According to the doctrine of assumption of risk, workers sold their labor in a free market and were therefore solely liable for accidents and injuries. Judges hailed this as the genius of free labor. Workers had the freedom to choose their places and conditions of employment. By agreeing to work, they therefore assumed the risk. If workers were concerned about conditions, they could simply quit and find a job more to their liking. The doctrines of contributory negligence and fellow-servant law also shielded employers from liability by declaring that if a worker in any way contributed to the accident or could be shown to have behaved in a way that caused death, then the fault lay solely with the employee, not the employer.[57]

These legal doctrines had emerged during the early stages of industrialization in the United States and did not accurately reflect the workplaces or economy that characterized the late nineteenth century.[58] The right to quit was a form of liberty, but quitting was a risky proposition in itself. As the business cycle created a seemingly perpetual army of the unemployed, there was no guarantee that another job with safer conditions could easily be found. Some workers therefore argued that their choices in the labor market were by no means free: they could work in danger or starve in safety.[59] Writing in 1906, George William Alger noted that the workers were right to observe the difference between the projection and experience of liberty. "His grievance is that in a multitude of instances the courts give him counterfeit liberty in the place of its reality." "Labor's right to get killed," he concluded, "is not highly esteemed by the people to whom this guarantee is given. The counterfeit liberty is no more satisfactory to its recipient than is the counterfeit dollar."[60]

Likewise, contributory negligence and fellow-servant law did not adequately consider the new hierarchical organizations of the workplace, the relationship between technology and risk, or the sheer size of some industrial workplaces. The courts projected relationships of equality onto work relationships and failed to recognize how foremen and managers could order, coerce, or intimidate their subordinates to take risks.[61] Accident tolls mounted, as supervisors shrugged off the significance of workplace accidents.

Anxious middle-class men and judges were not the only groups that represented work in romanticized terms. Some workers perpetuated the idea that they engaged in a daily life-and-death struggle that refined their physique and bolstered their notions of independent manhood. In 1884 Eugene V. Debs paid tribute to the mental acuity and physical prowess of railroad firemen. "[Firemen] are remarkable for common sense," he wrote. "They are bronze-browed, hard-fisted, noble-natured men. They are forever dealing with problems which demand and command serious thought. A locomotive fireman cannot, in the nature of things, be a dude." Historian Paul Michel Taillon points out that by contrasting firemen with dudes, Debs drew a distinction between working- and middle-class notions of masculinity. He "ridiculed 'unmanly' conduct of leisure-class men who did not work with their hands. By contrast, respectable working-class men not only earned a wage sufficient to support a family, they celebrated the risks, rewards, and ennobling effects of physical labor."[62] Railroaders were not alone. In other industries with reputations for danger, men displayed an ethic of "toughing it out" rather than risk having their manhood called into question.[63] In her 1895 study of workplace accidents, Katherine Pearson Woods found "public opinion among workingmen is to despise a man who takes precautions, perhaps even to call him cowardly, until he is killed or injured, when he is stigmatized as reckless."[64] Respectable working-class manhood combined physical strength and moral virtue to preserve ideals of manly independence. Tests of endurance, feats of strength, and risk taking made the man.[65] Risk taking also produced accidents.[66]

White male workers and middle-class reformers attempted to preserve the workplace as a male domain that could reinforce manhood. They launched campaigns to restrict women's access to wage-earning jobs or exclude them altogether. The American Federation of Labor (AFL) played a key role in resisting women's participation in the workforce. Trade unionists worried that the presence of women would adversely affect wages and challenge men's status as the breadwinner for the family. They also represented women as the weaker sex, best suited for being wives and mothers. Writing in the *American Federationist* in 1897, Edward O'Donnell argued that "masculine labor destroys the finer promptings and feelings of the sex, the necessary factors to happiness and prosperity, under the conjugal knot, are undermined, or they become totally undesirous of assuming domestic responsibility; and in either case our vaunted civilization receives a set-back."[67] Wage work, especially in the dangerous trades, was properly the domain of men, according to trade unionists and reformers alike. Equating dangerous work with the risk and reward of physical labor was a way to confirm the boundaries of masculinity. It also contributed to a representation of wage work as properly male and sufficiently risky.[68]

Sentiments such as O'Donnell's had been percolating through the United States during the 1890s, as labor reformers worked to restrict the number of hours women could work. Shorter-hours movements reinforced the idea that dangerous workplaces were the proper domain of American men, a point that was not lost on Jane Norman Smith of the National Woman's Party.[69] Smith rejected the professed humanitarianism of the shorter-hours laws. She believed that "male trade unionists saw shorter hours legislation as a way to 'drive women out of the trade as fast as possible.'" This preserved the male breadwinning ideology. It also reinforced the idea that dangerous workplaces would continue to be masculine contests between safety and danger.[70] The paternalist attempt to control women's work reinforced the primacy of the male body in the workplace.

Patterns of immigration to the United States also played a role in defining representations of workers and contributing to the industrial accident crisis. By the early twentieth century, it had become a prevailing assumption that immigrants met death on the job more frequently than did white native-born Americans.[71] This belief placed industrial work accidents within broader debates about immigration. Americans had debated the desirability of newcomers since the colonial period. Benjamin Franklin made a strong case as early as 1751 that North America should be limited to the "lovely White" to the exclusion of "all Blacks and Tawneys."[72] The revolutionary generation reinforced the linkage of color and citizenship in the 1790 naturalization statute by establishing "free white" and male as the necessary prerequisites. During the nineteenth century, waves of immigration from Europe and Asia ignited discussions about the meaning of citizenship, about who was fit to be an American, and who was not. These debates intermingled with industrialization, as immigrants provided the human motor to drive the nation's economy, often performing the lowest-paid and most physically exhausting work. Nativists could discount the importance of accidents because they believed that immigrants were the least important members of American communities.

Suspicion first fell on Irish Catholics, who immigrated in increasing numbers during the 1840s. Samuel Morse, inventor of the telegraph and a vocal nativist, worried that the Irish were part of a popish plot to subvert the American republic. Others suggested that the Irish did not possess aptitude for self-government or proper character to become citizens.[73] As nativists argued and sought to modify naturalization laws through political movements like the Know-Nothing Party, employers turned to the Irish to dig canals, expand the nation's railroads, serve as domestic workers, and perform a variety of other jobs that often combined danger, high mortality, and low pay. Their place near the bottom of the economic structure played into nativists' hands. They could use economic position to reinforce their arguments about the immigrants' character. As the Irish competed with free blacks for employment in the North, and southern employers preferred hiring the Irish in some cases rather than risking the lives of their slaves, native-born white Americans drew connections between the status of blacks and the Irish in America.[74] The Irish therefore occupied a complicated racial and economic position that intertwined questions about their citizenship with their status as workers. Although Irish immigrants gradually became accepted in American society, questions about the boundaries of citizenship and the connections to work persisted.

In the West, the Chinese became targets. Attracted to the West Coast first by the Gold Rush and then by the promise of industrial jobs, especially mining and railroad construction, the Chinese inspired a backlash that combined elements of class, race, and gender. White workers led the assault. They feared that the Chinese provided employers a source of cheap "coolie" labor that depressed wages and threatened whites' status as a "free" laboring class. California passed legislation taxing foreign miners in 1852. In 1854 the ruling in *People v. Hall* officially deemed the Chinese nonwhite and, as historian Tomás Almaguer writes, "legally restricted the Chinese to the same second-class status of blacks and Indians." Deemed nonwhite, the Chinese were ineligible for citizenship rights until the passage of the Federal Civil Rights Act in 1872.[75] The depression of the 1870s rekindled animosity toward the Chinese. Under the slogan "The Chinese Must Go!" the Workingmen's Party and Irish-born leader Denis Kearney inflamed anti-Chinese sentiment. In an 1877 speech, Kearney proclaimed, "We intend to try and vote the Chinaman out, to frighten him out, and if this won't do, to kill him out, and when the blow comes, we won't leave a fragment for the thieves to pick up."[76] Economic competition with the Chinese motivated white workers' opposition, but only in part.

European Americans in California united across the class spectrum to find much to dislike about the Chinese. The Chinese physical appearance, manner of dress, language, food, religion, and social customs led whites to describe them as heathens, childlike, lustful, and uncivilized.[77] Many of these criticisms were rooted in racial assumptions of the era. "Underlying the anti-Chinese movement was a larger campaign to impose and sustain white supremacy in the West," historian Erika Lee contends. "Californians had long envisioned their state to be an Edenic, unspoiled land where free labor might thrive." The Chinese threatened this vision. White Californians pronounced their views in 1876 when Congress dispatched a special committee to gauge public opinion on Chinese immigration. San Francisco attorney, and representative of that city's anti-Chinese association, Cameron H. King summed up the thoughts of many of the witnesses when he declared that the Chinese "spread loathsome diseases among our citizens, respect no laws, and acknowledge no God; who, filthy, vicious, ignorant, depraved, and criminal are a standing menace to our free institutions, and an ever-threatening danger to our republican form of government." Introducing the twelve hundred pages of testimony, the committee concluded that "there is not sufficient brain capacity in the Chinese race to furnish motive power for self-government. Upon the point of morals, there is no Aryan or European race which is not far superior to the Chinese as a class."[78] Later, in 1879, President Rutherford B. Hayes added his opinion to the growing consensus on the "Chinese Problem." The present "Chinese invasion," he argued, was "pernicious and should be discouraged. Our experience in dealing with the weaker races—the Negroes and Indians—is not encouraging. I would consider with favor any suitable measures to discourage the Chinese from coming to our shores."[79] The economic and racial arguments of the 1870s connected to decades-old attitudes about the Chinese "other" to form a growing consensus among whites in California and beyond.[80]

Congress addressed the matter in 1882, passing the Chinese Exclusion Act to restrict Chinese laborers from entering the country for ten years. Renewed in the Geary Act of 1892 and again in the Immigration Act of 1902, exclusion became a fixture of U.S. immigration policy until 1943. The exclusion period inaugurated what Erika Lee calls "gatekeeping ideology" in American history. "Americans learned to define 'American-ness' by excluding and containing foreign-ness. Through the admission and exclusion of foreigners, the United States both asserted its sovereignty and reinforced its identity as a nation."[81] Americans established a clear precedent of racializing undesirable immigrants and mounting a campaign to keep them away from American shores, all in the name of protecting the Republic.

Reflecting on the Chinese Exclusion Act in 1891, Henry Cabot Lodge confirmed the logic of gatekeeping. He said the Chinese had represented "a flood of low-class labor which would absolutely destroy good rates of wages among American workingmen" and that "threatened to lower the quality of American citizenship." The act might have been contested originally but contained "wisdom of which everybody now admits."[82] Exclusion had contained one threat, but new ones emerged in the 1890s for which the Chinese Exclusion Act served as a model for racializing newcomers and expanding the regimes of restriction.

With the Irish inching their way toward acceptance and the Chinese largely excluded, the focus shifted to immigrants from southern and eastern Europe. These transformations closely paralleled the thinking of Francis Amasa Walker, a professor of political economy at Yale and the superintendent of the 1870 and 1880 federal censuses. His work with the census put him in a unique position to popularize the notion that the immigration of allegedly racially inferior people brought with it the threat of racial degeneration in the United States.[83] By the 1890s, Walker had shifted his animus from the Irish to the "vast hordes of foreign immigrants" from southern and eastern Europe. He worried that these newer arrivals, whom he termed the "unlucky, the thriftless, the worthless," represented people who had "thus far remained hopelessly upon the lowest plane of industrial life," were "degraded below our utmost conceptions," and had "the least [hope for] possible adaptation to our political institutions and social life."[84] They were, Walker proclaimed in the *Atlantic Monthly* in 1896, "beaten men from beaten races; representing the worst failures in the struggle for existence." He used these ideas of racial inferiority to forecast doom for the United States. The very presence of the newcomers represented a "contact so foul and loathsome" that it shrunk Anglo-Saxon numbers and motivated native-born Americans to limit their family size. Walker's ideas formed the basis for the "race suicide" theories that emanated from the presidency of Theodore Roosevelt and found their way into the scholarly writings of pioneering sociologist Edward A. Ross.[85]

Fears about southern and eastern Europeans spread in the United States, as politicians, government officials, academics, and some leading Progressive reformers questioned the immigrants' desirability in the United States. Henry Cabot Lodge, who would later carry the agenda of the Immigration Restriction League in Congress, wrote in 1891 that "the shifting of the sources of immigration is unfavorable, and is bringing to the country people whom it is very difficult to assimilate and who do not promise well for the standard of civilization in the United States—a matter as serious as the effect on the labor market." In 1903 the U.S. immigration commissioner reflected the culmination of decades of assessing the desirability of immigrant workers when he wrote that they were "generally undesirable because unintelligent, of low vitality, of poor physique, able to perform only the cheapest kind of manual labor . . . and unfitted mentally or morally for good citizenship."[86] These arguments ultimately coalesced in Madison Grant's best-selling 1916 ode to racial hierarchy and white supremacy, *The Passing of the Great Race*.

The fears about unrestricted immigration in general, and immigration from southern and eastern Europe in particular, motivated Congress to explore new restrictive legislation during the early 1920s. They not only drew from the ideas of Madison Grant, but also solicited testimony and expertise from witnesses that ranged from general restrictionists such as John Trevor, a New York lawyer and associate of Grant, to avowed eugenicists such as Harry Laughlin, the director of the Eugenics Records Office at Cold Spring Harbor, New York.[87] Witnesses espoused racial theories during their testimony that posited the superiority of "Nordics" over the "Alpine" and "Mediterranean" races of southern and eastern Europe. After several decades of persistent worrying about the deteriorating quality of immigrants, their supposed inability to Americanize, and the threats of "race suicide," Congress passed the National Origins Quota Act of 1924 that virtually closed the gates against all immigrants who did not hail from northern and western Europe.[88]

This racial theorizing and the immigration restriction movements of the Progressive Era had a direct connection to the industrial accident crisis. As immigrants were "slotted" into the dirtiest, most dangerous jobs, anti-immigrant sentiments were mapped to workers' bodies. Native-born Americans could more easily dismiss the significance of industrial accidents if they primarily afflicted workers who were already deemed questionable for inclusion into the Republic. Americans who held more extreme anti-immigrant views could interpret immigrant deaths without concern because the industrial accidents removed a plague from the body politic. A dead worker did not need Americanizing, nor could he or she contribute to the racial replacement of "old" American stock with "new" immigrant blood.

The men who ran the country's industrial enterprises rarely supported calls for immigration restriction. They valued immigrants as a cheap source of labor that was, they assumed, more tractable than American-born workers. The opening of the West through the construction of the transcontinental railroad provides a good example of employers' attitudes toward immigrants and how ideas about race contributed to dangerous working conditions. To keep pace with the predominantly Irish track labor gangs working from the East, the Central Pacific Railway began to hire thousands of Chinese immigrants in 1865. Their motives were mixed. Company officials viewed the Chinese as a competent, tractable labor supply that could help control labor costs. As governor of California, Leland Stanford at first tried to exclude the Chinese—the "dregs of Asia," as he referred to them.[89] He had a change of heart as president of Central Pacific. Stanford considered the Chinese as "quiet, peaceable, industrious, economical—ready and apt to learn all the different kinds of work required in railroad building."[90] Superintendent Charles Crocker echoed Stanford: "They prove nearly equal to white men in the amount of labor they perform, and are much more reliable" because there was "no danger of strikes among them." Indeed, he used Chinese workers to discipline the white workforce. "We'll let you go and hire nobody but them," Crocker told white workers who protested the hiring of Chinese laborers.[91] Crocker's assessment of the Chinese being "nearly equal to white men" was reflected in the wage structure of the Central Pacific. Chinese workers earned approximately two-thirds the wages of whites, which historian Alexander Saxton estimates as saving the Central Pacific nearly five and half million dollars over three years. On payday railroad management insisted on paying Chinese labor gangs one lump sum rather than individual wages.[92]

The race to build the transcontinental railroads and managers' racial attitudes toward the workers combined to justify terribly dangerous jobs. Chinese handled explosives, traversed perilous cliff faces, and used their bodies where wooden supports were called for. Hoping to claim generous government subsidies for miles of track built, the Central Pacific forced its Chinese laborers to work through the winter of 1866. The extreme conditions featured snowdrifts more than sixty feet tall where workers lived and worked in tunnels underneath. The dangerous work turned deadly. "The snow slides carried away our camps and we lost a good many men in those slides," Central Pacific's head of construction, James Stobridge, remarked. "Many of them we did not find until the next season when the snow melted."[93] Stobridge's comments revealed broader attitudes about laborers in the nineteenth century. Managers regarded laborers in general, and the racialized bodies of African Americans, the Chinese, Italians, and Slavs in particular, as expendable.

From the completion of the transcontinental railroad to the end of the nineteenth century, industrialists and managers crafted a tradition of using ideas of inferiority to justify exploitation. Part of this was prefigured in the history of slavery that carried over into the New South. Hard, dangerous work was deemed "Negro labor" throughout the period.[94] The convict-lease system that developed in the South during the Jim Crow era led to horrendous working conditions and shortened life expectancies and produced high fatality rates for African Americans swept up in the pseudolegal nets of whites hungry for cheap labor.[95] Connections between race and management were integral to the management techniques of industrializing America. "Far from reducing labor to abstract and raceless inputs into the labor-process," historians Elizabeth Esch and David Roediger compellingly argue, "capital and management helped to reproduce racial differences over long stretches of US history and divide workers in ways that compromised labor's efforts to address race- or class-inequalities."[96] This insight has clear implications for explaining the industrial accident crisis. Managers felt justified in slotting groups they deemed inferior, such as the Irish and southern and eastern Europeans, into unskilled work that represented the "dirtiest and most despised urban US jobs."[97] As scientific racism developed, academics provided additional claims to link race and aptitude for work. Sociologist E. A. Ross claimed, "The Slavs are immune to certain kinds of dirt. They can stand what would kill a white man." The body of so-called knowledge created by Ross, Madison Grant, and others helped justify labor segmentation that exposed immigrants to the worst of industrial working conditions.[98] Employers could rationalize high fatalities, just as a member of the 1910 census team did, by suggesting the "best interests of society will be served by permitting the least valuable members . . . to be the victims."[99] These comments showed a contemptuous disregard for immigrant lives and diminished working people's contributions to industrial America.

It would be overly simplistic to suggest that only upper- and middle-class attitudes toward newer immigrants contributed to high fatality rates in U.S. industries. Native-born workers and English-speaking immigrants drew many of the same conclusions. They charged eastern European immigrants with being intellectually inferior or just plain ignorant. Steelworker John Griswold, a Scotch-Irish furnace boss who had decided to stay in the mills even though most of his Irish friends had found other employment, expressed his dismay at working with the newer immigrants. "They don't seem like men to me hardly," he confessed. "They can't talk United States." Their unfamiliarity with English could lead to acrimony. "You tell them something and they just look and say 'Me no fustay, me no fustay,'" Griswold noted.[100] Language barriers could lead to accidents in the mills. In *Blood on the Forge*, a novel documenting three African American migrants' journey to work in Pennsylvania's steel district, William Attaway portrays a similar sentiment:

"Hunkies don't talk nothin' but gobbler talk. Don't understand nothin' else neither. Foreman tell one old feller who was workin' right next to me to put leather over his chest. Foreman might jest as well been whistlin', 'cause when the heat come down there that hunky lays with a chest like a scrambled egg."[101] Attaway's work of proletarian fiction was not entirely an invention of the novelist's mind. Coroner reports from Allegheny County document fatalities attributed, in part, to communication breakdowns between English-speaking foremen and non-English-speaking immigrants.[102] In examples such as these, English-speaking workers challenged immigrants' intelligence and blamed accidents on the immigrant rather than any number of other causes that may have contributed to the incidents. Views such as these undoubtedly contributed to how English-speaking workers viewed the deaths of newer immigrant coworkers.

Native-born Americans from across social classes joined together to transform a word that originally referred to Hungarians into the racial epithet *hunky* to separate native-born and northern European workers from southern and eastern Europeans. It originated from immigrants' propensity for sustaining injury, or getting "hunked," on the job. The term defined new immigrants as both "physically strong [and] self sufficient," but also "intrinsically dull and stupid." "Thus," historian David Roediger writes, "'hunkie' described both the brawny and the broken, the inferior and the damaged."[103] The epithet influenced how managers and native-born workers interpreted eastern Europeans killed on the job. One foreman, for example, separated his list of industrial accidents for a month into two categories: "five men and twelve hunkies."[104] Discrimination embedded in *hunky* echoed broader currents of scientific racism en vogue in academic circles, as proffered by social scientists such as E. A. Ross and government bureaucrats like Francis Amasa Walker and Frank Julian Warne.[105] Some Americans viewed a foreign-born worker "as a human draft animal whose brawn could be enlisted to carry out the designs of the Anglo-Saxon intellect."[106]

Cultural representations of work and workers were key components of the industrial accident crisis. Middle-class Americans and some workers celebrated dangerous workplaces as proving grounds of masculinity. The widespread belief that deadly and disfiguring work accidents disproportionately impacted people of color and the so-called new immigrants meshed with broader notions of superior and inferior peoples. These attitudes combined with the lack of systematic reporting of workplace fatalities and the acceptance of the inherent risks of industrial production. Many Americans in the latter nineteenth century did not recognize the full extent of the industrial accident crisis.

Cultures of Reform: Creating Vulnerable Bodies

The turn of the twentieth century marked the beginning of an era when a cacophony of voices vied for the authority to raise awareness about the industrial accident crisis and provide solutions. Cultural norms and representations of work that had emerged during the era of industrialization came under closer scrutiny, as reformers sought to educate the public on the costs of workplace accidents. They turned to analogies with warfare. The "total number of casualties suffered by our industrial army in one year is equal to the average annual casualties of our Civil War, plus those of the Philippine war, plus those of the Russian and Japanese war," Social Gospel reformer and president of the American Institute of Social Service (AISS) Josiah Strong declared. "*Think of carrying on three such wars, at the same time, world without end!*" These astounding estimates demanded action for the likes of Strong and other reformers. The problem was, according to the *Independent* magazine, "The easy-going citizen reads of this slaughter with hardly a shudder. He accepts it as a necessary part of the daily struggle for bread."[107] Representations of work and the meanings mapped to workers' bodies that had developed during the nineteenth century had been used to justify the cost of economic development while facilitating public apathy. Reformers set out to combat public indifference by expanding social awareness of the problem, mobilizing public assumptions to pass protective legislation, and creating new narratives of work to press for safety.

Workers, of course, did not need such an education. They worked daily in the environments that produced the staggering statistics that middle-class reformers cited. They knew the dangers involved with industrial production. They were steeped in the traditions of the male-breadwinner ideology and the independence that could be derived from a fair day's work for a fair day's wage. The AFL worked within the boundaries of these ideas, as Samuel Gompers and other union leaders campaigned to reform employer liability laws. They hoped to tip the scales of justice in favor of workers by revising tort law so that workers seeking compensation for debilitating or deadly work accidents could receive a fair hearing. Modifying liability laws would increase their chances of receiving compensation, while also preserving the courtroom as a democratic space to confront the power relations enveloping modern workplaces. Workers relished the opportunity of using the witness stand as a secular pulpit to rail against dangerous working conditions and expose callous employers. Once reformed, the AFL believed, the legal system could empower workers, preserve their masculine independence, and bring a measure of economic justice—all without inviting the meddlesome involvement of the state.[108]

On this last point, keeping the state from interfering in labor relations, employers and the AFL were in tacit agreement.[109] They disagreed, however, on the role of the legal system. Employers viewed the courtroom as an undesirable venue for discussing accidents. They feared that crafty lawyers would depict manufacturers as predatory consumers of labor power who dismissed the human costs of industrial production. Workers' stories could play to the heartstrings of sympathetic jurors. The resulting verdicts could, and sometimes did, saddle a company with a costly settlement and tarnish the firm's public image. Such concerns motivated U.S. Steel, under the leadership of Elbert H. Gary, to inaugurate the company's pioneering Safety First program in 1906. The goal of the program was to promote safety in steel manufacturing and prevent accidents in the workplace. Accident prevention would keep workers off the witness stand and deny lawyers the opportunity to vilify the largest corporation in the world. In an unanticipated benefit, improved safety could also improve profits. Employers acted more out of self-interest to combat the accident crisis than concern for workers' lives.[110]

Although the American Federation of Labor and some of the nation's largest corporations offered solutions to combat workplace injuries, they did not lead the charge for workplace safety. On this issue, like many others during the Progressive Era, middle-class reformers angled for positions of power and influence. Josiah Strong, Florence Kelley, the members of the Pittsburgh Survey (especially Crystal Eastman), William Hard, and adherents to the Wisconsin Idea such as economist John R. Commons considered themselves working in the interest of a broader public good. The reform efforts to improve safety that emanated from this diverse cast resembled the broader Progressive Era itself.[111] Reformers came from an array of backgrounds and employed a variety of tactics to achieve their goals. Despite the variety of tactics and arguments, they worked toward a common goal. They confronted the notion, rooted in laissez-faire and social Darwinist ideas, that work accidents were the result of individual choice, inevitable, or solely the cause of careless workers. They sought to prick the public's social conscience and prove that a well-organized agenda of safety reform and new laws could lead to healthier, safer work environments.

Reformers first felt the need to amass a body of knowledge from which to educate the public. Private organizations like Strong's American Institute of Social Service, the American Association for Labor Legislation, and the National Consumers' League (NCL) exemplified these techniques. The AISS was formed in 1898 and worked to establish a clearinghouse of information on the main problems of the age by collecting data and establishing an international information network.[112] For two weeks in February 1907, the AISS hosted an Exposition of Safety Devices and Industrial Hygiene that brought awareness to accidents and methods for preventing them. The event attracted attention in newspapers and periodicals, as journalists reproduced Strong's claims about the severity of the problem and held the assumptions that facilitated America's accident crisis under the lens of scrutiny.[113] "The attitude of so many of our manufacturers, who maintain that a man foolish enough or careless enough to be injured in the pursuit of his vocation, deserves no sympathy and gets merely what he deserves, has been a great obstacle to the furtherance of industrial safeguarding of American workers," declared the *Scientific American*. The exposition showed how European countries had erected safeguards to diminish workplace accidents. Americans could do no less than keep up with their overseas rivals.[114] Some participants left the exposition with different ideas about the nature of industrial accidents. Instead of blaming workers, employers' justification for injuries seemed "more than shortsighted; it is almost negatively criminal."[115]

A two-week exposition was fleeting. Industrial work had become central to the U.S. economy. A brief display of safety suggestions and a flurry of news reports were perhaps a step in the right direction, but did not go far enough in confronting the assumptions and ideologies that framed the social relations of production. To effect change, reformers had to confront, or in some instances co-opt, the prevailing representations of work and workers. Through exposés and social-science investigations, journalists such as William Hard, social researchers such as those affiliated with the Pittsburgh Survey, and reform-minded academics and politicians recast the narrative of work and offered a new representation of workers. The careless and foolish workers were refashioned into victims of industrial violence. The worker's body that was impervious to pain and benefited from strenuous labor became a vulnerable body plagued by fatigue and threatened by overwork. Women became particularly susceptible to the rigors of work in reformers' eyes, but men were also key subjects. Vulnerable male workers created instability in communities due to lost wages and diminished productivity. Women were left to cope as best they could without male breadwinners. Children adjusted to life with a permanently disabled father or with merely memories. Reformers mobilized this new representation of the worker's body to call for the protective apparatus of state regulation and legislation that was informed by experts.[116]

Protecting women workers became an early battleground for combating the harmful aspects of freedom of contract and the individualistic ethos of the age. Working first in Illinois and later in New York as the National Consumers' League executive director, Florence Kelley led the charge. Her father, William "Pig Iron" Kelley, reportedly told her, "My generation has created industry, and your generation must humanize it."[117] The problem was identifying the proper method. Employers, the American Federation of Labor, and the freedom-of-contract doctrine erected roadblocks to passing laws that affected men in industry. Recognizing the forces arrayed against them, Kelley and other reformers hoped to use legislation for women as an "entering wedge" that would advance protective laws for all workers.[118] To be successful, they had to present a compelling argument that justified wielding the police power of the state to improve working life for women.

To press their cause, Kelley and the National Consumers' League emphasized women's vulnerability as workers and mothers. Women workers tended to be young, low paid, and unskilled, without the benefit of trade unions to negotiate on their behalf. They were, in the words of a club woman in 1910, "almost as helpless as the children in obtaining redress from oppression." Working mothers faced the classic double burden of combining factory work with household responsibilities. They were innately weaker than men, in reformers' eyes, physically and politically. The image of vulnerable mothers was a centerpiece to their argument for protective legislation. "The woman is worth more to society in dollars and cents as the mother of healthy children than as the swiftest labeler of cans," one reformer declared in a 1910 study of women workers.[119] Injuries and overwork could produce birth defects or lead women into prostitution, which threatened the welfare of the entire community. To solve these ills and protect the greater good, legislation was required.[120]

During the 1890s and early 1900s, the reformers' efforts advanced in fits and starts. State legislatures passed protective legislation only to have it challenged in court. Kelley's efforts as a factory inspector in Illinois led to an eight-hour law for women and children in 1893. Incensed at state interference, the Illinois Association of Manufacturers challenged the law, bringing it to the state supreme court. In *Ritchie v. People of Illinois* (1895), the court overturned the law, ruling that "the mere fact of sex will not alone justify the exercise of the 'police power' for the purpose of limiting the right of a woman to make contracts."[121] In the case of *People v. Williams* (1907), the New York Court of Appeals agreed. A factory inspector's discovery of Katie Mead still toiling at a book bindery at 10:20 at night led to charges against the employer for violating the state's law prohibiting women's work after 9:00 P.M. The court thought freedom of contract trumped the ill effects of overwork on women. "Under our laws men and women now stand alike in their constitutional rights, and there is no warrant for making any discrimination between them with respect to the liberty of person, or of contract," Chief Judge Gray opined. This reasoning led the court to rule that prohibitions on hours of work were unconstitutional. A woman should be "entitled to enjoy . . . her freedom to work for whom she pleases, where she pleases and as long as she pleases."[122]

Rulings such as these caused reformers to redouble their efforts. They repeatedly argued, as Josephine Goldmark did in 1912, that freedom of contract was a "legal fiction" because workers had little power in determining the conditions of their employment. Echoing a decades-old refrain from labor reformers, Goldmark proclaimed, "The alternative is to work or starve. To refuse means to be dismissed. Modern industry has reduced 'freedom of contract' to a paper privilege, a mere figure of rhetoric."[123] The state-by-state successes and failures represented the limitations of the federal system in reformers' eyes. Successes in states such as Pennsylvania and Nebraska were countered by defeats in Illinois and New York. In particular, the *Lochner v. New York* decision in 1905 provided a clear testament to the lingering power of the liberty-of-contract philosophy, as the court struck down a ten-hour law for bakers.[124] Reformers needed a precedent at the federal level to legitimate states' efforts.

The NCL's opportunity to use the vulnerable body and win a national precedent came from Oregon. Curt Muller, the owner of Grand Laundry, appealed his conviction of violating the state's 1903 ten-hour law that limited women's working hours in laundries, factories, and other places that operated mechanical equipment. As the case headed to the U.S. Supreme Court, Oregon's attorneys asked for the assistance of NCL officers Josephine Goldmark and Florence Kelley. Goldmark turned to her brother-in-law, the well-known attorney Louis Brandeis. Together, Goldmark and Brandeis prepared what came to be known as the Brandeis Brief. Brandeis and the NCL recognized the key features of the debate over shorter-hours laws that had developed between 1895 and 1907. State courts, such as in Pennsylvania and Nebraska, upheld laws where women were deemed to possess particular physical limitations as compared to men. Where courts focused on the "liberty of contract," judges routinely overturned shorter-hours laws. The path to success in the *Muller* case, therefore, seemed clear for the NCL. Brandeis had to convince the justices that women were a class apart from men, that they were weaker by nature, and that they warranted the protection of the state.

The Brandeis Brief presented 113 pages of sociological data, medical hypotheses, and legal precedent on these points. "Long hours of labor are dangerous for women primarily because of their special physical organization," Brandeis wrote. "In structure and function women are fundamentally weaker than men in all that makes for endurance: in muscular strength, in nervous energy, in the powers of persistent attention and application. Overwork, therefore, which strains endurance to the utmost, is more disastrous to the health of women than of men, and entails upon them more lasting injury." Brandeis and Goldmark culled stacks of medical studies, social investigations, and state reports to reinforce their points. Factory inspectors reported seeing "one by one girls drop out and die" from overwork. But the threats to women's bodies had a broader impact as well. Women working long hours had an "evil effect" on "the general welfare," Brandeis asserted, pointing to women's reproductive and mothering roles. "When the health of women has been injured by long hours, not only is the working efficiency of the community impaired, but the deterioration is handed down to succeeding generations. Infant mortality rises, while the children of married working women, who survive, are injured by inevitable neglect," he warned. Far from being an issue limited in scope to a single woman and her individual liberty, Brandeis argued, overwork was a broader problem that required the protection of the state. "The overwork of future mothers thus directly attacks the welfare of the nation," he concluded.[125] Working with the NCL, Brandeis had presented the vulnerable body of women workers to the Supreme Court.

With arguments for both sides concluded, the justices faced a decision. They could extend the logic of the *Lochner* ruling and accept the argument of Muller's attorneys: liberty of contract knew no distinction based on sex. Or they could establish a new precedent based on the Brandeis Brief's assertions that women were biologically inferior to men and that protection was justified due to the implications for the preservation of the welfare of the nation. Writing for the majority, Justice Brewer made clear that the Court found Brandeis's arguments of women's physical inequality compelling. "That woman's physical structure and the performance of maternal functions place her at a disadvantage in the struggle for subsistence is obvious," he wrote. Upholding the Oregon law would help ensure "healthy mothers," who were "essential to vigorous offspring." Therefore, the state's concern for women was justified, because "the physical well-being of woman becomes an object of public interest and care in order to preserve the strength and vigor of the race."[126] As the NCL had hoped, the *Muller v. Oregon* decision blazed a path for protective legislation, even while reaffirming the stereotypes of women as the weaker, and therefore the rightly subordinate, sex. Nineteen states passed shorter-hours laws between 1908 and 1917, and twenty more enhanced existing statutes.[127] The wedge for humanizing capitalism had been inserted. But it remained to be seen if protective legislation for women and the representation of workers' vulnerability would be the effective wedge that would open the space necessary to win gains for men as well as women.

For men, the debate was not about shorter-hours laws. Reformers hoped to revise employer liability laws or enact industrial insurance to stem the tide of workplace accidents. Some progressives marshaled the specter of a vulnerable male worker's body. Few did this better than Crystal Eastman. In her landmark 1910 study, *Work-Accidents and the Law*, a volume of the Pittsburgh Survey, she wielded the full array of tools in a reformer's arsenal to powerfully convey the human costs of wage work. Her social laboratory was Allegheny County, Pennsylvania, and the accident record produced from July 1906 to June 1907. Eastman's findings were grim: 526 fatalities for the year and more than 500 injuries for the three months of April, May, and June 1907. "This steady march of injury and death means suffering, grief, bitterness, thwarted hopes incalculable," she wrote. Eastman's mission was to explain the causes and consequences of workplace accidents. Her data, especially the visually striking Death Calendar in Industry, showed that dangerous workplaces were not isolated events, but were rather endemic to modern production. She identified three broad explanatory factors. About one-third of accidents could be chalked up as unavoidable due to the hazards of work. Another third could be attributed to individual actions because, Eastman declared, some "workmen are fools." The final third represented a form of depraved indifference. Accidents in this last category resulted from "an insufficient provision for the safety of workmen on the part of their employers."[128] Categorizing accidents in this fashion allowed Eastman to challenge the prevailing assumptions about the nature of accidents. Her work also led to the conclusion that accidents were a problem of social economy, as well as of justice, that required the "legislative interference" of the state.[129]

Eastman did not merely present statistics to make her point. "These things cannot be reckoned, they must be felt," she argued. To make the public feel the pain caused by workplace accidents, she documented the impact of fatalities and injuries through statistical analysis, case studies, and solemn photographs. She proved that accidents caused a ripple effect of hardship throughout the community, as the injury or death of a breadwinner created economic hardships for survivors. Widows were forced into jobs that meant "hard work, long hours, poor pay, and in most cases children neglected." A significant portion of the estimated 470 children left fatherless by industrial accidents left school in pursuit of work to make up for lost wages.[130] Photographic evidence provided faces to humanize the statistics. Workers missing hands, arms, and legs, some of them situated with their wives and children, looked grimly into the photographer's lens.[131] They bore silent witness to the dangers of industrial production and the families impacted by workplace accidents. Eastman's approach was not entirely unique, but it brought together the journalistic arts of muckrakers like William Hard, the social-science skills of academics like John R. Commons, the human-interest stories of novelists like Upton Sinclair, and the striking photography of Lewis Hine, who was behind the camera for several of the photographs she included. It was a piece of Progressive Era literature par excellence. Eastman joined with others to depict vulnerable worker bodies that needed protection for their own good and for the good of the community. The solution lay in the apparatus of the state—legislative reform.

Eastman added her voice to a growing chorus that established middle-class reformers as the proper agents of change to work through the state to implement reforms. These voices, along with those of employers and, eventually, the AFL, produced the workmen's compensation laws that spread state by state across the nation after a spate of disasters that stretched from the Monongah, West Virginia, mine explosion in 1907; to the Cherry, Illinois, mine fire in 1909; to the Triangle Shirtwaist Factory Fire in 1911. These accidents left more than 600 workers dead and provided stark reminders of workers' vulnerability during the Progressive Era.

Representing workers as vulnerable bodies in need of protection provided a key narrative of Progressive Era reform. Women workers served as the test case. Reformers' efforts sparked a national debate about the nature of industrial work and its dangers. They put the nation on a course that would ultimately, over several decades and in conjunction with changing technology and broader shifts in manufacturing, make traveling to work more dangerous than work itself. Yet it was also clear that middle-class progressives mobilized representations of workers and created new ones, such as the vulnerable body. Through industrial commissions and investigations, they sought to structure the narrative of industrial work toward their own ends. They empowered themselves, state agencies, and social-science institutions to speak for workers and represent their interests rather than creating the conditions that would empower workers to represent themselves.

These distinctions became clear through the work of the United States Commission on Industrial Relations, which investigated the source of labor tensions from 1913 to 1915. The commission eventually divided into two factions. Frank Walsh, a Kansas City attorney and chair of the committee, led a group of commissioners who hoped to use the investigation to give workers a voice to explain their hopes, desires, and grievances against the industrial system. The opposing faction, led primarily by John R. Commons, believed the commission should proceed as an investigation organized along the lines of a scholarly social-science study. According to this model, Commons and his cohort would organize the parameters of the study, choose the evidence, and produce results that they were happy with. The difference between the two approaches was that Walsh hoped to empower workers as a key group constitutive of American democracy in the twentieth century—perhaps, as historian Shelton Stromquist suggests, even leading to a new politics of labor. Commons, on the other hand, hoped to embolden state institutions and educated social scientists to offer solutions. Samuel Gompers vented his frustration at being brushed aside by the likes of Commons in the pages of the *American Federationist*. Workers were "not bugs to be examined under the lenses of a microscope by the 'intellectuals' on a sociological slumming tour," he fumed.[132] As Gompers's comment suggests, the Industrial Commission exposed the tensions between middle-class reformers and workers, as each group sought the power to shape the cultural politics of the industrial era.

Cultures of Protest: Workers' Resistance in the Machine Age

To the cultures of order, progress, work, and reform, working people created a counterculture of protest and resistance that sought to give different meanings to their lives and deaths. They argued that the working conditions slowly dehumanized the great multitude of men, women, and youth that provided the labor power.[133] While industrialists proclaimed the benefits of the factory and "labor saving" machinery, workers testified about intense paces, long hours, and hazardous conditions. Some workers despaired that the free-labor vision and the inspiring flame of republicanism were being snuffed. Instead of free and independent citizens, industrial capitalism produced wage slaves. They felt the iron heel of owners directly. "In the mad rush for wealth and political sinecure, humanity and morality have been forgotten; 'labor' has been humiliated and trampled in the mud," a group of labor organizations declared on July 4, 1886.[134] The International Working People's Association called industrial capitalism an "unjust, insane, and murderous" system.[135] Treating workers as mere tools of the production process raised the ire of the producing classes across the country. They did not accept the aspects of industrialization that threatened their sense of place in the Republic. After all, a dead body could not reap the benefits of increased production.

Workers did not passively accept the reorganization of work and the new regimes of discipline. They developed strategies to slow the pace—what David Montgomery calls "the stint"—or create moments when they might steal a moment's respite.[136] Welsh-born miner Tom Benyan called a form of the stint the secret to a long life: "Oh, they can't kill you with work if you have enough sense to go slow."[137] They also developed habits to blunt the effects of hazardous working conditions, long hours, and repetitive tasks. Brassworkers consumed whiskey and beer to "drown" the "breathing of the vapors" that pervaded their workplaces.[138] They were not alone. Workers in other industries turned to alcohol as a coping mechanism to shield their bodies and minds from hazardous and stultifying working conditions.[139]

Workers also turned to labor unions and radical politics to combat the industrial regimes of discipline employers hoped to erect to police their bodies. Throughout the late nineteenth century, labor reformers and trade unionists offered counterarguments to employers. Shorter-hours movements sought to reclaim greater control over their lives.[140] The Knights of Labor posed one of the most cogent challenges by forming coalitions around a shorter-hours movement in the 1880s. Their rallying cry, "Eight hours for work, eight hours for rest, and eight hours for what we will," provided a forceful declaration for greater control over their own lives. The Knights also challenged the social Darwinian assumptions that pervaded much of the capitalist arguments about the superiority of competition. When they proclaimed, "An injury to one is the concern of all," they made a powerful argument for solidarity and mutualism over individualism. They claimed dignity for the individual as part of a larger community.[141]

George E. McNeill, a member of the Knights and later a vocal labor reformer, cast the struggle firmly in terms of the body. He criticized working and living conditions that produced "the poor, ignorant, physically and mentally, and sometimes morally, deformed, unskilled worker." He wanted the labor movement to create new conditions that would facilitate "a well-built, fully equipped manhood."[142]

There is no doubt that workers resisted the industrial-era work discipline or that they developed arguments that countered the prevailing wisdom among capitalists. However, before World War I, they were largely unsuccessful in curbing the soaring casualty figures of industrialization. In part, their failure can be attributed to the blood-soaked pages of U.S. labor history. Whenever workers presented a bold challenge to employer control, they received rough treatment. The key confrontations include the 1877 railroad strike, the Haymarket Affair of 1886, Homestead in 1892, the Pullman Boycott of 1894, and the Ludlow Massacre of 1914. Numerous other clashes led to bloodshed. In each circumstance, employers called on the state to regulate and discipline workers' bodies beyond the workplace. Coercion, intimidation, and violence helped limit workers' effectiveness at resisting the reorganization of work and the new regulations and discipline imposed on their bodies. While employers and workers clashed over control over the work process, the casualties of industrialization continued to mount.

The cultures of industrialization shaped how Americans interpreted industrial work, which contributed to redefining the meanings of working people's lives and deaths. Cultures of order and progress served to marginalize workers' contributions to the economy and obscure their sacrifices. Cultures of work created representations of work and workers' bodies that celebrated risk and masculinity. Cultures of reform and protest demonstrated the contested terrain of workers' identities with middle-class reformers portraying the working classes as vulnerable and in need of protection. These crosscurrents of industrial America motivated working people to use the space of death to reflect on the meanings of their lives and deaths. Examining working people's rituals of death and dying adds another venue—to complement the shop floor, union hall, picket line, and neighborhood—to suggest how working people negotiated the changes unleashed by industrialization.

2   The Power of the Dead's Place

Chicago's Cemeteries, Social Conflict, and Cultural Construction, 1873–1913

The nature of the industrial accident crisis produced particular politics of death in which a number of groups—workers, middle-class reformers, politicians, lawyers, judges, and employers—competed to define the meaning of workers' deaths. The evolution of workers' responses to the violent, often sudden, death of the industrial era took many forms. Seeking a dignified burial was one.

The historical development of Chicago cemeteries serves as a case study to examine how broader tensions in industrial society were reflected in the processes of death and burial. Cultures of industrialization that had emerged to make sense of the sweeping economic changes of the nineteenth century found expressions in the landscapes of cemeteries. The wealthy oftentimes sought to control their burial spaces in similar ways as they had exerted influence over their business and civic interactions. Their cemetery plots projected symbolism of progress and order, while their appetite for real estate threatened to marginalize common people. The working classes of Chicago also turned to cemeteries to extend the terrain of contemplating the consequences of industrialization. The history of their struggles to find dignified burial space reflects that cultures of protest during the age spread beyond union organizing, strike activity, and political agitation.

Studying Chicago cemeteries reveals two important aspects of working people's experiences with death during the industrial era. First, it shows how diverse groups in the city turned to cemeteries as spaces to extend the debates of the age. Chicagoans projected notions about order, progress, and dignity through their cemetery policies, the monuments they erected, and the policies that dictated who could be buried where. Chicago's cemeteries were not unique in this respect. Other booming industrial cities negotiated similar tensions.

Second, the history of Chicago's cemeteries left a legacy that radiated far beyond the city. After the Civil War, workers engaged in a creative process of developing class-based rituals and attitudes toward death that sometimes overlapped with and sometimes challenged middle- and upper-class practices. Workers began to think more carefully about ensuring the dignity of a deceased worker due, in part, to the dehumanizing effects of industrialization. They also became more aware of the potential of funerals, memorials, and monuments to serve as another tool for educating working people. The Haymarket Affair provided a key marker in the development of workers' practices to commemorate the dead. The contested memory of the executed men, the expansive funeral, and the annual commemorations taught valuable lessons about the importance of funerals and burial spaces for ensuring dignity and using death to create a network of solidarity that could be a bridge to link the living and the dead. Labor leaders did not necessarily have to agree with the ideologies of the dead men to observe the value of such practices. The 1880s therefore became an important transition decade in the development of a working-class politics of death. Workers killed during the bloody battles of the 1870s accelerated the momentum of ritual creation such that workers killed in the clashes of the 1890s and early twentieth century were commemorated following scripts decades in the making. In important respects, the Haymarket legacy provided an important fulcrum toward new class-conscious burial practices, although it was not the first or the only one.

While perhaps unique in the pace of the changes, the city exhibited broader trends in industrialization, immigration, and urbanization that helped define U.S. history between the Civil War and World War I. The city's explosive growth was rooted, in part, in devastation. The Great Fire of 1871 reduced a large swath of the city to smoldering ruin. From these ashes, it rose phoenix-like to become the nation's second largest city by 1900. It earned sobriquets such as the "City of Big Shoulders" and the "City of the Century."[1] The city's rebuilt landscape featured hallmarks of industrialization that connected matters of work, life, and death. A peculiar battle for real estate, for example, accompanied the growth of one of the area's steel mills. Undertakers jockeyed for position on the street leading to the factory, each one trying to acquire a storefront closest to the gates. Their business acumen drove them to be nearest when accidents produced potential clients. Steelworkers passed these morbid vistas as they entered work, surely hoping the undertakers' services would not be needed.[2] Likewise, Chicagoans noticed that death traveled the streets of certain neighborhoods more often than others. One survey found that white hearses hauled babies through the streets of the stockyards district seven times more frequently than they did just a mile to the east, where wages and housing were better.[3] Regardless of the cause of death, Chicago's working people had to find a place to bury their dead.

Cemeteries played important roles in constituting the social and cultural landscape of the city. Burial grounds became urban spaces that reflected power relationships and the politics of death. The "ability to influence the production of space," geographer David Harvey notes, "is an important means to augment social power." Establishing rules for cemetery use, setting prices for burial lots, and controlling access to the city's cemeteries sparked clashes between diverse segments of the city's population. Some groups, such as Czechs and African Americans, used social confrontations as impetuses to organize their own burial spaces. Cemeteries also reflected what architectural historian Dolores Hayden calls "the power of place—the power of ordinary urban landscapes to nurture citizens' public memory, to encompass shared time in the form of shared territory."[4] As cultural places, cemeteries became repositories of meanings that combined various elements of people's lived experiences. They confirmed solidarities along lines of wealth, religion, and nationality. Cemeteries also exposed fissures in the late-nineteenth-century metropolis.

Chicago's cemeteries (see map), especially Graceland, Bohemian National, Forest Home, and Waldheim, reveal the ongoing relationships between class, religion, ethnicity, race, and urban space during the Gilded Age and Progressive Era. The burial spaces mirrored group affinities and schisms while also cementing them. That is, cemeteries both reflected and constituted elements in the creation of Chicago's diverse cultural and political landscape. Some cemeteries catered to the rich; others served the poor. Cemetery owners perpetuated discriminatory practices based on race and religion that impacted groups with large working-class constituencies who then sought creative solutions and brought legal challenges. One section of Waldheim Cemetery became a venerated space for working-class radicalism and a lesson for memorializing those who fought for the emancipation of the working classes.

The Cemetery in American History: The Rise of a Cultural Institution

Cemeteries acquired their place as important social and cultural spaces near midcentury, as attitudes toward death and burial evolved. During the colonial and early Republic eras, graveyards were places to be avoided, if possible, or endured as briefly as propriety would allow to bury a relative or acquaintance.

Before the 1830s, the family of the deceased washed the body and adorned it in a simple shroud. Religious and graveside services were often austere occasions where colonials and early citizens of the Republic reflected on the termination of the deceased's quest for salvation. Interment for city dwellers occurred in crowded, nondescript churchyard cemeteries amid the bustle of growing cities.[5] Many of the cemeteries, one critic complained, presented a view of "shapeless, ill-kept roads" and "a meaningless jumble of freakish, decaying headstones and dreary, moaning cedars, pines and spruces."[6] Few people cared about the landscape of death. The "dead [did] not care" about their surroundings, historian Neil Harris notes, "and the living—their eyes on a future life more glorious than any intimation of the terrestrial landscape—did not care either." As a frontier city with only a few thousand inhabitants, Chicago's citizens treated their dead in a similar fashion. Burials occurred in one of two burial grounds near Lake Michigan. The soil and terrain proved ill-suited to the purpose, and bodies sometimes refused to stay under the earth.[7]

Increasing urban populations in the North produced crowded graveyards and prompted calls for reform. Frequently "little more than stinking quagmires," the city graveyards elicited public health concerns and provided an obstacle to urban development.[8] City officials in New York City and elsewhere recommended creating "rural cemeteries" as early as the 1830s to develop a buffer from disease and to reclaim space for the living. Such concerns also surfaced in Chicago. In 1858 Chicago's sanitary superintendent, physician Joseph Rauch, worried that the proximity of the burial grounds to the city's water supply posed risks to public health.[9] The city council officially barred burial within the city limits by 1866.[10]

Evolving attitudes toward death also provoked calls for new burial spaces. People frequently complained about the "revolting" conditions of urban graveyards. In the 1820s, Washington Irving, author of the popular short stories "The Legend of Sleepy Hollow" and "Rip Van Winkle," recoiled at a grisly graveyard sculpture that represented the terror of death. Instead of invoking fear, he argued that "the grave should be surrounded by everything that might inspire tenderness and veneration for the dead, or that might win the living to virtue."[11] Fears of bodies contaminating urban environments and the desire to fundamentally reshape the landscape of death produced the rural cemetery movement in the middle of the nineteenth century and influenced the planning and implementation of Chicago-area cemeteries.

Advocates envisioned rural cemeteries providing places of beauty and tranquillity away from the commotion of the city. Visitors could escape the daily routines of urban life. Rural settings, organizers hoped, would facilitate interaction with nature while visitors paid respects for the dead and reflected on God.[12] Tasteful sculptures and monuments would add aesthetic appeal to provide tangible reminders of life and the nation's history; they might even foster patriotism. If executed well, contemporaries felt, the rural cemetery could inculcate morality and provide an outdoor "school of both religion and philosophy."[13] Established in 1831, Boston's Mount Auburn Cemetery led the movement toward rural cemeteries. It featured ambling footpaths that spread over seventy acres of undulating hills and flowing streams. In subsequent years, other cemeteries adopted features of the rural cemetery movement in cities across the Northeast and South.[14]

The proliferation of rural and landscape-park cemeteries transformed burial sites from forgotten spaces that colonial citizens treated with indifference, at best, into cultural institutions that played vital roles in lavish Victorian-era burial rituals. Thousands of visitors flocked to the cemeteries, treating them like "pastoral pleasure grounds."[15] Families purchased lots for their own and succeeding generations. Magazine and newspaper articles announced additions to the grounds and documented the unveiling of new monuments. Cemeteries like Mount Auburn provided spaces where visitors reflected on anxieties and came to terms with urban, industrial society. "Practical concerns such as overcrowded in-city burial grounds provided the catalyst [to rural cemeteries]," David Charles Sloane asserts, "but Americans were concerned about understanding the history of their communities and nation . . . and encouraging respect for the dead."[16] Many cemeteries in Chicago established in the last half of the nineteenth century were planned in the spirit of the rural cemetery movement. Graceland, Rosehill, the Bohemian National Cemetery, and Waldheim all featured parklike landscapes. These verdant vistas of death also reflected key urban areas divided along lines of class, religion, ethnicity, and race.[17]

Landscapes of Class: The Extremes of the Potter's Field and Graceland Cemetery

In many ways, nineteenth-century Chicago was a city of extremes. In boom times, an increasingly national economy consumed the city's McCormick reapers, Pullman palace cars, and the processed meat from the hulking packinghouses in the Union Stockyards. In lean times, especially the periodic economic downturns of the 1870s through the 1890s, armies of unemployed stalked the streets, looking for work. Mansions on Prairie Avenue stood in stark contrast to the crowded Italian tenements on Taylor Street or the ramshackle houses back of the yards. Yet neither millionaires nor working people could escape the stench and smoke that hovered over sections of the city. Nor could they escape death. Death, historian Joanna Bourke notes, "was a democratic fear: rich and poor alike trembled in the face of that eternal unknown."[18] Rich and poor may have shared similar fears of death, which established something of an equality of attitude between social classes, but there was less equality in the physical landscape of death. The last resting places of the bodies of the poor and rich inscribed symbols of economic difference on the city's landscape.

At one end of the spectrum lay the potter's field, the nondescript place where the city buried those without the financial means to provide for a funeral. Before 1911 the indigent were interred at the county's expense in the burial lot of the Cook County Cemetery at Dunning or in one of the common rows of other cemeteries. From 1911 to 1971, the county buried paupers in a county-owned plot at the Cook County Cemetery for the Indigent near Oak Forest Hospital of Cook County. Working people viewed such a burial with horror and went to great lengths to avoid such a fate, including spending accumulated savings and accruing debt. Poet Carl Sandburg, the great chronicler of turn-of-the-century Chicago, provided a glimpse of one stockyard worker's attempt to spare his daughter from a pauper's burial in his poem "The Right to Grief." He wrote:

> Now his three year old daughter
> Is in a white coffin that cost him a week's wages.
> Every Saturday night he will pay the undertaker fifty cents till the debt is wiped out.[19]

Such a funeral as Sandburg describes might have been simple, but it afforded the family an opportunity to mourn their loss. According to Jane Addams, Chicago's ward politicians exploited working people's fears of a state-supported funeral in exchange for votes. "The alderman saves the very poorest of his constituents from the awful horror of burial by the county," she wrote in 1892.[20] Chicago aldermen's attention to funerals of the poor reflected the fears that pervaded working communities.

Interment in a potter's field anywhere in the United States stripped individuals of even such a modest memorial as Sandburg's stockyard worker provided. Such burials were performed devoid "of all symbols which classify them as human beings," sociologist William Kephart has observed. The poor were buried, often naked, without ritual or flowers in mass graves where ample quantities of quicklime hastened decomposition. Many potter's fields across the country used numbers on wooden paddles to identify the locations of remains. In the end, the poor were stripped even of their names. Policies at Philadelphia's potter's fields mandated that bodies not claimed within ninety days be disinterred and burned in the crematory to make room for new bodies.[21] Those who failed to snatch their relatives from the fires of the crematory might worry that such disrespect would prompt the departed's spirit to haunt them. "There were no rites capable of placating the lingering ghost of a pauper," Bourke notes.[22]

In Chicago the potter's field at the Cook County Cemetery for the Indigent provided the final, though perhaps tormented, resting place for Chicago's poor.[23] Rows of mass unnamed graves, clouded with the noisome fumes of quicklime, evoked a different experience of death than did the elaborate monuments of the wealthy across town.

Graceland Cemetery on the North Side became the cemetery preferred by the elite in Chicago. Its manicured and landscaped lawns contrasted sharply with the crowded single lots of nearby Wunders Cemetery and the anonymity and ignominy of the potter's field. Lavish floral displays produced a decidedly different aroma than quicklime. Founded on 119 acres two miles north of Lincoln Park in 1860 by attorney and entrepreneur Thomas Bryan, Graceland became known as "the resting place of the city's founders and heroes."[24] It attracted affluent clientele with its professional, parklike design. Some of Chicago's elite embraced the opportunity to spend lavishly for the right to rest under Graceland's verdant vistas. Over the course of the late nineteenth and early twentieth centuries, it became the final resting place of some of Chicago's wealthiest and most powerful individuals. Within the cemetery gates, famed reaper inventor Cyrus McCormick shared deathly repose with railcar magnate George Pullman, meatpacking mogul Philip Armour, brewer Peter Schoenhofen, department store giant Marshall Field, architect Daniel Burnham, five-time Chicago mayor Carter Harrison, Illinois governor John Peter Altgeld, and others.

With clientele such as this, Graceland became an ostentatious display of Chicago's wealthy citizens. The grounds included families from a range of economic positions, but cemetery management carved out the most desirable sections near Lake Willowmere and applied inviting names such as "Lakeside," "Bellevue," "Fair Lawn," "Maplewood," and "Ridgeland." Space in these sections sold from $1 to $1.25 cents per square foot during the early 1890s, and the wealthy purchased lots that ranged from five thousand to twelve thousand square feet. People spent lavishly to adorn such prime real estate.[25] Lumber merchant Henry Harrison Getty commissioned famed architect Louis Sullivan to design the Getty family tomb. Sullivan's plan consisted of a cube shape, where smooth limestone covered the lower half of the mausoleum. Finely carved arches and ornate octagons decorated the upper half. Referred to as a "symphony in stone," the Getty tomb stood near the top of the list of expensive family monuments that occupied the lawns at Graceland.[26]

For some, Graceland reflected Chicago's fractious class politics and beheld the promises and perils of capitalist society. A business-friendly *Chicago Tribune* reporter lauded Graceland's, and other Chicago cemeteries', opulence as indicators of how wealth produced beauty. "Many of the cemeteries of Chicago are beautiful in the extreme," the reporter averred. "At those where lie the representatives of wealth stately monuments of bronze and marble and charming flower bordered paths greet the eye at every turn. . . . Tombs worth hundreds of thousands of dollars rear their classic lines in the sky and guard grimly the ashes reposing in their depths."[27] Carl Sandburg did not share the *Tribune*'s infatuation with the pomp of the city's cemeteries. They masked the circumstances of accumulation of wealth, albeit with the elegant "perfume and color" of flowers, as he wrote in his poem "Graceland":

> Tomb of a millionaire,
> A multi-millionaire, ladies and gentlemen,
> Place of the dead where they spend every year
> The usury of twenty-five thousand dollars
>   For upkeep and flowers
> To keep fresh the memory of the dead.
> The merchant prince gone to dust
> Commanded in his written will
> Over the signed name of his last testament
> Twenty-five thousand dollars be set aside
> For roses, lilacs, hydrangeas, tulips,
> For perfume and color, sweetness of remembrance
> Around his last long home.[28]

Few individuals better embodied the competing interpretations of Graceland Cemetery than one of its residents, George Pullman. Pullman became a leading Chicago businessman based on the success of the Pullman sleeping car and the Pullman Palace Car Company. His successful entrepreneurial efforts seemed to model the mad rush toward industrialization in Chicago. Pullman, Illinois, the company town that took his name, became a tourist stop during the 1893 Columbian Exposition. Yet Pullman was "always controversial," historian James Gilbert points out, "reviled and admired by commentators who visited the company town."[29] He earned part of this reputation by slashing workers' wages in the spring of 1894. The act precipitated one of the defining strikes of the 1890s, featuring a nationwide boycott of trains pulling Pullman cars, the arrest and imprisonment of American Railway Union leader Eugene V. Debs, and the use of federal troops to quell the tumultuous strike.[30] A federal commission later condemned Pullman for exploiting his employees in the midst of a deepening economic depression and failing to hear their grievances.[31]

Drained mentally and physically by the strike and its aftermath, Pullman died of heart failure in 1897 in the midst of a legal battle with the state's attorney that threatened his corporate empire. Worried that disgruntled workers might vandalize the remains, Pullman's family lowered the casket into the grave at Graceland at night under the cover of darkness. Cemetery workers spent two days encasing the casket in concrete and covering it with steel rails. Aboveground, Pullman's tomb is marked by a soaring Corinthian column designed by architect Solon S. Beman.[32]

Sandburg's biting commentary on Graceland and the Pullman family fears represented the competing images of burial space in Chicago. Industrial capitalism contained the potential to produce both paupers and princes. The Ragged Dicks who failed to realize the rags-to-riches life of Horatio Alger's fiction ended in a grave much feared by working people. Both physical space and wealth divided the potter's field from the gates of Graceland, as the wealthy poured their money into the landscaped lawns, architectural embellishments, and fragrant flora to sanitize the relationships of production that allowed their accumulation of wealth. "Upon the one side," socialist George Schilling wrote, "we find the propertied classes. . . . They are in possession of the earth. Upon the other side we find a large army of workmen who have nothing on earth except their labor."[33] Schilling's opinion of Chicago's labor relations extended to how the indigent and affluent were interred upon death. A worker with no savings or other way to provide for burial received interment in the potter's field in exchange for his or her life's work. Schilling's "propertied classes" maintained their "possession of the earth" by purchasing prime real estate in one of the city's most esteemed spaces for the dead. How many bodies lying in Chicago's potter's field swept blood in the packinghouses, applied the finishing touches to the plush Pullman palace cars, or pushed lumber in the yards?

Monuments like Getty's and Pullman's engraved the legacy of class struggle on the landscape of Chicago and revealed how cemetery spaces reflected access to the city's real estate. Only "persons blessed abundantly with this world's goods can think of buying" a coveted cemetery lot, according to one contemporary observer. Membership in the "brotherhood of riches" was a prerequisite to obtain and properly adorn it.[34] One of Chicago's famed old settlers, "Long" John Wentworth, spared little expense in Rosehill Cemetery. A sixty-five-foot obelisk constructed of white Hallowell granite imported on two train cars from Maine marked his grave. The family lot cost the

Wentworth estate ten thousand dollars and the obelisk another thirty-eight thousand dollars.[35]

Large family lots of Chicago's elite contrasted with working people's efforts to secure burial space. In his 1893 study of the city's cemeteries, Andreas Simon found that German workers found it difficult to amass enough wealth to buy family lots. Insufficient funds meant that many people could afford only single graves that in some cases had "to be used over and over again." By the early 1890s, Wunders Cemetery, located just south of Graceland, no longer permitted the purchase of single grave sites and mandated that all interments be made in family lots. This decision, which other cemeteries in the area later adopted, placed a financial barrier to burial. Without the means to acquire a family parcel, workers had to find a cemetery that allowed single burials, which often meant traveling to one of the suburban cemeteries on the fringe of the city. "It is sometimes regretted," Simon concluded, "that man is dependent even in death upon the prices asked for land, and that people of small means must content themselves with burial places in the out of the way corners of the cemeteries. The adage, that in death all are equal, is therefore not true."[36] The average Chicagoan rested in crowded cemeteries at the turn of the century rather than under the expensive real estate of Graceland near the Gettys and Pullmans.[37]

Landscapes of Equal Rights: Cemeteries and Battles of Religion, Ethnicity, and Race

Wealth may have determined whether a body found its way to Graceland Cemetery or the potter's field, but in the late nineteenth century factors of religion, ethnicity, and race proved more important in the establishment and use of Chicago's cemeteries. In the 1850s, three cemeteries served Chicago—a public cemetery, a Jewish cemetery, and a Roman Catholic cemetery. As the city's population grew and diversified through successive waves of immigration, the need for additional burial space, desires for separate burial spaces because of religious or nationalist affiliation, or outright segregation spurred the establishment of new cemeteries. By 1900 twenty-seven cemeteries covering twenty-six hundred acres served the city.[38] In both design and reputation, they occupied the middle ground between the extremes of the Cook County Cemetery for the Indigent and Graceland Cemetery. Many were founded by or targeted specific ethnic groups. While religion played a key role in burial in other parts of the country, ethnic identity added another variable in the dynamic of death in Chicago, where, as one historian notes, "ethnicity has always inflected religion."[39] Both Protestant and Catholic cemeteries became identified with specific ethnicities, while some commercial cemeteries sold entire sections to Armenians, Latvians, Serbians, and other ethnic groups.[40]

The creation of Roman Catholic cemeteries, in particular, reflected the tensions between established hierarchies of the diocese controlled by the Irish and others from a variety of backgrounds. The Irish dominated the Roman Catholic Church in Chicago during the nineteenth century. All the bishops of Chicago were either Irish born or of Irish descent from the appointment of the first bishop, William Quarter, in 1844 to the death of Archbishop James Quigley in 1915. This remarkable period of Irish influence ensconced them in the role of overseers, as the diocese grew to include forty-seven territorial churches and sixty-three national churches by 1902.[41] The predominantly Irish Catholic hierarchy clashed at times with lay Germans, Poles, Czechs, and Lithuanians. The establishment of one new Catholic cemetery was a by-product. Inspired by an unwillingness to share burial space with their Celtic brethren in the Calvary Cemetery, a group of German Catholic churches consecrated their own burial space in 1863 when they founded St. Boniface Cemetery.[42]

Desires for intraethnic solidarity and the growth of the city produced other Chicago-area Catholic cemeteries, such as St. Adalbert Cemetery, founded in 1872 by Polish and Czech Catholics, and the Roman Catholic Lithuanian cemetery, St. Casimir, established in 1903. Some Roman Catholic cemeteries were born from ethnic pride, while others reflected the desire of Catholics to have a cemetery closer to their parishes and neighborhoods as the city expanded. Both factors led to the consecration of new cemeteries to serve Chicago's Catholics.

While some Chicagoans chose to work within the Catholic Church, a group of Czech freethinkers and benevolent societies established a nondenominational cemetery to challenge clerical control over burial. In 1876 Father Joseph Molitor, the pastor of St. Václav Parish, clashed with the fraternal St. Václav Society when he refused to allow the burial of Mrs. Marie Silháneck, a lifelong Catholic, in St. Adalbert Cemetery. Silháneck had not confessed before her death, and Molitor cited this fact to justify denying her access to the church's consecrated ground. Czech freethinkers, led by Frank Zdrubek, the editor of the Czech-language daily newspaper *Svornost*, called for "a Bohemian National Cemetery where any Bohemian, regardless of creed, could be buried among his fellow countrymen without begging a priest for permission."[43] The freethinkers' appeal found a receptive audience among the city's Czech population. Contemporaries estimated that only 25 percent of Czechs affiliated with the Catholic Church, and historian Bruce Nelson suggests that irreligious Czechs outnumbered the religious by a ratio of six to one.[44]

Anger with Father Molitor and the Catholic Church inspired a new cemetery. Responding to Zdrubek's call, a group of fraternal societies collected donations, purchased land, and opened the Bohemian National Cemetery in the summer of 1877. Within its gates, "the pilgrim who has arrived at the end of life's journey, can enter without being questioned about his religion, color, or nationality. Equal rights are accorded to all."[45] Although the cemetery eventually implemented a series of restrictions that banned some burials, such as those of people who had died of smallpox, and gave priority to fellow Czechs through discounted pricing of grave lots, occasions arose that allowed them to honor their freethinking heritage. In 1902 several prominent individuals requested burial for F. Vonásek, "a Catholic who had always used abusive language when he talked about Freethinkers." Although the cause is unclear from the records, the Catholic Church had refused Vonásek's access to the consecrated burial ground of a Catholic cemetery. Twenty-five years after its founding as a result of a similar case, the Bohemian National Cemetery welcomed one of its critics who had been denied burial by the church. Not only did they admit Vonásek to their garden of the dead, but they also did so free of charge.[46]

Initiated from a battle with the church, the Bohemian National Cemetery became a symbol of ethnic pride to which Czechs pointed as evidence of their collective character. Chicago's Czech community became the target of sustained criticism from native born and immigrant, particularly Germans, alike. "We Bohemian citizens of this town have been abused several times by the [German-language newspaper] the *Staats-Zeitung* without reason and it is time that it was stopped," two Czechs wrote to the editor of the *Chicago Tribune* in 1879.[47] The *Tribune* affirmed that "there was a dedicated prejudice against them on the part of American workingmen and capitalists."[48] The English and German press, the *Svornost* complained, cast Czech immigrants "to a basis below that of the Polish or Russian Jew" and scurrilously charged that "the Bohemian working masses are very low in every way."[49] Such attacks emanated in part from competition between immigrant groups in local labor markets. Germans feared competition from Czechs in the lumberyards and tailoring houses.[50] Native-born Chicagoans tapped into deeper distrust of immigrants that percolated throughout the late nineteenth century and made pejorative generalizations about the foreign born a standard feature of the era's discourse.

In this context, Czechs seized the success of the Bohemian National Cemetery as evidence to counter unfavorable comments by other groups and challenge a culture of industrialization that sought to marginalize immigrants. As with other garden cemeteries, organizers worked diligently to maintain the parklike appearance of the cemetery to spark visitors' awe for natural beauty. The Bohemian Cemetery Association's success at manicuring the lawns and planting a variety of flora attracted praise from visitors, both native and foreign born. Judge O. H. Carter remarked after a visit that he had "not seen a cemetery more beautiful in the vicinity of Chicago." The Czech-language newspaper *Denni Hlasatel* interpreted Carter's comments as implying "praise for the National Cemetery Association and for all of those who have devoted their honest endeavor to the building up of the institution."[51] Czechs used the cemetery's success as a testament to their character. The cemetery provided a tangible space that Czechs could "be and are proud of by every right." It marked their place among other immigrant groups and, its patrons hoped, would deflect anti-Czech sentiment in the area so that "no one can any longer censure us" as an undesirable ethnic group, as *Denni Hlasatel* editorialized in 1911. Bohemian National Cemetery symbolized the Czech immigrants' alacrity for entrepreneurship and their ability to sustain successful enterprise. "The present economic strength of the Bohemians in Chicago," J. E. S. Vojan wrote in the midst of the 1920s campaigns to restrict immigration, "shows that they belonged and still belong to the most desirable immigrants, and that the best policy for the United States is to receive these sturdy self-made men with open arms."[52]

Perhaps more important than testifying to Czech character, Bohemian National became a space where Czechs reflected about their immigrant experience, celebrated their national heritage, and claimed a stake in the American Republic. After the founding of the cemetery, Czechs held annual celebrations near or in the cemetery that attracted thousands of people. They paid homage to national heroes such as John Huss and Karel Havlícek and in 1884 began erecting a monument to honor Ladimir Klácel, "a teacher and awakener of the Bohemian people of America, a pioneer of the Free Thought and Rationalism."[53] Czechs used the cemetery as a national park, albeit over the graves of the dead, to reflect on traditions and national heroes.

Bohemian National also became a bridge for Old World traditions to commingle with the politics of the United States. On May 29, 1892, Czechs dedicated a monument in the cemetery to the memory of Bohemians who fought in the Civil War. They did so amid a period of intense memorialization of the sectional conflict, where soldier reunions and a flurry of monuments proved the contested legacy of the war.[54] In the context of the Bohemian National Cemetery, however, the monument did not evoke the debates over slavery, emancipation, and states' rights. It reflected the immigrant experience. The unveiling ceremony brought Czech fraternal societies together with the Grand Army of the Republic, Chicago police, prominent attorneys, and former and future mayor Carter H. Harrison. H. S. Dietrich, past senior vice commander of the Department of Illinois, GAR, dedicated the monument by commending the Czech soldiers' immigrant trajectory and lacing his comments with hopes for assimilation. "Our Bohemian citizens responded bravely when our country was assailed and left their homes to preserve the flag of their adopted country," he said. "This monument is not only a memorial to your heroic dead, but it will hereafter teach all men that in this country there can be but one government and one flag."[55]

Unlike Dietrich, the five thousand Czech participants at the unveiling emphasized national pride rather than assimilation. For *Svornost*, the monument "gave a practical answer to the American press for all the maligning which we [Bohemians] have endured in recent years." It signified that Czech immigrants contributed to their new country and were not simply parasites on the body politic feasting on its freedoms. "Even if we are not as strong numerically as other nationalities, still the American people must realize that the Bohemian element is one of the strongest pillars in the foundation of this republic," *Svornost* concluded.[56] Appeals to assimilation such as those made by the Grand Army of the Republic, revealed a tension evident in the daily lives of Czechs in Chicago. For the editors of *Svornost*, cries for assimilation were out of place in such a national space as the Bohemian National Cemetery, which was founded, in part, to recognize and honor a distinct national heritage and immigrant experience.

In years after the dedication of the soldiers' monument, Czechs continued to express the complicated relationships between their ethnicity and citizenship through participation in Decoration Day festivities. Every year at the end of May, the Czech community joined the rest of the nation in spending the day memorializing the dead. Befitting such a purpose, cemeteries provided the primary space to host events. Czechs visited St. Adalbert and Resurrection, but the Bohemian National Cemetery consistently drew crowds in the thousands. On Decoration Day, Bohemian National "was transformed," in the words of the Czech-language newspaper *Denni Hlasatel*, "as by a magic wand, into a sea of blossoms."[57] The broad popular participation during the 1890s prompted the cemetery's board of trustees to impose order on the events. They passed a resolution in 1901 that authorized the board to make all preparations for the festivities, which included inviting speakers, arranging for military and other societies, hiring bands, and providing all necessary decorations.[58] A typical celebration featured a morning parade in the Pilsen neighborhood from which people boarded street- and train cars for the cemetery.

Once inside the cemetery's gates, a range of speakers addressed the crowds, and the day concluded with two keynote speeches, one by a native English speaker and one in Czech.[59] These speeches typically reiterated the tensions displayed at the unveiling of the soldiers' monument. American-born speakers tended to dwell on the soldiers' sacrifices and the meaning of freedom in the United States. The foreign-language speakers touched on similar themes, but also took advantage of Decoration Day to reflect on the immigrant experience. "It is mainly due to the merits of the immigrants that America has become a great and powerful country," M. M. Mangasarian boldly proclaimed in 1911. "Europe sent to our country young, enthusiastic, industrious, and energetic people of robust blood and healthy minds, and all this intelligence and strength united in one whole, raised this country to an unforeseen degree of industrial and social progress."[60] On a day saturated with significance for the nation, Czechs used the cemetery to honor not only the exploits of men in uniform, but also the daily contributions of the immigrant workforce that contributed to propelling the nation's economy. From its founding in 1877 though the turn of the century, the Bohemian National Cemetery became a space integral to the experiences of Chicago's Czech community. It provided a unique place to perpetuate traditional practices and come to terms with urban industrial life in the United States.

While the exclusionary practices of the Catholic Church prompted the formation of a separate cemetery that promoted ethnic distinction, Chicago's African American population grappled with an expanding regime of de facto segregation. Hopes for equality drew many African Americans to Chicago after the Civil War, just as dreams of Chicago as the "promised land" free of Jim Crow segregation combined with the lure of industrial jobs to spark a long period of exodus out of the South, beginning just before World War I.[61] African Americans constituted less than 2 percent of Chicago's population from 1880 to 1910, although their numbers grew from 6,480 in 1880 to nearly 44,103 in 1910. Residential patterns "might loosely be called" integrated during this period, as whites still lingered in black neighborhoods.[62] However, 78 percent of African Americans already concentrated on the South Side on a narrow strip known to whites as the "Black Belt," bounded by Twelfth Street on the north, Wentworth Avenue on the west, and Fifty-Fifth Street on the south.[63] As the black population increased, white racial attitudes hardened. African Americans increasingly confronted discriminatory practices in employment, housing, health care, and schools.[64]

Cemetery policies paralleled the broader evolution of race relations in Chicago and provided a stark reminder of racial prejudice. Cemeteries became increasingly exclusive such that by the 1880s, "the problems of Jim Crow had crept northward into Chicago."⁶⁵ Thomas Harris publicized the inequality of service he received, based on his color, at Mount Greenwood Cemetery in 1890. Arriving at the cemetery on the funeral train, Harris's son had been unloaded first, and Harris paid the burial fee first. The cemetery workers ignored the cemetery's first come, first served policy, according to Harris, and set his son's casket aside while they buried the whites. When Harris protested, the manager replied, "If you don't like the way we do things here, don't come." Upon receiving Harris's letter, a *Tribune* reporter visited Mount Greenwood to investigate its policies. While waiting to interview the manager, the reporter recounted hearing two clerks discuss Harris's situation. "Did you see the crazy coon who was in here? He was on the warpath and after somebody's scalp because they wouldn't bury his kid first at the cemetery yesterday," one clerk said, mixing racialist metaphors. His conversational partner replied, "Lots of good it will do him," seeming to substantiate a past record of unequal service provided to blacks. The past president of the cemetery company dismissed Harris's protests by claiming he misrepresented the facts. "The white people may have made earlier arrangements which entitled them to precedence," he told the *Tribune*.⁶⁶ Harris's experience provides one example of how the color line operated before the turn of the century. African Americans experienced unequal service or outright denial of access to graves, while cemetery administrators denied that such racial discrimination occurred.

As the black population increased after 1900, some cemeteries openly advertised their segregated burial practices. The *Chicago Defender,* one of the most important African American newspapers in the country, reported seeing advertisements for the Mount Hope Cemetery on the city's streetcars that boldly proclaimed their grounds were "exclusively for the white race." The *Defender* predicted that financial necessity might, in the end, equalize access. "In this day of sudden financial wreck, crash or embarrassment, the high muck-a-mucks of Mount Hope may find final resting place among the people whom they now reject."⁶⁷ The *Defender* took solace in the possibility that hard economic times might necessitate a revision of the cemetery corporation's policies of segregation.

Other black Chicagoans did not intend to wait for an economic resolution. They responded to increasing segregationist burial policies by drawing on a long history of black self-help and community organizing. African Americans in Chicago, even before the Great Migration, "organized constantly, and successfully," historian Christopher Reed argues. "As soon as a need was encountered, it was met with a plan of resolution. From churches to fraternal orders to social clubs to civil rights groups, as part of a 'larger, national culture,' associational life made life more bearable in an often-hostile setting."[68] Blacks transferred organizing skills from their experiences organizing churches like Olivet Baptist, newspapers such as the *Conservator* and *Defender*, and various civic clubs to securing access to burial space. They purchased a large section in Oak Hill Cemetery, black businessmen established Mount Glenwood Cemetery in 1908 with an explicit nondiscrimination clause in its charter, and a coalition of fraternal lodges founded Lincoln Cemetery in 1911.[69] Purchasing sections of cemeteries intended for African Americans or founding their own represented one strategy for confronting segregation in death.

African Americans also protested discriminatory burial practices in the Illinois Legislature and the courts. Although Illinois led the nation in passing the Civil Rights Act in 1885, which barred discrimination in public places, private businesses openly discriminated without fear of legal repercussions. Physicians advertised for "white patients only" on the edge of the Black Belt, landlords frequently charged higher rents to African Americans, and insurance companies either shunned black policyholders entirely or charged them higher premiums.[70] Price differentials filtered into the area's cemeteries as well. In 1911 Edward D. Green, a state legislator whom, according to famed antilynching crusader Ida B. Wells-Barnett, black Chicagoans "sent to Springfield to represent our race," introduced an amendment to the Illinois Civil Rights Act that outlawed discriminatory practices in the sale of cemetery plots.[71] The *Defender* applauded Green's "brilliant fight" for equality. The paper claimed that African Americans routinely paid fifty dollars for plots, while whites paid only ten dollars, and that equalizing prices would finally leave carfare in blacks' pockets to return from the cemetery. Green's bill passed in the spring of 1911, effectively amending the state's Civil Rights Act.[72]

Green's success might have equalized prices for burial lots, but it did not prevent racial discrimination in the city's cemeteries. In 1912 John Gaskill brought a lawsuit against Forest Home Cemetery for refusing to bury his wife, Pinkie, because of her color. As Pinkie's body waited in a holding room, the case worked its way to the Illinois Supreme Court and revealed the ongoing racially based impediments to burial in Chicago. Mr. Gaskill had buried four of his children at Forest Home before 1912. Between his last child's burial and the death of his wife, Forest Home had passed a resolution in 1907, making it a segregated cemetery that would accommodate whites only. In a letter to Gaskill stating the rationale for denial, Forest Home maintained they held no prejudice toward African Americans, but the fate of their business depended on exclusionary practices. "If the colored people did buy lots," the letter stated, "it would only make the neighbors angry and kick and remove to some other part of the cemetery or possibly some other cemetery."[73]

Cemetery administrators had reason to worry that white racism would adversely affect business. White property owners enforced residential segregation in the 1890s through organized resistance to black tenants. Woodlawn property owners met in 1897, for example, and "declared war" against African Americans living in the neighborhood. Landlords who rented to blacks were labeled "enemies" who "should be tarred and feathered." Labor relations in Chicago, especially in the 1904 stockyards and 1905 teamsters' strikes, also featured racial hostility, as white workers attacked black strikebreakers. Only four years before Gaskill brought suit, Springfield, Illinois, had erupted in a race riot that produced a significant casualty toll and virtually destroyed the African American neighborhood. The Springfield riot reverberated in Chicago by inspiring instances of white-on-black violence and threatened lynchings.[74] Open hostility toward African Americans and racism thrived in Illinois and influenced Forest Home's decision to segregate the cemetery as a sound business practice.

Gaskill's case challenged the legacy of racism in Illinois, but his cause met defeat at the hands of the court. In its ruling in favor of the cemetery, the supreme court held that Forest Home, as a private enterprise, was not subject to the Civil Rights Act and therefore did not have to provide equal access. Such discrimination, the court ruled, "did not infringe any right of the widower under the Constitution of the State of Illinois," nor did Mr. Gaskill have any "right respecting such burial under the Fourteenth Amendment, which only applied to acts of the State."[75] Refusing to accept the ruling, Gaskill appealed to the U.S. Supreme Court, which failed to hear the case, citing lack of jurisdiction.

Gaskill's defeat before the bar of justice stunned the *Chicago Defender*. "This is happening in Chicago, some little distance above the Mason and Dixon line," the newspaper fumed. "This self-styled 'superior race' not only legislates to keep you aloof from them while living, but [also] after you have passed away. No doubt they will want a part of heaven—if they should be fortunate enough to get there—set aside for their especial benefit. Wonderful people, the Caucasian race."[76] For the *Defender* and African Americans in Chicago, segregated cemeteries belied the proverb that death was the great equalizer. Racial hostility pervaded the realm of the dead, just as it did the living. As late as 1950, while new battles over residential segregation raged, more than two-thirds of the city's non-Catholic cemeteries restricted burial by color.[77]

A Landscape of Radicalism: Waldheim Cemetery and the Haymarket Monument

As cemeteries became imprinted with particular attributes across Chicago, one section of Waldheim Cemetery, ten miles west of the city on the Des Plaines River, became a space that linked anarchism, the labor movement, and radicalism in Chicago to similar movements across the globe. Waldheim became, not entirely willingly, connected to the epic national struggle for shorter hours that produced the great upheaval in Chicago's streets in the spring of 1886. The May 4 bomb in the Haymarket sparked a melee that killed seven policemen and an unknown number of others. The bomb ignited a quest for vengeance that, after a lengthy trial, resulted in the convictions of eight men. The court sentenced five of those men to death. Louis Lingg took his own life in his Cook County jail cell by biting into a dynamite blasting cap. August Spies, Albert Parsons, George Engel, and Adolph Fischer were executed by strangulation when the hangman's noose failed to perform its function of snapping their necks on November 11, 1887.[78] The defense committee that had fought for the men's freedom turned from their campaign for amnesty to looking for burial lots for the dead men. They turned to Waldheim Cemetery.

Waldheim seemed a likely place to inter the men. A group of German fraternal lodges had purchased part of Haase's Park, a popular leisure spot for Chicago's Germans, to found a nonsectarian cemetery in 1873. "Within its limits there can be no distinction of race, color position, nationality, or religion," Francis Lackner said during his dedication speech. All "become citizens of the democracy of the dead, the ground idea of which is absolute equality."[79] These were the principles Spies, Parsons, and the rest had argued should be afforded the living, which, when combined with the ethnic heritage of the cemetery and the likely refusal of other cemeteries to accept the bodies, prompted the defense committee to turn to Waldheim.

On Sunday, November 13, 1887, Chicagoans witnessed a funeral of unprecedented size in the city's history. Two hundred thousand people filled the streets to observe the procession. Not even Lincoln's casket had drawn such a crowd.[80] Mayor John A. Roche, Carter Harrison's successor, granted permission for the funeral procession but insisted on a set of restrictions. He forbade banners, flags, and the displaying of arms. Only the musical notes of dirges could accompany the bodies, and the procession would be subject to police surveillance.[81] There would be no confrontations on that day, however. As one of Albert Parsons's pallbearers, James Buchanan, later recalled,

"I marched through three miles of crowded streets that day, and upon every one of the thousands of faces I saw about me there was a look of sorrow. I noticed that some of the policemen bared and bowed their heads as the hearses passed them." Mary Harris "Mother" Jones, who lived in Chicago at the time, recalled, "Thousands of workers marched behind the black hearses, not because they were anarchists but they felt that these men, whatever their theories, were martyrs to the workers' struggle."[82] The procession wound its way to the Wisconsin Central Station, from which the bodies were transported to the temporary vault at Waldheim.

As the sun sank low, the bodies arrived, and Waldheim became a key space for anarchists and other radicals. The funeral services marked a new phase in the work of the defense committee that had been originally organized to win clemency for the accused anarchists. After the execution ended the campaign for freedom, they sought to construct a "countermemory" of the men that suggested their lives should be celebrated rather than reviled. The families and friends of the executed men "organized mass actions, giving expression of emotions, particularly emotions of love and grief, an important role in radical politics as the glue that held masses of individuals together in struggle," scholar Rebecca Hill notes.[83] The speeches at Waldheim on November 13 initiated this process. "They were called Anarchists," said Captain William Perkins Black, who served as the defense attorney at the trial. "They were painted and presented to the world as men loving violence, riot and bloodshed for their own sake. Nothing could be further from the truth. They were men who loved peace, men of gentle instincts, men of gracious tenderness of heart." The mourners were not "beside the caskets of felons consigned to an unglorious tomb," he continued. "We are here by the bodies of men who were sublime in their self-sacrifice, and for whom the gibbet assumed the glory of a cross."[84] Other speakers echoed Black's sentiments. Since they could not save them from the gallows, the mourners attempted to save them from the harsh judgment of history, anointing them martyrs to the labor movement.

Execution, however, did not confer amnesty, nor did the impressive funeral guarantee burial space. Despite a reputation of being "open to all" and making "no distinction between the believer or unbeliever, between Christian, Jew or Heathen," the cemetery's administration begrudgingly, and only after negotiation, agreed to provide burial for the controversial corpses.[85] Even before the funeral, John Buehler, the president of the Waldheim Cemetery Association, worried about anarchist sympathizers staging demonstrations at the cemetery, which may have played a role in placing the bodies in the temporary vault on November 13.[86] In subsequent negotiations between the cemetery and the defense committee, administrators twice rejected the committee's offer to purchase large lots. They justified their refusal by pointing to the potential large crowds that might visit Waldheim yearly to mark the "Black Friday" of the hangings.[87] Then, without explanation, Buehler sold a burial lot for the Haymarket anarchists on December 5.[88] Even with the successful sale, politics had made burial space in Waldheim Cemetery contested terrain.

With a lot secured, families and friends gathered to commit the bodies to the earth on December 18. Reporting from the scene, a *Chicago Tribune* writer hoped that the event also marked the more symbolic "burial of anarchy" in Chicago. Speaking at the grave, anarchist Albert Currlin offered a different assessment. He suggested that the execution represented a Golgotha for radicalism and charged his audience with the task of going forth to create an Easter of resurrection and redemption for anarchism. "If at any time you become soul-weary or discouraged," Currlin exhorted, "make a pilgrimage to this hallowed spot and be reinvigorated for the strife. . . . Let us struggle for the right, for justice, freedom and true fraternity . . . until the peoples are regenerated and clean hands and clean hearts have authority to rule."[89] The *Alarm*, a radical publication once edited by Albert Parsons, called for the grave site to be the "future Mecca of all good socialists."[90] In many ways, anarchists heeded Currlin's and the *Alarm*'s directives.

November 11 became observed yearly as a revolutionary memorial, and Waldheim Cemetery became the key space that Chicago radicals visited. Workers across the country invoked the cemetery in mass meetings in Boston, New York, Philadelphia, St. Louis, San Francisco, and other cities.[91] Radicals such as Voltairine de Cleyre penned poetry to the site that balanced grim stanzas on death with unbridled hope for new dawns of freedom.[92] "By reliving the martyrdom" at the annual memorials, historian Blaine McKinley observes, "the anarchists could see themselves as participants in, and successors to, a noble sacrifice."[93] The Haymarket anarchists' grave at Waldheim provided a crucial cultural reference point for anarchism and served purposes both didactic and motivational.

Tributes to the memory of the radicals did not occur without incident, however. Harassment at the November 11 commemorations drew a direct line from the martyrs at Waldheim and the events of May 1886 to those who sought to remember them in subsequent years. In 1889 the mayor of Philadelphia closed the Odd Fellows' Temple to prevent a Haymarket commemoration. Police prevented famed anarchist Emma Goldman from speaking in Providence in 1892, forcing her to the train station and out of town.[94]

Conflict provoked by the November 11 commemorations struck closer to Waldheim as well. Police disbanded a meeting at the Vorwaerts Turner Hall in Chicago in 1891.[95] Lucy Parsons seemed to perennially attract the attention of the police. For several years, Parsons hung a red flag, or planted one on the roof of her house, only to have policemen forcibly remove the symbol of anarchy.[96] Never intimidated, Lucy continued to agitate. At an 1896 meeting, Chicago Commons director Graham Taylor remembered in his autobiography, Parsons rose to speak at the demand of the audience. "I am the widow of Albert R. Parsons and the mother of his son," she began. "I charge the police and the court with murdering my husband. I live to bring up his son to take up the work which was stricken from his father's hand." A police captain promptly arrested Parsons, escorted her to the police station, and charged her with disorderly conduct.[97] Police intimidation further cemented bonds between the executed anarchists and those who hoped to work in their memory.

Block N of Waldheim attracted attention as anarchists planned a monument to memorialize the martyrs soon after the burial. A monument, according to the *Alarm*, would serve two related functions. First, it would organize: "it will prove the surest way of encouraging faint hearted workers in the cause," the *Alarm* wrote. Second, a monument in Waldheim would provide "liberty loving radicals of Chicago" a permanent meeting place.[98] Planning and fund-raising proceeded slowly, however, until the dedication of a police monument in the Haymarket provoked radicals to action.

In 1889 Chicago police dedicated a monument to the officers who lost their lives in the Haymarket. Depicting a police officer with his hand raised in a halt position, the monument embodied allegiance to law and order. In his popular 1888 book, *The Rise and Fall of Anarchy in America*, George McLean penned a tribute to Chicago's police that echoed the sentiments that inspired the monument. The peace-loving citizens of Chicago, he wrote,

> will with me thank God for the blessings of peace secured to us by the prompt and steady action of our brave and noble police on the night of May 4, 1886. When forgetful of their own personal safety in their devotion to the cause of liberty, over the prostrate forms of mangled and dying comrades they charged this treacherous band of alien outlaws, beating down the red hand of anarchy which was reaching out its tentacles to usurp the birthright of this nation bequeathed to it by our ancestors and made sacred to every loyal heart by a baptism of the blood of our sires and grandsires in 1776.[99]

When city officials dedicated the monument on May 31, 1889, they hoped it would symbolize the authority of the police and pose a visual deterrent to any groups who sought to threaten rule of law. With the dedication, city officials offered a public interpretation of the events in the Haymarket that heroicized police actions against the "unruly mob."[100]

The dedication of the Haymarket monument on June 25, 1893, countered the narrative offered by the police monument and further solidified Waldheim as a landscape of radicalism. Sculpted by Albert Weinert and inspired by "La Marseillaise," the monument to the martyrs featured two life-size bronze figures in front of a sixteen-foot granite shaft on a two-step base. A female figure, variously interpreted as Justice and Liberty, struck an aggressive posture as she gestured toward a recumbent male figure. Spies's last words from the scaffold adorned the base: "The day will come when our silence will be more powerful than the voices you are throttling today." The unveiling precipitated a parade that retraced the martyrs' funeral procession and drew eight thousand people to Waldheim. They watched as thirteen-year-old Albert Parsons Jr. removed the red curtain to reveal the monument.[101] The next day, Chicagoans' thoughts again turned to anarchism and Waldheim. Governor John Peter Altgeld pardoned the three Haymarket anarchists who still sat in prison: Samuel Fielden, Michael Schwab, and Oscar Neebe.

The Haymarket memorial anchored Waldheim Cemetery as a key site in the hearts and minds of radicals in America. In the year after the 1893 Columbian Exhibition, one author estimated that "almost as many visitors came to [the Haymarket monument] in the course of twelve months as to the statue of Abraham Lincoln in the park which bears his name."[102] For anarchists and other radicals, it served, as Lucy Robins Lang recalled in her memoir, as "the sacred center" that drew the hearts and thoughts of American radicals at the end of the nineteenth century. The bronze statue meant as much to them "as the Church of the Holy Sepulcher means to the Christian, or Mecca to the Moslem, or the Wailing Wall to the Jew."[103] The Haymarket monument became a shrine to which socialists and other pilgrims came from all over the world to reflect on life, freedom, and oppression.[104]

The Haymarket Affair became a key episode in the contested meaning of space in Chicago, and Waldheim Cemetery played a leading role. Mainstream press accounts hoped that anarchism had been buried along with the anarchists. Even George Schilling, who had worked to elect Altgeld and then pressured the governor to pardon Fielden, Schwab, and Neebe, ultimately associated the men at Waldheim with misguided tactics. "At Waldheim sleep five men," he wrote to Lucy Parsons. "They worshipped at the shrine of force; wrote it and preached it; until they were overpowered by their own Gods and slain in their own temple.... The public mind, terrorized by fear ... swept away the safeguards of the law and turned its officers into pliant tools yielding to its will."[105] For people who agreed with Schilling, those buried near the monument at Waldheim represented the perils of immigration and radical politics. Those Chicagoans preferred to gaze upon the police monument that stood in Haymarket Square until 1900.

Others labored to perpetuate a countermemory of the Haymarket tragedy that transformed Spies, Parsons, Engel, and the others from villains into martyrs. "In the cemetery of Waldheim, the dead were buried," Mother Jones later recalled. "But with them was not buried their cause. The struggle for the eight hour day, for more human conditions and relations between man and man lived on, and still lives on."[106] Haymarket drew a number of people such as Emma Goldman, Alexander Berkman, and Voltairine de Cleyre to the anarchist cause.[107] Still others found inspiration in the martyrs' protests and chose to make their final resting place near the Haymarket monument. Next to the likes of Lucy Parsons, de Cleyre, Goldman, and William Z. Foster rest lesser-known radicals Frank Zoellner, Anton Johannsen, and others.[108] Waldheim became a symbolic space that perpetuated a countermemory of the Haymarket tragedy and fostered a democratic sympathy with radicals of subsequent generations.

Cemeteries and the Fault Lines of Civic Culture

As the Haymarket memorial in Waldheim attests, Chicago's cemeteries provided a rich tableau of the contested meanings of life and death as the nation marched into the twentieth century, "with the trumpets of militarism and imperialism blaring in Cuba and the Philippines, and with the engines of corporate capitalism roaring from Pittsburgh to Chicago."[109] Chicagoans united to show the world the promise of industrial urbanism through Daniel Burnham's famed "White City" at the Columbian Exposition of 1893. They joined forces on projects large and small during the Progressive Era to forge "civic culture"—"the desire to foster a shared sense of local identity and social engagement that had the potential to transcend boundaries of ethnicity, race, religion, and class."[110] Progressives hoped to replace the fractious politics of the past with a vision of a triumphant future that transcended, or at least masked, divisions in society.[111] Space, specifically professionally planned urban landscapes, played a central role in this project.

The history of Chicago's cemeteries reveals that the fissures that divided the city could not simply be buried under the rhetoric of progressive renewal. Indeed, Chicagoans developed and used cemeteries as spaces to cement solidarities and reify differences. The potter's field served a melancholy, but necessary, function. Its existence as both physical and cultural space drove many working people to miserly extremes to avoid it. Yet in profound ways, the potter's field made possible the luxuries of Graceland and Rosehill Cemeteries. Some of the bodies that lay covered in quicklime under a numbered wooden paddle made possible the opulent memorials to wealth that topped the graves of the Wentworths, Gettys, Pullmans, and Fields. Chicago's elite lived in mansions. Upon death their remains rested in elaborate mausoleums—mansions for the dead. As many contemporary commentators revealed, equality of condition did not rule the cities of the dead.

Between the extremes of the potter's field and the upper-class lots, Chicago's cemeteries also displayed how common people and the middle classes negotiated religious, ethnic, and racial factors. Cemeteries became badges of ethnic pride, but they also produced religious and racial ghettoes. "Observant Jews, Catholics and Mormons rest in the sacred ground of their separate faiths," historian Kenneth Jackson observes, "while black and white Americans have been separated in death even more than in life."[112] These divisions pervaded the landscape of death in Chicago. Ethnic and racial hostility proved creative, as groups answered restrictions by establishing their own cemeteries. These new cemeteries became spaces where immigrant groups reflected on their experiences and African Americans ensured dignity to their deceased. With both positive and negative ramifications, religious, ethnic, and racial friction enshrined difference in the landscape of the city.

The development and use of Chicago's cemeteries reflected anxieties of an urban population grappling with the pleasures and perils of a burgeoning industrial city. Intense population growth combined with fears of disease to push the city's burial grounds to the periphery. Yet in significant ways, the cemeteries were central to how Chicagoans experienced urban life. They provided grim, though not silent, testaments to the fault lines that undergirded the modern metropolis.

The historical development of Chicago's cemeteries produced a politics of death that was laden with class overtones. Considered as a period of historical development, the way working people interacted with cemeteries suggests change over time. Cemeteries became reflections of the divisions of post–Civil War society, and working people, whether in ethnic neighborhoods like the Czechs or more broadly, used them to reflect on life. The cemeteries also became a focal point for resistance. The Haymarket Affair served as an important turning point in the way workers politicized death in the late nineteenth century, with the grave at Waldheim becoming sacred space and a model for other workers in the coal regions of Illinois, the steelmaking valleys of Pennsylvania, and beyond.

3 Every New Grave Brought a Thousand Members

The Politics of Death in Illinois Coal Communities, 1883–1910

In the late nineteenth century, a poem and folk song, "Only a Miner," circulated through U.S. mining communities. It began, "Only a miner killed; / Oh! Is that all?" These opening lines betrayed a powerful irony. Although miners performed labor vital to fueling the country's economy, the poem suggested that Americans did not appreciate the risks involved. The last stanza reinforced the point. "Only a miner killed!" it read, "Bury him quick, / Just write his name on / A piece of stick."[1] This and subsequent versions of "Only a Miner" criticized public apathy. More significantly, it placed ideas about workers' bodies at the heart of understanding the social relations and cultural meanings of the industrial United States. Examining Illinois coal mining communities' attitudes toward death and the meanings they mapped to dead bodies demonstrates how experiences with death shaped miners' beliefs and, in some instances, motivated their activism.

Illinois coal miners met death from a variety of causes. This chapter examines three. During the 1880s and 1890s, the haunting possibilities of mass-fatality disasters, the seemingly ubiquitous deadly perils in everyday mining, and the violent confrontations between miners and employers profoundly shaped miners' experiences with death. Miners developed consistent political and cultural responses to the deaths their coworkers encountered and fashioned cultural responses to memorialize the dead and embolden the living. These practices were not hermetically isolated. Mining communities created hybrid deathways that commingled with religious, ethnic, and fraternal rituals. The nature of coal mine labor, the evolution of the social relations of production, and the broader tensions in the United States over labor and citizenship meant that miners' experiences with death were part of broader cultural debates during the industrial era. By the time of the 1909 Cherry mine disaster in which 259 workers perished, Illinois coal miners had established patterns of political activism and a repertoire of ritual that reflected their economic and social positions in the United States.

A miner's death carried the potential to inspire among the living an array of emotions—from grief to relief, from anger to joy. This emotional gamut was mediated by aspects of class, race, gender, and religion. A worker's death did not produce the same response from every onlooker because Americans mapped a variety of meanings to dead working-class bodies. In the 1880s and 1890s, Illinois miners endeavored to attach dignity to the dead. Their efforts underscore the fact that work during the industrial era was both a bodily experience and a cultural construct whose meanings were up for debate. Illinois miners' encounters with mass tragedies, the daily dangers of their occupations, and the labor relations of industrial production provided three distinct venues for reflecting on the meaning of life and death in the United States during the late nineteenth century.

"Such Fearful Loss of Life": Mining Disasters in 1883

Dangers lurked in coal mines and other workplaces across the United States in the late nineteenth century. Although casualty figures in occupations such as railroading outpaced those in coal, coal mining alone produced mass fatality accidents that killed scores of workers at once and fundamentally altered traditional rituals of death and dying. In the early months of 1883, two disasters struck Illinois coal mines. On January 8, an explosion claimed the lives of ten men in Coulterville. A little more than a month later, on February 16, accumulated rainwater and melting snow rushed into the works at Diamond, flooding the mine. Sixty-nine miners perished. Both events captured headlines and became fused together as striking examples of the deadly potential of mining coal. The Coulterville and Diamond mine accidents connected Illinois coalfields to other deadly disasters, such as the Avondale, Pennsylvania, mine fire that claimed 110 lives in 1869, and demonstrated how miners risked their lives daily. At Coulterville and Diamond, survivors could not mourn the dead in the way they might have in other circumstances. The scale of the tragedies, the control mine owners exerted over the scenes, and community relationships of power influenced the death rituals that followed the disasters.

Emergency signals in coal communities raised the alarm and marked the first stage of experiences with death during a disaster. Two sharp whistles pierced the afternoon air in Coulterville, located about fifty miles southeast of St. Louis. Residents rushed to the mine shaft to look for loved ones or gain information about the nature of the accident. The explosion had reduced parts of the mine shaft to rubble. Noxious fumes stymied early attempts at rescue. Survivors and relatives could only stand in the bitter cold or return home to await news of the fate of their husbands, fathers, and friends. Around nine that night, after the smoke had begun to clear and the gases dissipated, the rescue party hoisted the corpses to the top of the mine. The bodies were washed, their legs tied together, and wagons carried them to town. By midnight an "awestruck calm" punctuated the frenzied excitement of the day as the "strangled and burned bodies" were laid out in the assembly room of the Band Hall.[2]

Similar scenes unfolded in Diamond, a small town about sixty miles southwest of Chicago. Approximately 300 miners were at work on February 16 when a worker noticed an unusual amount of water flowing into the bottom of the main shaft. Alarm spread through the tunnels and rooms of the mine as men raced to safety. Water rushed into the mine like an "Alpine torrent," according to one survivor.[3] Within a half hour, the mine had flooded. "Tongue nor pen," one reporter proclaimed, "can never describe the horror of those poor men, with water on one side and death on the other, and shut out from the light of day."[4]

As miners fled for their lives, those on the surface witnessed harrowing efforts at survival and rescue. Alerted to the accident by three sharp whistles from engines near the mine, women, children, and others in the community raced to the scene. Around the main shaft, the crowd assisted miners who reached the surface. "Women wrung their hands," the *Chicago Tribune* reported, "as, one by one, they anxiously viewed each new face that appeared above ground, but found not the father or son who was missing, and for whom some fell down upon their knees and prayed."[5] One woman suffered the heartrending experience of seeing her husband emerge from the mine with their dead son in his arms. She "was doomed to disappointment," a reporter observed, "for the man, worn out with the desperate struggle which he had undergone to save the body of his son, fell back into the pit a lifeless corpse, and has not since been seen."[6] Another group near the air shaft lent assistance to workers as they emerged from below and watched as two miners, Harmon Unger and Blazius Shatzel, entered the shaft in a futile effort to rescue trapped miners. They never returned. A half hour after the initial breach, a sea of water had taken "possession of the more remote recesses of the mine at its own deadly leisure."[7] The assembled crowds looked with hope into the water that had risen to within five feet of the surface for any last survivors. By dusk all rescue attempts were halted, and the small mining community began coming to terms with the grim reality. Sixty-nine men and boys had drowned in the No. 2 shaft of the Diamond mine.

More than the Coulterville accident, the Diamond mine disaster disrupted the possibility for traditional rituals of burial. The tragedy captured national headlines over the next days and remained in the news for the next month. After the final attempts at rescue, the work of reclamation began. The general manager of the coal mining company ordered steam pumps to the mine to begin removing the water. An estimated 3,000 coal miners in the area refused to work "in sympathy with their entombed brethren."[8] Some of the miners arrived at the Diamond mine to assist recovery efforts by building a dam to hold back water from the shaft. Others assembled at their choice of one of eighty-five saloons in the nearby town of Braidwood. "Grief is notoriously thirsty," one reporter remarked, "and no exception to the rule can be made here."[9]

Alcohol consumption was common at working-class wakes and funerals, but mourning such large numbers was not. In fact, little about the miners' deaths in the Diamond mine could have been classified as normal, even in an era when violent deaths were frequent. The massive tragedy disrupted conventional rituals of dying and burial. Europeans had been thinking about the art of dying and the characteristics of a good death since the publication of *Ars moriendi* in 1450. A good death was an anticipated death where the process of dying would allow an individual to put his or her worldly affairs in order, accept visits from the community, pray, and die surrounded by family and friends.[10] Variations on a good death included these elements and added "peaceful death" to the criterion with the hope of a painless passing.[11] Sudden, violent deaths would, by definition, constitute bad deaths, because the dying person would pass without the opportunity to practice the art of dying. Deaths away from family or homelands and deaths due to the incompetence of others could also define a bad death.[12] Americans during the nineteenth century clung to these notions of a good death, and the soldiers who fought in the Civil War and the families on the home front went to great lengths to maintain aspects of the good death.[13]

The tragedy prevented the men and boys from dying a good death, and the flooded mine threatened to deprive the community the opportunity to perform traditional burial rituals. As long as the mine remained flooded, families could only mourn over an empty space where the body should have been. They could not practice the rituals consistent with the era that helped ease the separation of the living and the dead. No one could wash and prepare the body, open their house for a viewing or wake, or conduct the remains to a final resting place.[14] These anomalies added to the emotional burdens of the traumatic situation. The living might fear that a soul thus scorned would haunt relatives as a form of retribution. Others surely felt pangs of guilt for not properly honoring the dead. For these reasons, a body—even a mangled one—was preferable to none at all.[15]

With these concerns weighing on them, widows at the Diamond mine called for recovering the bodies even as the pumps worked to rid the water from the mine. They frequently visited the mine to monitor the pumps' progress. Dispatched to the scene by the governor, Illinois adjutant general I. H. Elliott reported that the widows seemed "to care for, and think of, nothing else, and it is most deplorable to see them moving about making this inquiry of every one they meet," he reported.[16] The disaster left a sizable group to voice their concerns. Thirty-nine women became widows, and ninety-three children were left fatherless.

As widows and orphans waited for their loved ones' remains to be rescued, two events memorialized the miners. On the morning of Sunday, February 25, 1883, miners and their families crowded into Braidwood's Music Hall along with a number of "the best citizens of the place" for a memorial service. They sang hymns from Moody and Sankey songbooks and listened to ministers deliver sermons and offer prayers.[17] Reverend Adams, a Presbyterian minister at the only church in Diamond, framed the accident as a local and national calamity but praised the afflicted families for meeting the tragedy with "the greatest Christian fortitude," as "more than one poor heart was breaking with agony over the loss of some dear one who had been caught by the destroying water and carried to his death." Reverend Adams's remarks moved several women in the large audience to tears before Reverend Brunell, a visiting minister from Chicago, closed the service. Many of the same scenes recurred at an afternoon service in Diamond but were, according to one onlooker, "more affecting" because nearly all of the women and children directly affected by the accident had gathered to mourn.[18]

The memorial services continued a spectacle where prescribed rituals of burial did not fit the circumstances. Some in attendance may have previously participated in funeral services where more than one life was remembered, more than one body laid to rest. Surely, none had performed the task simultaneously for sixty-nine recently departed. Less likely still would such an event have occurred without the bodies, a point to which the widows testified. For these women, the prayers, hymns, and sermons at the memorial service allowed spiritual reflection on the souls of those still under the Illinois prairie, but it was not enough. A memorial without a body would have been like a wedding without a groom. Just like the women made widows by the Civil

War twenty years before, the women made widows by the mine accident demanded a last look at their loved ones.[19]

The widows could only wait as the pumps worked day after day to rid the water from the mine. February passed into March, and March neared its end before the mining company predicted they would soon be able to reach the bottom of the shaft and commence a mission of reclamation. The Wilmington Coal Mining and Manufacturing Company employed men to build a fence around the mine to keep relatives and curious onlookers at a distance, because "the widows and children exhibit a morbid interest in everything new that comes regarding the preparations for the recovery of the bodies."[20] Anticipation of entering the mine set the relief committee, a group from the community that had been formed to manage some of the details of the funerals and collect funds for the widows and children, into action. They ordered the cleaning of the company's blacksmith shop where the bodies would be laid out for identification, hired three barbers to clean the bodies, and contacted the Chicago & Alton Railroad to furnish two flatcars and three coaches to transport the bodies the eight miles from the mine to the cemetery.[21] A committee of women from Braidwood used crepe to decorate the flatcars and a specially constructed bier.[22] Undertakers began building coffins, and the coroners of Will and Grundy Counties argued about which one held jurisdiction to hold inquests over the dead bodies and collect the fees. The county line bisected the mine such that the bodies were thought to lie in Grundy County, while the water entered the mine in Will County.[23] After more than thirty days of incessant pumping, the plans were finally ready to be implemented.

On March 24, a team exploring the mine for the first time since the accident discovered the first two bodies. In a room adjacent to the mine shaft, the search party's flickering safety light revealed a dead miner, still clutching his dinner pail, near the center of the room. The man's face bore a vicious scar, as though he had smashed headlong into a sharp rock in his attempt at escape. Advancing a few feet farther, the party found another body in a similar position. Without disturbing either corpse, the searchers retreated to hold a meeting with mine officials. Discovery of the first body initiated a process whereby the coal company carefully controlled how the remains would be reclaimed and who could have access to the bodies. Mine managers withheld information that a search party had entered the mine for twelve hours. They feared that a sizable crowd would gather upon learning the news and hoped to forestall emotional scenes at the mine. Coal officials contacted the local sheriff to assist in the transportation of the bodies. They probably also hoped that the presence of law enforcement would preserve strict order on coal company property.

The company's attempt at secrecy failed when one official leaked the news of the impending retrieval of the bodies to a *Chicago Tribune* reporter.[24] The news attracted miners, widows, children, and other people to the mine. "Train-loads of people pouring in from all directions" swelled the crowd of waiting people to perhaps as many as four thousand.[25] Around midnight on March 25, the waiting onlookers saw the first victim exhumed. The sheriff and men he had enlisted to preserve order walked to the mouth of the shaft and almost immediately pulled the first coffin from the depths.[26]

The sight of the remains caused excitement to ripple through the assembled crowd, as the sheriff's men struggled to transport the coffin to the makeshift morgue near the mine. Onlookers desperately wanted to see the corpse in hopes of identifying the miner. Following strict orders, the sheriff's posse spirited the body to the morgue and locked the doors behind them. This maneuver made the crowd go "wild with excitement," according to one reporter. People climbed the sides of the building, hoping to peer in windows that had been covered with curtains. Some men knocked at, and others kicked, the doors, hoping to gain entry. They resorted to hurling threats at mine officials when their attempts failed. Only when three more bodies had been exhumed, washed, and arranged in tiers were the doors opened so that the process of identification could begin.[27]

The coal company's careful scripting of the reclamation and near-complete control of the access to the bodies had prompted outrage and fury. Once identification of the bodies began, authorities again asserted their power of mediating survivors' access to the bodies. As the first members of the crowd filed into the building, a woman bent down to examine one of the corpses. After carefully looking at the clothing, she nearly walked away before noticing a ring embedded in the man's swollen flesh. "With a piteous moan," a *Tribune* correspondent reported, "she threw herself upon the coffin, and with heartrending utterances identified the body as the remains of one of her relatives." The woman's display of grief, combined with her reluctance to leave the body, caused the sheriff and mine officials to forbid women from viewing the corpses. Instead, men identified the remains and then sent notice to the next of kin.[28]

After the first bodies emerged, search parties raised remains to the surface approximately every thirty minutes for the rest of the night. From two until six in the morning, mine officials did not allow anyone access to the corpses. When they opened the doors at seven, the remains of twenty-two miners had been prepared for identification. The exclusion of women did not prevent emotion from entering the temporary morgue. The local newspaper, the *Wilmington Advocate*, reported, "Many a miner brushed his sleeve across his eyes and turned away from the sickening sight, of one whom he had recognized, saying: 'Yes, it's Paddy, boys—thair's no mistake.'" Nineteen of the bodies were identified in this manner, with friends or relatives recognizing coats or hand-knitted socks as belonging to a dead miner. Relatives of five miners carried their remains away, likely intent on performing a more private, individual burial. The other seventeen bodies were transported to flatcars that stood near the mine, awaiting their grim cargo with tall biers decorated with black cloth and large white diamond-shaped figures on the side. Before the train departed for Braidwood, women were once again permitted to look at the remains of the bodies that rested in "cheap, but very decent" coffins to perhaps identify the last of the unknown.[29]

After these last looks, the train departed for Braidwood. Relatives of the deceased interrupted the coal company's plans for the procession and burial. Mrs. Redmond, a woman whose son had died in the accident, stopped the train and demanded that she be allowed to take possession of her son's body. With one less body on board, the train chugged into Braidwood to find a crowd intent on viewing the corpses before they were carried to one of the two cemeteries in town, one Catholic and one Protestant. Two of the men on the train—a "brawny Scotchman" and a "strong . . . Yorkshire lad"—attempted to deter the crowd by informing the people that the remains had already been exposed to view and identified. The crowd ultimately prevailed and convinced the men to do the "fair thing." One by one, the coffin lids came off, and "the people crushed and jostled around to catch a glimpse of the blackened, distorted forms." One widow sat on her husband's coffin and refused to move. She maintained her one-woman wake until the hearses came to take her husband to the cemetery, at which time she had to be physically lifted from the coffin and carried away.[30] From the train depot, four hearses transported the bodies in a procession to Braidwood's two cemeteries in town, where small piles of dirt "marked the place where many earthly hopes would be buried."[31]

In all search parties recovered twenty-eight bodies from the No. 2 shaft of the Diamond mine, leaving forty-one forever entombed. The precarious condition of the mine convinced the mine's manager to abandon it. At a mass meeting to discuss whether to continue reclamation efforts, Braidwood mayor Daniel McLaughlin and miners who had worked on the recovery efforts spoke in favor of ending the search. At least one miner in the crowd argued that the work should go on and that "the company should spend their last dollar on it." These comments brought shouts of "Hear! Hear!"

In the context of this debate, miners voiced their belief that their coworkers' remains represented more social and emotional capital than the coal company's solvency. They asserted that people, in this case the bodies of the recently departed, were more important than profit.[32] Ultimately, the miners and community members agreed with the company; no more lives could be risked in the search for those already lost. Thus, the "fires were drawn from the furnaces, the pumps ceased, the shaft gradually again filled with water, and the late populous mine became simply the silent sepulcher of the unrecovered dead."[33]

These details reveal important elements of how the mine accident transformed rituals of death for the coal mining community around Diamond and Braidwood. The disaster initiated a contest for power over the bodies between the coal company and the miners' relatives. The officials of the Diamond mine carefully scripted the process of reclamation, identification, and burial. Had the deaths occurred under more typical circumstances, prevailing rituals of the nineteenth century that placed the power in the hands of the family would have prevailed. Here at Diamond, employer power trumped familial prerogative.

In the context of catastrophe, gendered notions of emotion excluded women from processes normally considered female work in the emotional division of labor in grieving. Women routinely prepared bodies for burial and assumed the burden of public displays of mourning.[34] At Diamond men inverted traditional roles, citing emotional fortitude and masculine rationality to exclude overwrought women from the identification process.[35] Men, miners and others alike, manipulated the gendered ideas of rationality and emotional fragility to legitimize their power. It seems onlookers justified men's displays of emotion that occurred as they identified bodies as part and parcel of the extenuating circumstances rather than failures of manly self-control.

These two points of contest between the coal corporation and the mining community and men and women also reflected the broader context in which the Diamond disaster was rooted. Press coverage of the mine flood inadvertently revealed that a growing disparity of wealth between the rich and poor in industrial America led to radically different experiences of daily life. The popular *Frank Leslie's Illustrated Newspaper* included a page in the April 7, 1883, issue with two drawings illustrating newsworthy events of the previous two weeks (figure 1). The top image displayed the scenes of wealth and leisure as the artist depicted a ball at the opulent New York Fifth Avenue mansion of William K. Vanderbilt, Cornelius Vanderbilt's grandson. New York's elite dined in an immaculate supper room and danced in a spacious

Figure 1. Drawings of newsworthy events from the April 7, 1883, issue of *Frank Leslie's Illustrated Newspaper* included the accident at the Diamond mine

ballroom. An illustration below the images of the ball re-created the scene at the Diamond mine. Far removed from multicourse meals and the latest fashion, women formed a line in Illinois to identify recovered bodies. Perhaps editorial happenstance rather than social commentary, the illustrations nevertheless revealed what many working people began to observe in the late nineteenth century: the wealthy waltzed over working people's graves.[36]

Coal miners' responses to the Coulterville and Diamond accidents suggest that they were not content to bury coworkers for the benefit of the industrial elite. They seized the initiative to press for enhanced safety measures in order to "never again be called to the sorrowful task of recording another such catastrophe [as Diamond]."[37] Miners felt that stronger safety laws and state oversight were necessary to equalize power between miners and operators.

They argued that Illinois's 1872 mine law, passed in the wake of Pennsylvania's Avondale mine fire, made it too easy for mine managers to attribute accidents to miners' incompetence or acts of God.[38] Many Illinois miners feared that, without protection of a law, they would surely be fired if they spoke against unsafe working conditions or petitioned employers directly for change.[39] According to labor activist John McLaughlan, the disasters provided the nettles to workers' consciousness necessary to arouse Illinois miners "from their Rip Van Winkle sleep" and prodded them to stand up and defend their own lives by agitating for safety reform.[40]

On March 4, 1883, miners met in McArthur's Hall in Braidwood to organize a delegation to lobby for stricter laws in Springfield. The group framed a resolution that highlighted coal miners' importance to Illinois's economy and demanded equal protection under the laws. They bemoaned the 1872 law as being "very insufficient, and in some respects wholly ignored [by coal operators] and becoming, in fact, a dead letter," which resulted "in such fearful loss of life as the Diamond disaster and Coultersville [sic] catastrophe." The miners resolved that each man contribute five cents per month to fund lobbying to pressure their representatives in Springfield. With these funds, an elected delegation would push for compulsory escapement shafts with adequately maintained roadways leading to them, establish a statewide system of inspection, and clearly delineate fines for operators not in compliance with the state's mining laws.[41]

The Coulterville and Diamond accidents prompted an extensive overhaul of the state's mining laws, with many of the miners' demands being met. Miners ensured that the new 1883 law addressed escapement shafts and mandated clearer paths of egress. The new law also created the office of the State Inspectors of Mines, led to the first statewide system of mine inspection, and mandated uniform inspection of the mines for safety issues.[42] Both miners' activism on this issue and the legislature's willingness for reform were driven by the grief, anger, and public spectacle that followed the Coulterville and Diamond accidents. While a step toward making Illinois mines safer, the 1883 law did not completely ameliorate the risks of mining coal.

"The Revelry of Death Goes Constantly On": Everyday Death in the Mines

After the Coulterville and Diamond disasters, Illinois miners confronted the inherent dangers of their craft without a mass-fatality accident. Between 1883 and 1903, no accident claimed more than five lives.[43] Without the spectacle of a massive tragedy, the public gave little thought to the perils of the state's mines. "In the dark recesses of the coal mine the revelry of death goes constantly on, and practically unnoticed," the Illinois Bureau of Labor Statistics observed. "Few there are indeed, who, while enjoying the light of their firesides, are ever disturbed by the thought that with the consumption of every quarter of a million tons of coal, there is burned the flesh and bones of some unfortunate man."[44] While Americans enjoyed the warmth from their fire and some benefited from the expanding coal-fueled industrial economy, Illinois miners extracted coal and buried their dead.

During the 1890s, miners drew on traditions of interpreting death and ritualizing the dead that had been cultivated through several decades of occupational lore, religious practices, ethnic traditions, and fraternal benefit societies. In the increasingly class-conscious environment of the late nineteenth century, they also established trade unions to work for safer working conditions, defray the financial and emotional cost of death, and fight for the living. More common than mass tragedy, the specter of individual accidents loomed as a daily possibility. Miners' responses to everyday death demonstrate that they developed traditions and cultivated institutions to cushion death's impact while at the same time claiming dignity for working people. For Illinois miners, the turn of the century represented a period of ritual consolidation better suited for the class-derived social tensions of the industrial era. They invented traditions that blended prevailing ideas about a proper funeral in the nineteenth century with evolving ideas about the meanings of solidarity so that funerals became another venue for navigating the politics of industrial society.

Between 1883, when reliable statistics first began to be compiled, and 1910, Illinois mines produced millions of tons of coal, while thousands of miners died from work accidents. More than 3,000 men and boys died instantly in the mines or later as a result of their injuries. More than 12,500 miners sustained serious injuries. The death rate averaged 2.43 deaths per 1,000 workers, with disaster-year peaks of 5.6 in 1883 and 5.4 in 1910. Between 1901 and 1911, U.S. mines were the most dangerous among all of the major coal-producing countries in the world.[45] Before a series of mass-casualty disasters—initiated by the Cardiff mine explosion of 1903 that claimed 5 lives and punctuated by the Cherry mine fire in 1909 in which 259 miners perished in Illinois's deadliest accident—Illinois coal communities buried their dead in ones and twos.[46] As these statistics suggest, danger lurked in every nook and cranny of a coal mine.

Between 1888 and 1910, falls of rock and coal represented the number-one cause of fatalities and serious accidents, causing more than 46 percent of all fatalities. Inspectors' reports reveal the pervasive danger of falling rock and coal that occurred without warning. Seventeen-year-old James Hall was crushed only minutes after his partner had tested the roof and found it safe. While Hall likely had labored in the mines only a few years or less, forty years' experience did not save J. W. Broadbent, who died after being crushed by a piece of rock measuring eight feet long, four feet wide, and three feet thick. Other fatal accidents exemplified the complete unpredictability of death in the mines.[47] Fourteen-year-old Otto Barnes died from a fall of slate in 1891 while visiting his father in a Coulterville, Illinois, mine. Barnes's curiosity to see how miners worked drew him to the mine and cost him dearly.[48] In Illinois mines, men saw their coworkers crushed, and sons stood by as falls claimed their fathers.

Accidents caused by falling rock and coal also revealed the grim economic calculus miners computed while plying their craft. They earned an income based on the amount of coal they mined, usually measured on a per-ton basis. Any other work necessary to extracting the coal, such as laying track or stabilizing corridors and workrooms with wooden props, was unpaid work, which most miners called "dead work."[49] Inspectors reported that some miners chose to load an extra car rather than securing a seemingly unstable roof. In an occupational irony, failing to complete the dead work could lead to death. On March 11, 1898, Jon Stanhouse remarked to his partner that he would erect props to secure the roof of their workroom as soon as he finished loading a substantial pile of loose coal. Before he could finish, a piece of slate fell, crushing Stanhouse's head between the rock and coal car. He died instantly.[50] Other miners, such as Anthony Ellena, were crushed as they set the props that they hoped would ensure their safety. As Ellena cleared a spot in which to place a prop, the roof fell, killing him immediately.[51] These two examples show how some miners faced life-or-death decisions when making decisions about dead work.[52] Fatalities caused by falling rock and coal claimed more than 1,200 lives in Illinois mines.[53]

After falls of rock and coal, blasts and explosions claimed the second-highest number of lives in Illinois during the late nineteenth and early twentieth centuries, killing almost 500 miners and representing 18 percent of all fatal accidents. Underground miners risked igniting accumulated gases with their lamps. On the morning of July 25, 1890, Joseph Shober entered an abandoned room of the Lincoln Coal Company in Lincoln, Illinois, igniting what miners termed "fire-damp." While fighting to leave the room, he "swallowed considerable flame," according to the mine inspector's report, "which burned him worse internally than externally." Shober lived for three days before succumbing to his injuries.[54] Other miners died from premature blasts—when a drilled-out hole packed with blasting powder exploded before the worker was prepared—or from miscommunications between shot firers and miners. Peter Miller left a widow and six children when a shot exploded on October 13, 1893, striking him with flying coal.[55]

Falling rock and coal and various explosions represented the vast majority of fatal accidents in the mines, but did not encompass the full array of dangers. Miners could be crushed by pit cars, trapped by ascending and descending cages in the mine shaft, or, in 95 cases between 1888 and 1910, fall to their death down the mine shaft, sometimes hundreds of feet. In one utterly macabre case, an empty cage beheaded the unfortunate William Coleman on January 17, 1893. Coleman had leaned over the shaft to call to some men below when a descending cage sheared his head from his body, causing the head to tumble 333 feet to the bottom of the shaft.[56] Fatalities due to cages, pit cars, and falling down the shaft constituted 17 percent of all fatal accidents.[57]

Such dangerous workplaces provided ample opportunity for mining communities to develop specific rituals for remembering the dead and to reflect on their roles as citizen workers. Broader social and cultural debates informed the meanings behind the practices, with clear social relations informing their development. Miners used wakes and funerals as a space to perform commentaries in ongoing discussions about social worth in industrial society. They often countered employers' attitudes about safety and the value of workers' lives. These clashes shaped the development of rituals in the 1890s.

Miners' rituals intersected directly with debates about risk and liability. Mine owners, and many mine inspectors, insisted that individual miners carried the responsibility for their own well-being.[58] One Illinois inspector observed in 1886 that accidents resulted from "lapses of personal watchfulness rather than the criminal negligence of proprietors." For him, only "individual prudence"—not laws or state inspection—could curb the increasing danger in the mines.[59] Managers also blamed individual miners for risk taking, while some went so far as to generalize about coal miners, as legal scholar Earl Beckner did, calling them prone to recklessness and carelessness as a class.[60] Individualizing the danger in the mines allowed operators to obscure management decisions that imperiled miners, such as hiring inexperienced workers, failing to provide escapement shafts or adequate wood for timbering, and insisting on twelve- to fourteen-hour workdays in some Illinois mines.[61] The Illinois Bureau of Labor Statistics commented on the practices of hiring unskilled and inexperienced miners, writing, "Incompetent miners not only constantly endanger their own lives, but continually jeopardize the lives of others." Managers who hired incompetent men bore responsibility that amounted "to criminal carelessness and liability."[62]

Miners accepted a certain amount of risk involved with the occupation in a discerning exchange of danger for a measure of independence and modest wages.[63] They never reconciled themselves, however, to charges of carelessness from mine managers, owners, or other commentators. Indeed, miners and newspapers sympathetic to mining communities and those sympathetic with the labor movement did not equivocate about responsibility for unsafe working conditions. When analyzing the "appalling" number of accidents in the early 1880s, the *National Labor Tribune* could only wonder that the number was not greater due to "the domineering methods of pit bosses." "We believe that more than half the casualties are directly caused by overwork and long hours in the damp and foul air of the mine, and if the present system of working twelve or fourteen hours per day were removed by the enforcement of a national eight hour law there would be fewer accidents in the mines," the paper argued. Speaking before Congress in 1901, United Mine Workers of America president John Mitchell declared that accidents "were often the fault of the mine owners" and thought that legislation ought to be enacted to ensure mine safety. Further reflecting the Progressive Era turn toward advocating state intervention and legal reform, journalist Robert Watchorn demanded change. "Every preventable death in a coal mine is equivalent to a case of manslaughter or homicide," he wrote, "and it is the State's business to put an end to the shocking travesty of dependent local juries presenting their monotonous verdicts of 'unavoidable accidents.'"[64]

Debates about liability extended beyond the narrow confines of legal theory. Some miners interpreted operators' decisions about safety as revealing a social commentary on how the owners viewed the human worth of their employees. Illinois miner Jack Battuello was born into a coal mining family in 1899 and entered the mines at the age of thirteen. He felt employers cared more for the mules who pulled the coal to the shaft than the miners who extracted it. "It was not unusual," Battuello recalled in an oral interview in 1973, "for the mine executives to come to the mine and conduct an investigation if a mule was injured or killed, but no such investigation ever took place when a miner was killed."[65]

Ideas about race and attitudes toward immigrants added another hue to the lenses with which employers viewed workers. Immigrants historically worked the coalfields of Illinois, and the evolving composition of the workforce paralleled broader immigration patterns. English, Irish, Welsh, and Scottish miners dominated the coalfields through the 1890s. In that same decade, southern and eastern Europeans—especially Italians, Poles, and Czechs—began arriving in significant numbers.[66] Employers' attitudes toward miners' deaths were influenced by the high number of immigrants in the workforce, according to Lyman Beecher Stowe, a Progressive Era author and Harriet Beecher Stowe's grandson. He reported that one corporation executive responded to the large loss of life by saying, "Yes; but, after all, it's not so serious, because most of the men killed are ignorant foreigners who can be easily replaced."[67] Foreign-born workers constituted more than half of the workforce in Illinois mines throughout the state, and concentrations could be as high as 80 or 90 percent in some towns.[68]

Attitudes such as those Stowe reported challenged the human and social worth of miners and working people generally. Wakes, funerals, and other tributes to dead workers provided a way to combat these callous assessments and offer alternative arguments. Well-attended funerals and accompanying rituals provided a way to claim human worth and mark social place. The social and cultural ramifications of a proper burial produced a persistent fear of the opposite: a pauper burial. A state-sponsored funeral or burial in a potter's field became a paramount concern for working people. Such an end offended workers' sense of independence and seemed like a final insult at the end of a hardscrabble life near the bottom of the social hierarchy. Worst of all, an anonymous burial seemed to confirm employers' arguments about workers' expendability. To avoid such embarrassment, miners and other working people developed extensive networks of mutual aid. They inculcated the values of a respectable burial to successive generations. Miners joined fraternal associations that offered burial benefits as well as burial and sick societies and purchased life insurance policies where available.[69]

Given their high fatality rates and proclivity to meet death on the job, miners often met exclusive membership policies from some organizations and insurance companies. Some life insurance companies refused to enroll miners or did so at an inflated rate.[70] The Independent Order of Foresters had banned miners from joining their organization by 1905, largely out of fear that they would quickly drain their life insurance funds. Similarly, in their 1908 constitution, the Security Benefit Association denied benefits for any claim caused by "a mob, riot, or insurrection, or as a result of being engaged in committing any offense against the laws of any State or Nation."[71] Violence proved a persistent feature of economic relations in Illinois communities and likely gave corporations like the SBA reasons to refuse to insure miners or deny their claims.[72] More broadly, patterns of discrimination through fraternal societies and insurance companies angered miners and served as a marker of their occupation and class. Although many organizations accepted miners, the exclusion they met prompted them to form class-based alternatives to traditional fraternal organizations. They turned to union organizing.

Unionization efforts in coalfields in the nineteenth century revealed persistent concerns about issues of health and safety, care for the dead, and support for widows and children. Illinois miners from the Belleville area initiated the first attempt at a national miners' union in 1861. English immigrant Daniel

Weaver brought political skills honed from the Chartist movement to organizing coal miners, urging them to create an "electric sympathy" for solidarity to prevent the "insatiable maw of Capital" from devouring "Labor's rights."[73] His leadership led to the founding of the American Miners' Association.[74] The constitution commented on the "manifold dangers" of the mines as a key reason for the union "as well as . . . accidents arising from other causes consequent upon the parsimony of employers, whose objects would seem to be the increase of their capital, without reference to the fearful loss of life, limb and health, which is the cause of such increase."[75] The AMA quickly acted to improve working conditions in Illinois; in 1863 union miners presented safety legislation to the general assembly that passed the senate but "was killed by legislative trickery" in the house.[76] Internal dissension among the leadership and strikes in 1867 and 1868 caused the AMA's dissolution.

The AMA might have enjoyed a brief history and few successes, but the union set a pattern that subsequent miners followed when organizing. Miners' unions in the 1870s held a similar focus on pressuring for safety legislation and added clauses to their constitutions to provide burial funds. In its short tenure between 1871 and 1873, the Illinois Miners' Benevolent and Protective Association used dues money to provide five dollars a week for injured miners and forty dollars for the burial of members. Illinois workers helped elect John Hinchliffe to the state legislature, where, aided by a committee of miners chaired by Walton Rutledge, he was successful in winning support for the passage of the state's first mining law in 1872 that regulated ventilation and implemented an inspection system. Miners agitated for stronger legislation in every session between 1872 and 1883, when the Diamond mine disaster made the political climate amenable for a stricter inspection regime.[77]

Miners' unions of the 1880s continued to argue for the economic and social importance of the nation's miners. The National Federation of Miners, which competed with the Knights of Labor for members during the 1880s, listed as one of its key objectives "the protection of [miners'] health and their lives" and hoped to "obtain legislative enactments . . . whereby the lives and health of our members may be better preserved."[78] In a call to operators for a joint conference to negotiate, the union connected health and safety on the job to the rights of full citizens who ought to realize the benefits of the industrial economy. On the latter point, the miners argued:

> The freedom hitherto enjoyed in this country by our well rewarded labor and the intelligence and dignity of the American workingman have been matters of congratulation alike gratifying to our civil pride and conducive to our national glory. Our industrial progress, the continuance of our unexampled prosperity,

the peace of society, and security of our free form of government, each and all demand that the American workingman shall receive just and liberal wages and decent treatment. The workingmen in our mines, in our factories, and in our farms compose not only a vast array of citizenship, but constitute our mighty standing army, which is ever ready for the defense of our country's rights and our country's honor.[79]

Unions like the Illinois Miners' Benevolent Association and the National Federation of Miners provided a discourse on health, safety, and social worth. Rituals of death in coal mining communities that coalesced at the end of the nineteenth century had roots in these earlier efforts to protect miners' lives and argue for the importance of miners to the economy.

The United Mine Workers of America was a product of the history of short-lived local and national unions. The union emerged in 1890 from a merger of the National Federation of Miners and the Knights of Labor Trade Assembly No. 135. The founders established a clear set of principles in the constitution, arguing that "those whose lot it is to toil in the recesses of the earth" made possible the "grand achievements, privileges, and blessings" of the industrial era and demanded the "just fruits of [their] toil."[80] To win respect on the job and in society, the UMWA formulated eleven objectives of the new union that included banning child labor, calling for the eight-hour day, and abolishing company stores and payment in scrip. Issues of safety also featured prominently in the objectives. Miners advocated stricter safety laws and the introduction of "any and all well-defined appliances for the preservation of life, health, and limbs of all mine employees."[81] They founded the UMWA on principles of inclusion. They organized all workers in the mine on an industrial basis, irrespective of skill or particular craft, and forbade discrimination on the basis of race, color, creed, or nationality.[82] Some Illinois locals levied fines for violating the nondiscrimination clause.[83] At the turn of the century, the UMWA served as an important institution in Illinois miners' lives that fought to improve working conditions and win respect for the occupation.

They worked toward these goals, in part, by helping miners negotiate experiences with death. Like its predecessors, the UMWA established accident funds, funeral benefits, and funds for surviving relatives. Each local determined the amount of a death benefit, with $50 seeming to represent the norm in Illinois in the 1890s.[84] The UMWA in Illinois distributed $132,620 in 1899 for relief to injured workers and to provide for widows and children of dead miners.[85] By the end of the decade, union miners had developed a set of rituals to remember their deceased coworkers that included a union graveside burial service, well-attended funerals, resolutions of respect, and, in some rare cases, elaborate monuments. These rituals emerged in collaboration with religious practices and cross-class fraternal organizations of the period such as the Independent Order of Odd Fellows (IOOF) and built on traditions that nourished immigrant communities.[86] As the UMWA's membership numbers grew and the union strengthened, becoming a union miner prevented an ignominious pauper's burial.

A well-attended funeral became a badge of honor that sent messages to the miners' families and to the broader community that the individual's life had meaning. UMWA locals suspended work and turned out en masse to attend memorial services "in a body."[87] Miners staged conspicuous funeral processions that could include thousands of community members, bands, and various forms of transportation. When Fritz Hubert died on September 19, 1898, as a result of an accident in the No. 10 mine near Mt. Olive, Illinois, Local 728 marched his body to the grave in order to "pay [their] last respects to a United Mine Worker." They did so, according to one onlooker, to "show their sympathy to the bereaved ones" and also to "show regret that he should be so suddenly taken from our midsts."[88] In another case, one hundred miners accompanied the King Humbert's band of Herrin to escort the bodies of four coworkers killed in an explosion in a Murphysboro mine back to Herrin for burial. Of the four, two were interred in Illinois. A delegation from the Independent Order of Odd Fellows traveled with the other two bodies to Coal Creek, Colorado, where the deceased miners had lived before seeking work in the Midwest.[89]

Once the funeral processions reached the intended cemetery, the UMWA constitution provided a script to be read graveside. After reciting a brief biography of the deceased miner, the text led miners to think about their mortality, their networks of coworkers and friendships, and the possibility of afterlife. "Again, brother workmen," the burial service read, "we are reminded that we too are but mortal and will soon break the tenement of clay and soar to the flowery fields of the sweet hereafter; and it behooves each of us here today to follow a line of conduct that will bring about a closer friendship, one that is true to God and man." Before closing with prayer, miners paid "the last sad rite and tribute of respect" by placing evergreens on the grave "as a token of respect, that thy memory shall be with us always, though thou hast paid the debt and hast gone to the realms above."[90] Although brief, the union burial service directed miners' thoughts vertically through realms of life, death, and heaven beyond. The ritual also connected miners horizontally to the mining communities that they hoped to unite with a spirit of brotherhood and fellowship.

In a broader society that regarded miners "as almost beyond the pale of well-ordered civilization," miners used these rituals to insert their human losses into the public sphere and claim human dignity.[91] Each funeral procession provided a grim reminder of the cost of coal. The evolution of codified union rituals of death and dying around the turn of the century showed that their lives would no longer "become a sacrifice to their ignorance" of the social relations that enveloped the industry.[92]

A "Baptism of Blood": Reanimating the Union Movement

The 1890s was a pivotal decade for the UMWA in Illinois. The union melded previous burial practices established by churches, fraternal societies, and other unions to lay the foundations for a coherent set of ritual practices for union coal miners. This repertoire of rituals did not, by itself, ensure the vitality of the union in the Land of Lincoln. A battle between union coal miners and coal operators served as a congealing agent that made the rituals essential to bridging workplace, home, and community and cementing the bonds of solidarity.

From its promising beginning in 1890, the UMWA in Illinois found its ranks depleted as the country clawed its way out of the economic depression that plagued the middle years of the decade. In 1897 the union claimed fewer than 400 members out of a workforce that numbered nearly 35,000.[93] The low membership figures did not adequately reveal the miners' discontent, however. When UMWA president Michael Ratchford called a strike for July 4, 1897, to resist "the cruel, heartless, and inhuman conditions" imposed on workers by "unscrupulous employers," northern Illinois miners answered.[94] They joined an arc of idle miners that stretched westward from western Pennsylvania to the Midwest and comprised an estimated 150,000 workers. Ratchford called the strike the action of "an enslaved class" forced to protest their "overworked, underpaid," and "semi-starved" existence.[95] Strikers' peaceful protest garnered widespread public support with heart-wrenching tales of deprivation and declining living standards in coalfields. Operators were forced to the negotiating table. Union leaders and operators reached a compromise agreement in Columbus, Ohio, in September that provided a slight wage increase and a promise to resuscitate an interstate trade agreement. Miners from Pennsylvania, Ohio, and Indiana went back to work. Northern Illinois miners did not. They held out a bit longer, hoping to win their demands on wages and working conditions without the compromises of the Columbus agreement. Operators' threats to import replacement Chinese workers motivated a settlement at Joliet on November 22 that established an average wage increase of ten cents per ton, which was slightly higher than the Columbus agreement.[96]

The union victories in Joliet paved the way to Chicago, where operators and miners met in January 1898 for the first interstate conference in more than a decade. UMWA officials arrived emboldened by the surge in membership generated by the successes of 1897; in the four months since the Columbus agreement, the national membership increased from 10,000 to more than 30,000.[97] While union leaders entered with confidence, both sides hoped to stabilize the fractious labor relations that had plagued the industry.[98] They agreed to an average wage increase of ten cents per ton, an eight-hour day, and a six-day week. Operators reversed their long opposition to shorter workdays as a way to prevent overproduction from driving down the cost of coal. They also promised future negotiations with the UMWA.[99] Onlookers hailed the conference as a model to solve the labor problem in the United States. "The Chicago convention was . . . perhaps the most remarkable gathering of employers and their workmen ever held in this country," Harvard economist John E. George proclaimed, because both operators and miners recognized their mutual interests.[100] George's optimism had boundaries, however. Not all coal operators were satisfied with the growing influence of the UMWA or the terms of the Chicago agreement.

Two of Illinois's largest operators, the Chicago-Virden Coal Company and the Pana Coal Company, protested the agreement. The Chicago-Virden Coal Company locked out its workers and in August began advertising in the South for replacement miners. "Wanted—one hundred and seventy-five good colored miners for Virden, Illinois," the circular declared. The company enticed African American miners with the promise of thirty cents per ton and a paycheck every two weeks.[101]

The advertisements failed to mention the maelstrom of labor conflict that awaited the southern miners if they boarded a train bound for central Illinois. In September Fred Lukens, the manager of the Virden mine, ordered the construction of a stockade around the shaft and hired fifty armed guards to police the property. Miners from across the state traveled to Virden and braced for a confrontation. One reporter compared the festering tensions to those in Cuba during the Spanish-American War. "Virden to-night is like a town occupied by an army of men. All that is needed is the uniforms of soldiers of the United States and a visitor here might believe himself at Santiago or some other place where battles have been fought lately."[102] Strikers drew similar parallels. They interpreted the stockade as an arrogant display of the company's property rights and nicknamed the barricaded mine shaft Moro Castle, a reference to the Spanish fort that guarded Havana, Cuba.[103] Like U.S. soldiers who had recently taken a stand against despotism in the form of the Spanish empire, Illinois strikers prepared to fight to defend their homes and ways of life from the threats posed by the coal company and their tactics of importing strikebreakers.

The allusions to the recent war were apt in other ways as well. Notions of manliness and race motivated strikers just as they had influenced American interpretations of the war in Cuba.[104] At a community rally in support of the miners in Springfield on October 11, speakers extolled the respectability of hardworking coal miners who were not awarded fair compensation for their labors. UMWA vice president John Mitchell drew on producerist rhetoric reminiscent of the Knights of Labor and the recently defeated Populist Party, as he reminded listeners that the miners made the Chicago-Virden Coal Company the most productive in the state. Mitchell and other speakers went to great lengths to make the Virden strike and the threat of imported strikebreakers about economics rather than race. Referring to the UMWA's constitution, Mitchell declared, "We know no color or creed in our union. A colored man is as welcome to join as a white man and will have our support." Therefore, he concluded, the union did not resist on the grounds of prejudice. Rather, miners refused "to be driven from their homes and have imported ex-convicts take their places."[105] Mitchell framed the miners' motivations as protecting their livelihoods.

Although Mitchell emphasized the miners' manly duty to protect their homes and paychecks, racial commentary also played a role in uniting the miners and inspiring community support for their stand against imported labor. Mitchell and other speakers at the rally couched their remarks in a broader discourse of white working-class respectability and cast the southern black miners as their counterparts. He reminded the audience that the Illinois miners "have broken no laws and do not intend to." He contrasted the law-abiding union members with the "imported ex-convicts" who threatened their jobs. "We believe it has come to a bad state," he argued, "when the women of Pana are afraid to go on the streets owing to the fact that armed negroes are on them starting fights and defying laws."[106] By the end of his speech, Mitchell had defined the black workers as threats to miners' paychecks, to their laws, and to their women. He declared that white men had the duty of resisting these challenges.

Mitchell's audience agreed with this analysis. Before the meeting disbanded, they passed a resolution criticizing the mine managers for "importing a lawless set of men," a tactic that represented a "menace to society."

The resolution referred to the black workers as "an undesirable class" and a "body of cheap, ignorant laboring men."[107] In a decade in which Jim Crow laws were spreading across the South, people of central Illinois employed a similar rationale that white southerners used to legally segregate the races and form lynch mobs. Illinois strikers cloaked themselves in the rhetoric of job security, manliness, and white working-class respectability. While Illinois miners stayed vigilant to defend their jobs and homes, African Americans boarded trains in Alabama with dreams of steady pay and decent work.[108]

These competing visions collided at Virden just before noon on October 12. As the train steamed near the mine, a shot rang out from an unknown source, and the battle commenced. Company guards fired at miners from the train and from behind the wooden pickets of the stockade. Miners flanked the opposite side of the tracks and returned fire. One of the guards stationed on the train later commented that the class warfare was "hotter than San Juan Hill."[109] As men fell dead or wounded, the train engineer pulled away from the mine with all Alabama miners on board. As many as forty-seven union miners had been shot, eight fatally. Nine company guards sustained wounds, of which four died.[110] At least one black miner was wounded in the firefight. This brief skirmish left a long casualty list and an even larger impact on the history of unionism in Illinois. The battle at Virden propelled the UMWA to unprecedented heights of membership and influence in Illinois coal mines and across the country. The UMWA's ascent began with the deaths at Virden—what one Illinois man claimed was a "baptism of blood"—and was sustained by the rituals that Illinois miners practiced to commemorate those who sacrificed their lives for union principles.[111]

The scenes that unfolded after the guns fell quiet displayed a tightly knit extended coal mining community that came to the aid of fellow workers and preserved the dignity of the dead. Father Clancey, a local Catholic priest, rushed onto the battlefield to administer extreme unction to the dying. Local women scoured the battlefield for husbands and fathers while hurling invectives and shaking their fists at the stockade. Teams with wagons carted the wounded to nearby houses, and women such as Mrs. O'Neill and Mrs. McWhinney performed triage. With all of the doctors called to the stockade, Mrs. O'Neill opened her house. Her office became a hospital, and her parlor was transformed into a temporary morgue. Women dressed wounds for the living. They washed the bodies of the dead and respectfully laid them out to await an undertaker.[112] The governor of Illinois, John Riley Tanner, ordered the state militia to Virden to ensure that no other bodies were added to Mrs. O'Neill's parlor or to the list of dead guards protecting the coal company's property.[113]

Rage at the Chicago-Virden Coal Company transitioned into grief and mourning for the dead miners. After John Mitchell reported the battle to UMWA president Ratchford, Ratchford telegrammed: "The union miners who fell in yesterday's riot must have a decent burial."[114] This reply represented a value system that stood at the center of union miners' beliefs about life and death. The UMWA and the miners of central Illinois drew on a repertoire of ritual that had developed during the nineteenth century. They passed resolutions of respect in their local union halls, draped their union charters in mourning, and planned funerals in which all area miners were required to attend. These practices inserted miners' voices in the broader currents of the cultures of industrialization. They demanded an accounting of workers' dignity and place in the Republic.

Illinois miners used these rituals to steel their resolve in the struggle against the Chicago-Virden Coal Company and to elevate the dead to the status of martyrs to the cause of the labor movement. The first order of business was to bury the dead. Frank Cartwright, likely the president of a UMWA local near Springfield, Illinois, issued a public call to all miners to attend the funerals of two of the Virden dead, Edward Welch and Frank Bilyeu. He requested that miners in central Illinois attend the funerals rather than reporting to work.[115] Miners answered the call. An estimated two-thousand-person funeral procession accompanied the body of Edward Welch, making it "one of the largest [funerals] that has occurred" in central Illinois, according to Springfield's *Illinois State Register*.[116] The size of the procession clearly made an impression in a town that had hosted one of the largest public memorials in American history when Abraham Lincoln's funeral train made its final stop there.[117] Miners also heeded the call to remain idle for William Harmon's funeral. They traveled to Sorento from Mount Olive, Staunton, Virden, Litchfield, Girard, and Coffeen to pay their last respects.[118]

Perhaps the most remarkable of the funerals occurred in Mount Olive, as Illinois miners laid to rest Ernst Kaemmerer, Joseph Gitterle, and E. W. Smith. One funeral service remembered the three men, in which the traditions of each man's religious denomination played a role. Protestants mourned alongside Catholics as they buried the three men together in one grave. This last act was the ultimate symbol of solidarity for the *United Mine Workers Journal*. "We think," the author opined, "it is the most beautiful act that could be done by the living to proclaim to the world that though we differ as to the forms of religion, differ as to its ceremonies, that these differences do not prevent us from acting in unison when such is necessary for our industrial welfare, nor does it prevent us from bearing our heads and bowing in respectful deference [sic] when the last sad rites are being performed over the bodies of our departed comrades." Surviving family members of those killed at Virden shared the spirit of gratitude for the solidarity Illinois miners displayed to the deceased. They sent thank-you letters to local newspapers, expressing appreciation to union locals for the "display of true friendship [that] was not lost sight of in our sorrow."[119] The funeral services for the dead men thus united central Illinois coal mining communities in their grief for the dead and motivated the living to improve working and living conditions for the living.

While the funerals provided powerful symbolism of solidarity, the graves also became catalysts to reassert beliefs central to union culture and to ensure that the lives were not sacrificed for a lost cause. Miners passed resolutions praising their fallen union brothers. People sympathetic to the miners' struggle wrote poems commemorating the battle, and miners took relics from the battle site that were later awarded as special prestigious tokens of honor.[120]

These behaviors paralleled traditional rituals of death and dying, but they also bore the stamp of class struggle and constituted the process by which the dead from the battle were elevated to the status of martyrs. While it was customary by 1898 for unions to drape their charters in mourning for thirty days after a member passed, it was not common for the locals to pass resolutions with harsh rhetoric. After the battle at Virden, one union local took the opportunity of the ritual draping of the charter to criticize the Chicago-Virden Coal Company for hiring "thugs and assassins." The local also praised their fallen brothers for "nobly defending rights and liberty against greed and oppression."[121] The editors of the *United Mine Workers Journal* proclaimed that the story of the Virden struggle would be passed from generation to generation so that the blood spilled on the soil would grow the union, just as "the blood of the martyrs is the seed of the church." Miners' struggles at Virden served as the "seeds of unionism" that were "well watered by the blood and fertilized by the suffering of our fellow miners, who died that our opportunities may become enlarged and our heritage more sacred." The newspaper promised that "Remember Virden" was destined to become as popular and emotionally significant as the call of "Remember the *Maine*" had been in the days before the United States declared war against Spain.[122]

As the outcome of the strike hung in the balance, Murphysboro, Illinois, resident George Bagwill powerfully evoked the connection between the miners' deaths and the duty of the surviving union members in a November letter to the *United Mine Workers Journal*. "All honor to our heroic dead," he wrote. "Their graves are a legacy of which we may well be proud, but their courage has left us responsibilities that will tax our noblest manhood to fulfill. So let us wreath our graves with flowers. We will be grateful for their sacrifice, and proud of their courage and above all we will seek to be worthy of our union and our dead."[123] Bagwill likely had two meanings of manhood in mind. One centered on the labor conflict between the miners and operators. Bagwill exhorted the strikers to victory. Defeat would be a demerit on the miners' manhood and would devalue the sacrifice of the dead miners. The other meaning of manhood applied to union brothers caring for the wives and children affected by the deaths. While union locals across the state collected funds to bury their dead, they also collected money to house the widows and educate the children. One local miner referred to this act of union paternalism as a "sacred duty."[124] Illinois miners followed through with their perceived obligations. By September 1899, they had collected thirty thousand dollars for the widows and children. Buttressed by this large sum and the prevailing gender norms of the nineteenth century that cast women as dependents and men as breadwinners, the UMWA became the guardian of the women and children. The union purchased houses for two widows and bestowed ownership so long as the women did not remarry. It also took responsibility for educating the children in "useful trades" and declared that "the union acts as guardian for them."[125] Establishing the UMWA as the authority over widows allowed union men to act on ethos of mutualism inherent in trade unionism, while also perpetuating the idea that the domestic sphere was the proper one for women. Widows could also serve as grim reminders of how the capitalist relationships of production threatened workers' family life.[126]

Much like the sinking of the *Maine* rallied the country to war in the spring of 1898, the lowering of miners' caskets inspired the Illinois miners' union to stand firm in the fall. Governor Tanner's ordering of the National Guard to Virden prevented any additional attempts at importing replacement workers. By mid-November, the Chicago-Virden Coal Company conceded defeat and agreed to honor the conditions of the Chicago agreement. Miners reveled in victory, but most onlookers recognized that the cost had been high. The *Mount Olive Herald* declared that it was "not until bloodshed and the sacrifice of human life" occurred that the mine manager considered negotiating.[127] The newspaper held the company responsible for the loss of life. Public sentiment in central Illinois favored the striking miners. Economic arguments, racial prejudice, and the emotion of burying local men contributed to the miners' victory.

Although the strike ended successfully, labor peace did not linger. Two conflicts erupted in 1899 that once again featured violent race relations. A riot broke out in Pana in April when Governor Tanner removed the National Guard. Five hundred white miners attacked a nearly equal number of blacks.

Six people died, five of whom were African Americans, and fourteen were wounded.[128] Later in the year and farther south, five black miners fell dead after a gunfight with white union miners at Carterville.[129] These incidents demonstrated the persistence of racial conflict and reflected a tension between the UMWA's nondiscrimination clause and the practice of race relations in Illinois coalfields.

Ironically, as white miners battled blacks in 1898 and 1899, they shared particular attitudes toward respectable burial and bringing dignity to the dead that had historic roots in African American culture. Before the Civil War, slaves placed great importance on providing dignified burials for their dead, even if it meant holding funerals in the dead of night beyond the watching eyes of masters.[130] Freedmen persevered in the struggle to provide dignified burial to community members during Reconstruction and beyond. Blacks banded together to form burial organizations that paid death benefits. Discriminated against in local cemeteries across the country, black fraternal and religious groups purchased land and established African American cemeteries.[131] In 1876, to cite just one example, the black working-class fraternal society Sons of Zion established Zion Cemetery in Memphis, Tennessee, to provide its members guaranteed access to respectable burial grounds.[132] Racial prejudice and economic oppression made honorable burials a central feature of African American culture from slavery to freedom.

In the fall of 1899, UMWA miners followed a path blazed by earlier African American fraternal and religious organizations. The union miners sought to erect a monument in Mount Olive Cemetery to the memory of the Virden dead. It was meant to be a token of respect and "a tribute to the memory of these martyred heroes."[133] As the miners' plans became public, the donor of the land for the Mount Olive Cemetery objected to both the intended monument and the ceremonies that would honor the dead. Union miners turned to the adjacent Immanuel Lutheran Cemetery, but were again rebuffed. The churchmen refused to allow the dead miners to be buried in their cemetery. They interpreted the men as "murderers," not martyrs.[134]

To ensure the proper respect for the Virden dead, the UMWA purchased one acre of land adjacent to the other two cemeteries in Mount Olive. They created the Union Miners Cemetery, the only union-owned burial ground in the United States.[135] With their own land, the miners had the power to determine how their fallen union brothers would be remembered. Local Union No. 728 held a memorial-day ceremony on October 12, 1899, to remember the battle at Virden and unveil a monument dedicated to E. W. Smith, Joe Gitterle, Ernst Kaemmerer, and E. F. Long. The *Mount Olive Herald* reported that eight thousand people participated in the event that featured a parade, ornate wreathes, bands, singing, and speeches. Undoubtedly attempting to add solemnity to the occasion, organizers invited Mrs. Lucy Parsons to speak. Parsons's presence drew a literal and symbolic connection to the Haymarket martyrs and their monument in Waldheim Cemetery that lay just west of Chicago—another burial space held sacred by the labor movement in the United States and beyond.[136] The cemetery and the festivities of the memorial day offered a clear argument to those in Illinois who might suggest that the union miners interred in the Union Miners Cemetery were murderers. The monument, parade, and speeches testified that the men were "heroes" who died fighting for "the principles of their noble cause."[137]

The founding of the Union Miners Cemetery erected a symbolic landmark to labor in Illinois and facilitated the creation of new traditions. Miners declared October 12 Union Miners Day in Illinois, and they organized commemorative events each year between 1899 and the mid–twentieth century. Thousands attended each year between 1900 and 1904. Eminent labor movement figures such as Eugene Debs, John Mitchell, and Mother Jones traveled to Mount Olive to participate.[138] Mother Jones, that iconic figure of labor struggles during the Progressive Era, requested to be buried in the Union Miners Cemetery alongside those who died at Virden. An estimated crowd of fifteen thousand laid her to rest on December 8, 1930.[139] In the midst of another series of labor battles in central Illinois in the 1930s, the Progressive Mine Workers of America erected a monument to Mother Jones and the Virden dead.[140] Although more than thirty years had passed since the battle at Virden, the miners lined the base of the monument with epitaphs for Gitterle, Kaemmerer, and Smith to emphasize the values that sustained their organization. Kaemmerer's read, for example, "He thought it better to be dead to die for liberty and his friends than live in bondage or just for bread." The epitaphs, the monument, and the cemetery enshrined the memories of the Virden martyrs on the landscape of Illinois.

The battle at Virden and subsequent scenes of community mourning, mass funerals, memorialization, and union victory led to a precipitous growth in UMWA influence in the state and nation. Miners rallied to the union that demonstrated a commitment to improve wages and working conditions. They also responded to a union that honored its dead. Membership in District 12, the district that encompassed Illinois, ballooned from fewer than four hundred before the 1897 strike to seventeen thousand in 1899. By the early years of the twentieth century, the UMWA had organized locals in every part of the state and claimed nearly fifty thousand members, which constituted nearly 20 percent of the national membership. From the brink of dissolution, union members had battled, bled, and died to become the most powerful district of one of the most influential unions in the United States.[141]

The events at Virden and Pana provided a third way Illinois coal miners experienced death during the industrial era: violent confrontation with employers and strikebreakers. This form of death had more layers of social meaning than did dying from a massive accident or the everyday instances of death that pervaded the industry. The struggle at Virden was a microcosm of the labor question that dominated the later decades of the nineteenth century. Illinois miners viewed their struggle as one of social class. Workers pitted themselves against mine managers and absentee owners. Miners who fell as a result of the violent conflict at Virden became heroes, indeed martyrs, to the cause of unionization. Their acts represented manly deeds of defending homes and livelihoods. Their deaths became powerful symbols of the stakes involved. Whereas some other instances of class violence in the nineteenth century broke the backs of strikes and demoralized workers, the Virden strike steeled the miners' resolve and catalyzed the entire union. It also became a central part of the historical memory of coal miners' ideas about death that spanned backward to Avondale, Pennsylvania, and would extend forward to future accidents and conflicts that characterized the history of coal mining in the United States.

From "Only a Miner" to "Every New Grave Brings a Thousand Members"

Looking at Illinois coal miners' experiences with death and dying provides the opportunity to assess the human and emotional impact of industrialization. Miners daily negotiated the risks associated with their profession. They reached for solace in their religious faiths and in their family and community relationships. They refused to accept dangerous working conditions as inherent to the job and beyond remediation. Nor did the Diamond miners, or later the Cherry miners, accept mass-casualty accidents as unavoidable or as merely acts of God. Illinois miners used death as a means of interpreting their lives in the context of an evolving national economy. They used their experiences in the mines and their attitudes about death to launch political reform movements and organize unions that were central to the culture of protest during the industrial era. The grave became a symbol for the dignity of labor. The 1879 version of the poem "Only a Miner" made this point explicit, declaring that miners, buried in a plain grave, could be heroes just "As any who sleep / In a marble-top grave."[142] Miners and their families joined together in cemeteries and union halls to claim dignity for those who picked, blasted, and hauled coal.

Some UMWA leaders at the turn of the twentieth century, such as UMWA secretary W. C. Pearce, tended to focus on the economic incentives for joining the union. Testifying before Congress, Pearce argued that when the UMWA gained "a little advance in wages . . . our membership increased." Wage increases and other improvements on the job certainly played a role in the UMWA's growth. But so too did miners' rituals of death and dying. In the middle of the twentieth century, folk singer Woody Guthrie recorded "Union Burying Ground," in which he sang, "Every new grave brings a thousand members." By correlating the number of graves to union membership, Guthrie suggested the intermingling of a broader array of motives for unionization than did Pearce. In his song, Guthrie tapped decades of mining lore and community history that showed coal miners were concerned with much more than economics.[143] He could have easily drawn some inspiration from Illinois. Illinois miners created a repertoire of rituals during the 1880s and 1890s that were a hybrid of religious, fraternal, and immigrant traditions. Making symbolic gestures, attending funerals en masse, and positively memorializing the dead created a culture of solidarity that buttressed the economic calculus of craft unionism.

4 As Close to Hell as They Hoped to Get

Steel, Death, and Community in Western Pennsylvania, 1892–1919

Like coal, steel manufacturing served as a barometer of industrialization in the United States. In contrast to Illinois coal miners who built a strong union and exercised a vast degree of autonomy on the job, steelworkers labored in a starkly different atmosphere in western Pennsylvania. The defeat of the Amalgamated Association of Iron and Steel Workers (AAISW) at Homestead in 1892 ushered in the nonunion era in the steel mills. Expanding strata of managers and foremen sought to control an ethnically diverse semi- and unskilled workforce. Steel corporations extended their control into communities. They used their economic might to cement the loyalty of municipal governments and funded philanthropic projects like sports teams and public libraries to foster fealty among workers. Relationships between work and community influenced how steelworkers and their families interpreted and experienced death at the turn of the century.

Reformer Crystal Eastman explored these connections while conducting research for the Pittsburgh Survey in 1906 and 1907. She found that, in the midst of the "daily tyranny of hard work in their lives," steelworkers and their wives had "little time for pondering the 'Why?' of sorrow." She concluded that working people did not have the "luxury of grief."[1] Eastman's observations contained shades of truth. The nature of life in and around the steel mills certainly shaped working people's interaction with death. Yet Eastman's commentary inspires questions that go beyond the purview of her study. How did people working in the mills and living in their shadow reflect on death and express their grief? How did skill, ethnicity, race, gender, and religion interact in producing rituals, institutions, and attitudes about dangerous working conditions and deleterious living environments?

Death hovered over Pittsburgh as thickly as the black smoke that belched from the mills and foundries. Seven workers sacrificed their lives in defense of unionism during the epic battle at Homestead in 1892. Thousands died on the job or as a result of occupational injuries. Even more met death in the streets and rooms of Pittsburgh's working-class neighborhoods. This chapter begins with an analysis of death in the Homestead strike and then examines working people's experiences with death and dying on the job and in their neighborhoods during the first half of the nonunion era. Dreams of freedom and social mobility fired immigrants'—and later African American migrants'—imaginations, pulling them to labor in the heart of the U.S. steel industry. Death prompted reflection on how aspirations fared against daily lived experiences.

The Monongahela Valley steel industry warrants attention because it encapsulates broader emerging trends in the industrial economy. Iron and steel mills of western Pennsylvania modeled larger factories lorded over by foremen and controlled by largely absent wealthy owners or stockholding companies. Owners launched a multifaceted campaign to increase profits and stabilize production. They sought to discipline workers through a division of labor, time-management studies, and the stern surveillance of a burgeoning corps of foremen. Some employers openly desired to diversify the ethnic and racial composition of the workforce to exploit workers' existing, and in some cases growing, prejudices against other groups. Such economic, social, and cultural changes meant that rituals of death became infused with commentary on industrial life and reveal working people's strategies for coping with it.

Death acquired layered meanings in places like Homestead, Braddock, and McKees Rocks depending on social position. Class, race, and gender shaped the constructed meanings of death and occupational accidents. Superintendents, native-born skilled white workers, and the legal system viewed immigrant workers' deaths and bouts with disease through dominant racial discourses. At best, "new" immigrants occupied a racial "inbetweenness" in the United States at the turn of the century that meant they were not black, but not necessarily white either.[2] More invidious forms of academic and popular discourse characterized them as occupying the border between human and subhuman. One white native-born skilled worker, for example, likened eastern Europeans to "cattle," while northern European laborers called themselves "white men" to differentiate themselves from the southern Europeans they worked beside.[3] Such attitudes shaped the meanings attached to the dead bodies of southern and eastern European steelworkers and their family members and were echoed, sometimes amplified, up the social scale.

For their part, working people labored to thwart dehumanizing tendencies of industrial production and racialized thinking. "Our people ain't never goin' to stop [demanding industrial democracy]," a Slovak woman in Youngstown explained during the organizing drives around World War I, "until our fathers can be home sometimes and not be just like a horse—take out of the stall and put back in the stall."[4] Even when death ended the monotony of twelve-hour shifts and twenty-four-hour turns, steelworkers did not stop demanding dignity. This pursuit represented a persistent theme in the history of western Pennsylvania from Homestead in 1892 to the 1919 steel strike.

"A Town Bathed in Tears": Homestead, 1892

Steelworkers had dealt with death before the battle of Homestead in 1892. But the confrontation that summer represented a collision of opposing belief systems. Workers clung to an older republican ideology that bestowed honor on a hard day's labor. Andrew Carnegie and Henry Clay Frick were pioneers, among others, of an emerging corporate ideology that prized efficiency, control, and profit over the dignity of work. These two positions clashed on the banks of the Monongahela River on July 6. Seven workers and three Pinkerton agents died in a battle that pitted the wealthy owners of the Carnegie Steel Company against one of the most powerful unions in the United States, the Amalgamated Association of Iron and Steel Workers. The stakes of the conflict could not have been higher. The strike at Homestead enacted "a nationwide debate on the meaning of democracy and republican values in an age of rapid technological transformation" and concentration of wealth.[5] The dead bodies represented, as funeral orators would make clear, the corporate onslaught against a republican value system that granted skilled workers dignity and social place because of their labor. The battle became a focal point for the country because the labor movement, the press, and capitalists wondered if the deaths on the banks of the Monongahela signified a birth of new social relations in steel manufacturing. At Homestead, as during so many other key moments in U.S. labor history, workers' bodies and the community's responses to violent death played a key role in the immediate interpretation of events and the lasting lessons of the conflict. The July 6 confrontation and subsequent government-ordered occupation of the town by the state militia cast a long shadow over life and experiences with death in western Pennsylvania steel communities.

The trouble that descended on Homestead in the summer of 1892 had been brewing for three years. Andrew Carnegie and his chief of operations, Henry Clay Frick, had tried unsuccessfully to break the union at Homestead during the previous round of contract negotiations in 1889. Carnegie and Frick wanted to expel the AAISW from the works and freely dictate the terms of production. The Carnegie Steel Company had not fallen on hard times.

Carnegie's secretary claimed that the company capitalized for twenty-five million dollars in 1892, made four million dollars in profits in 1891 and 1892.[6] Before leaving for vacation to Scotland, Carnegie advised Frick to stand firm against the union, which he did. Frick locked out thirty-eight hundred men on June 29, one day before the contract expired. Homestead's workers responded by seizing the mill and securing the town to prevent scabs from replacing them in the works.

These belligerent actions reflected the high stakes of the standoff. Carnegie initiated the conflict on the principle that owners should operate their businesses without interference from wage earners. "The road to Homestead," historian Francis Couvares remarks, "was clearly marked by a singled-minded intention to usher in the age of steel by burying once and for all" the skilled craftsmen who had been "the champions of the age of iron." Carnegie and Frick bristled at the power skilled workers wielded before 1892.[7] They sought to reconfigure relations on the shop floor such that wealth and property, not knowledge and skill, bequeathed control. The resolution of these matters held dramatic implications for conditions of life and death in steel manufacturing.

Workers resisted the dictatorship of the millionaire steel magnate. Reflecting broader concerns in society, they warned that concentration of capital into the hands of a few owners represented "an enormous and despotic power over the lives and the fortunes of their employees and subordinates—the great mass of the people; a power which eviscerates our national constitution and our common law." Such concerns stoked workers' fears of having their bodies reduced to their labor power. This possibility heightened anxiety about life beyond work. If their voices were stifled in the workplace, would they still command full participation in the Republic? If Carnegie, and others like him, prevailed, would there *be* a Republic? Such thoughts led the Advisory Committee of the AAISW to conclude that they were duty bound "as American citizens to resist by every legal and ordinary means the unconstitutional, anarchic and revolutionary policy of the Carnegie Company."[8]

These issues prompted Frick to order three hundred Pinkerton agents, a quasi-mercenary force, to retake the Homestead Works and inspired the steelworkers and their wives to resist the invasion. Alerted to the advancing Pinkertons by lookouts in Pittsburgh, Homestead's workers stormed the corporation's wharf to prevent the imported force from landing. The standoff erupted into a battle when a shot rang out. Pinkertons fired their Winchester rifles. Workers retaliated with small-arms fire and, as the skirmish continued throughout the morning, a Civil War–era cannon, dynamite, and other weapons to keep the Pinkertons penned to their barges. Casualties mounted on both sides. On the shore, John E. Morris, a Welsh skilled worker in the blooming mill, died instantly from a shot to the forehead. Peter Fares, a semiskilled worker in the open-hearth department, and Joseph Sotak, a Hungarian, also received fatal gunshot wounds to the head. Silas Wain, a common laborer in the Bessemer mill who was engaged to be married, died when an errant shot from the cannon blew his head off. Henry Striegel, Thomas Weldon, and George Rutter died from gunshot wounds that were a combination of accidental discharges, friendly fire, and Pinkerton sharpshooting. In all, seven workers and three Pinkerton agents—Thomas J. Connors, J. W. Kline, and Edward A. R. Spear—lay dead when the smoke cleared and the Pinkertons raised the white flag of surrender.[9]

AAISW leaders negotiated the terms of surrender, promising the Pinkertons safe passage from the barges to Homestead's Opera House. As the agents disembarked, a waiting crowd formed two lines, six hundred yards long, through which the defeated men passed. As the Pinkertons made their way through the gauntlet, Homestead's rage at the attempted invasion and the resulting deaths exploded in "a fierce carnival of revenge." Men beat them with fists and clubs. Women, "converted for the nonce into veritable furies," used their fists, "clubs, stones, bricks, broomsticks, mophandles and any missile upon which they could lay their hands." Children threw mud and stones.[10] Some widows of the slain men joined the fracas in an effort to exact blood for blood. As the Pinkertons drew near the Opera House, a large group of eastern European immigrants, including friends and relatives of Joseph Sotak and Peter Fares, stood in wait. Two immigrants assaulted one of the agents. One man grabbed the agent by the throat, "while a stoutly-built woman belabored him with a club."[11] Only the intervention of a union man escorting the defeated Pinkertons saved the agent from the ultimate wrath of the enraged crowd.

The Pinkerton gauntlet horrified newspaper reporters, much of the mainstream reading public, and some trade union sympathizers. Yet in the emotionally charged atmosphere, Homesteaders felt justice was on their side. The lockout had wounded their pride. The Pinkertons had done more than that. The agents had killed men who had been defending workers' rights. With the battle temporarily won, Homesteaders exacted retribution by striking the bodies of those sent to threaten their livelihoods. They were not participating in mindless violence. By beating members of Frick's proxy army, they hoped to strike a blow at corporate tyranny.

These points became clearer the day after the battle, as the sounds of brass bands playing funeral dirges replaced the reports of Winchesters in Homestead. Rage transformed to grief, as the community, "bathed in tears," turned their thoughts from armed resistance to burying the dead.[12] Burial services for John Morris, Peter Fares, and Silas Wain on July 7, and those for Joseph Sotak, Thomas Weldon, and Henry Striegel on July 8 illustrated how the battle affected different ethnic and occupational groups in Homestead and how rituals of last rites served as a solemn reminder of the stakes of the struggle.

The funerals exhibited the social networks that sustained Homestead's citizens during times of crisis as well as peace. Families brought the remains of their loved ones to their homes, where they prepared the bodies for the rituals of burial according to ethnic and religious traditions. They opened their doors to receive condolences from well-wishers. Members of fraternal societies assembled to perform the tasks associated with their particular orders. Ministers and priests made ready to officiate over funeral services and prepared orations fit for the circumstances. Six freshly dug graves waited on the hill high above town in the Catholic and city cemeteries.[13] The scenes of July 7 and 8 ultimately reflected the nature of living in Homestead in the early 1890s, as the diverse population turned from the extraordinary events of the battle to the traditions of providing a respectable burial for the departed. Homestead's citizens had joined together in one determined group to repulse the Pinkerton invasion. Now they separated according to ethnicity and religion—factors that also tended to reflect skill and nativity—to bury their dead.

With passions still racing, the funerals for the six dead workers attracted large groups of mourners. The largest crowds assembled for the dead men whose wages allowed them to join one or more fraternal organizations. John Morris, a Welsh skilled worker in the blooming mill who had been in the country for two years and left a wife, prompted one of the most elaborate funerals. He had maintained membership in the Amalgamated Association, the Independent Order of Odd Fellows, and the Knights of Pythias. He regularly attended the Methodist Episcopal Church, although he was not officially a member. These details of Morris's life shaped how the community responded to his death. At two o'clock, as the Golden Eagle band played the slow notes of a funeral march, six of Morris's coworkers from the mill transported his modest coffin to the hearse, as a crowd of nearly 1,000 mill hands and fully uniformed members of the Odd Fellows and Knights of Pythias stood "with tearful eyes and drooping and uncovered heads."[14] Led by the band, the procession advanced to the Fourth Avenue Methodist Church, as his mother, widow, and brothers and sisters followed in carriages. Once at the church, Morris's body rested on a bier surrounded by floral tributes. If not for the bullet hole in Morris's forehead, which the undertaker had attempted to conceal with plaster, these scenes would have resembled funeral processions held under more ordinary circumstances. After the church services, the Golden Eagle band struck the notes of the Decoration Day dirge and led a procession to the cemetery that included 225 members of the Odd Fellows, Homestead Lodges 1040 and 479 of the Knights of Pythias, and the L. W. Stoker band of Homestead. The procession swelled after it crossed Fifth Avenue, when 300 men from the Amalgamated Association and the Excelsior band fell into line.[15]

Two of the other decedents received similarly lavish processions due, in part, to their membership in fraternal organizations. Henry Striegel, who was of German descent and worked as a teamster, belonged to the Eintracht Saengerbund Society and a local Turnverein, a German American organization focused on athletics and physical fitness. A delegation of Turners arrived from Pittsburgh dressed in their athletic suits, and the Germania band of Pittsburgh provided appropriately dour music. Both the leader of the band and a member of the Turners carried American flags draped in mourning.[16] Likewise, Thomas Weldon's funeral attracted 1,000 people and a score of carriages. His wages as a roller in the mill afforded him membership to the Amalgamated Association, the Hibernians, and the Homestead Beneficial Association. Guided by the music of the Germania band, hundreds of workmen, "neatly dressed and wearing white gloves," guided Weldon to his final resting place.[17]

The workers killed in the attempted Pinkerton invasion who worked on the lower rungs of the town's occupational ladder received well-attended funerals, but lacked some of the adornments provided by the various fraternal societies. Joseph Sotak, a Slovak immigrant and a leader of East European steelworkers; Peter Fares, a Slovak immigrant who worked as a semiskilled helper in the open-hearth department; and Silas Wain, a recent English immigrant who worked as a common laborer in the Bessemer mill, all received honorable burials.[18] Historical accounts of these funerals do not detail elaborate processions, as was the case for Morris, Striegel, and Weldon. Instead, the funerals for Sotak and Fares were rooted more firmly within their ethnic communities and corresponding churches. The Amalgamated Association marshaled ranks of workers to pay tribute to the sacrifice each man made; 800 members of the Amalgamated Association attended Fares's funeral.[19] As for Wain, who suffered the macabre death from the shot of the GAR cannon, the Reverend John B. Glass conducted funeral services from the Free Methodist Church, but extant records reveal neither the content of his sermon nor the details of the funeral procession. Occupation and ethnicity for each of the men, like for the others killed in the battle for Homestead, determined the details of their funerals and the constituents in the processions. Whether elaborate or simple, however, the immediate context of the funerals garnered each dead man the respect of the community. Part of the legacy of Homestead, especially the class fragmentation it bequeathed to subsequent generations of steelworkers, meant ethnic and religious differences would carry more weight in subsequent years. On July 7 and 8, 1892, however, Homesteaders viewed death through the lens of class struggle.

Various church services for the slain workers focused on the conflict between the Carnegie Steel Company and the Amalgamated Association. Although the services varied according to the prescriptions of the denomination, each minister or priest framed the funeral service in terms of the labor relations that had just exploded with life-taking volatility. Two of the most notable orations came at the services of John E. Morris at the Fourth Avenue Methodist Episcopal Church and at the funeral of Thomas Weldon at Homestead's St. Mary's Catholic Church.

The Reverend J. J. McIlyar, "the venerable and white-haired pastor" of the Methodist Episcopal Church, delivered a fiery oration that reminded the congregation of the extraordinary circumstances of Morris's death. He recounted the history of the conflict and heaped condemnation on Henry Clay Frick. "There is no more sensibility in that man than in a toad," McIlyar said.[20] He accused the Carnegie Steel Company of trying to destroy the Amalgamated Association. "Why should men who are piling up millions upon millions shed the blood of men who are earning at the best but a mere pittance and seek to increase that by a few cents?" McIlyar wondered.[21] For him, men like John Morris justifiably protected their homes and families. With the sobs of Morris's widow audible to the church, and her grief finding "a sympathetic echo in the hearts of all present," McIlyar motioned to the corpse and professed beliefs that had motivated the resistance.[22] "This blessed man lying here; this mortal man, an affectionate husband, sober and industrious, gentlemanly in manner," he said, "was killed because a conflict provoked by the Pinkerton clan made it necessary for him and his fellow-workmen to protect their homes and families."[23] McIlyar used the circumstances of Morris's death to interpret labor relations in the 1890s, warn against the excesses of wealth, and reinforce the manly ideals of protecting hearth and home. In dying for the cause, Morris had performed his masculine duty. Women had participated in the action as well, but most of their actions had not conformed to the gendered expectations of the late nineteenth century, and McIlyar cast them as passive participants in need of the paternal protection of men.[24]

Father Bullion preached on similar themes the next day over the remains of Thomas Weldon at St. Mary's. He echoed the Amalgamated Association's rhetoric of workers' rights, suggesting steelworkers properly defended their jobs because they produced the mill's wealth "by virtue of long service." "The men here have a right to permanent employment," Bullion proclaimed. "They have helped make this property, they have a right to own part of this property, and we hope there will come a time when laws will be passed which will make unnecessary such riotous conduct as we have witnessed within the past few days." Bullion linked his remarks about workers' rights with those expressed by Senator John Palmer of Illinois in a speech the day before. Palmer had expressed concern about a manufacturing aristocracy wresting control of the Republic and governing through the nobility of wealth. For Father Bullion, Thomas Weldon, and working people like him, represented the antidote to power derived from wealth. Bullion concluded by lauding Weldon's life as meriting "to the last moment . . . the holy sacrament of extreme unction" and asking the assembled congregation to "be ever mindful of his soul."[25] These last words linked the Catholic faith, and its rituals and beliefs about death, to the Homestead struggle. Catholics believed the fate of the soul was not determined immediately upon death but could be influenced by the intercession of the living, especially by prayer. The battle at Homestead likewise represented a contest where the stakes were high and the outcome not predetermined. The fate of work relations in Homestead would require the continued agency of the living.

Funeral orations connected the broader stakes of the conflict to the deceased, but the dead men's sacrifice accrued additional meaning for their coworkers as the conflict continued. On July 10, Pennsylvania governor Robert E. Pattison ordered eighty-five hundred militiamen to Homestead to "restore the right of law."[26] Initially, Homesteaders welcomed the news. Confident in their interpretation of their rights as workers and citizens, some Amalgamated leaders argued that the militia would not assist Frick in reopening the mill with scab labor. They prepared to meet General Snowden with a parade and brass bands.

Homestead's workers soon found out that the militia arrived not to uphold the principles for which their coworkers had died, but to ensure the rights of private property. As the militia occupied Homestead on July 12, Carnegie Steel Company officials reoccupied their offices. They laid plans to import replacement workers and launched legal salvos intended to reframe the terms of the conflict and subvert the political arguments sustaining the steelworkers. The interpretations of the conflict could not have been more polarized. On one side, Amalgamated leaders such as Hugh O'Donnell argued that steelworkers were fulfilling their civic duty by protecting the Republic against the "despotic power" of unrestrained capital.[27] On the other side, the company branded the workers as criminals of the most depraved species—traitors. Philander C. Knox, the company's lead attorney and later U.S. attorney general and secretary of state, prepared hundreds of indictments, charging the workers with conspiracy, murder, and treason. Were the men just buried with such adoration American heroes or treasonous murderers?

Interpreting the meaning of the deaths at Homestead became part of the growing divide in the late nineteenth century between wage earners and captains of industry. In 1892 William W. Delaney captured the attitudes of many working people in one of the most widely known labor songs, "Father Was Killed by Pinkerton Men." The song compared the lives of America's wage earners to the country's business elite and condemned politicians for pandering to corporations. "Ye prating politicians, who boast protection creed," Delaney wrote,

> Go to Homestead and stop the orphans' cry.
> Protection for the rich man ye pander to his greed,
> His workmen they are cattle and may die.
> The freedom of the city in Scotland far away
> 'Tis presented to the millionaire suave,
> But here in Free America with protection in full sway
> His workmen get the freedom of the grave.[28]

As Delaney's verse suggests, Homestead raised questions about the relations between wage labor and basic freedoms. Wage labor devalued workers' human worth, as evolving regimes of labor discipline sought to manipulate workers' brawn rather than acknowledge their brains.[29] Wealth dictated the types of freedoms Americans could access. While Andrew Carnegie enjoyed the freedom to vacation in Scotland, workers endured the freedom of hunger, disfigurement or death from workplace accidents, and the ability to catch a life-taking bullet from a Pinkerton Winchester. Some workers, secure in religious faith, may have embraced death as an end to earthly toil.[30] Many wage earners, however, surely thought the "freedom of the grave" was one freedom of which they would rather not avail themselves.

The resolution of the lockout and strike added another layer of meaning to the life and death of workers. Not wishing to provoke a violent confrontation with eighty-five hundred militiamen, steelworkers watched as the state's military force occupied the town for several months and the company enticed nearly two thousand nonunion workers to fire the mill's furnaces and eventually break the strike. In November, after the drama of courtroom trials, evictions, and months of living with the pangs of hunger, the unskilled workers voted to go back to work. The Carnegie Steel Company blacklisted most of the Amalgamated leaders, and each man who returned to work had to sign an individual contract with the company. The defeat crushed the union in Homestead and emboldened other steelmakers in the Pittsburgh area to jettison negotiated contracts. One of the largest trade unions in the United States, with twenty-four thousand members before the lockout, the Amalgamated Association was left after the battle at Homestead with only "the shell of a union," with members concentrated in a handful of the western mills.[31] A once mighty union had fallen.

"Making Steel and Killing Men": The Meaning of a Life in the Nonunion Era

After the defeat at Homestead, steelworkers' experiences with death were shaped by an array of factors. Work life changed, as union strength and corporate power developed in an inverse relationship. As the AAISW was weakened and driven out of Pennsylvania, workers lived and died in the shadow of increasingly larger and more powerful corporations such as Carnegie Steel and, after 1901, U.S. Steel. Life outside of work changed as well. Corporate power did not stop at the mill gates, but extended into mill villages and towns to shape community life. Life under the aegis of such power shaped deathways in western Pennsylvania. The changing demographics of the workforce also contributed to ideas about life and death. Attitudes about race framed work relationships and established something of a hierarchy of human dignity. Native-born workers attempted to claim the top spots among the working classes and sometimes joined forces with employers to look dismissively at the human suffering immigrants endured. Workers in western Pennsylvania were divided by an array of factors, such as skill and ethnicity. These divisions influenced steelworkers' deathways, as the AAISW declined and gave way to the nonunion era. Workers memorialized their dead in their ethnic, religious, and fraternal communities rather than in overtly class-based organizations, such as the AAISW. Although fragmented along many lines, steelworkers and their families clearly made a priority of respecting the dead.

Dignity had been at the heart of the AAISW's union philosophy and had been at the center of the battle at Homestead. The union's defeat led it on a path of declining membership and increasing impotence to counter the growing power of employers. From a peak of more than twenty-four thousand members in 1891, the union's ranks dwindled to ten thousand in 1898. It was driven from one mill after another, until the strikes of 1901 and 1909 resulted in the union's expulsion from most steel mills in the East.[32] Whereas workers in other industries, especially coal miners in the UMWA, could count on the financial and philosophical support of their unions when dealing with grief and loss, steelworkers in western Pennsylvania had to pursue alternatives.

It is unclear if the AAISW would have been a key factor in steelworkers' experiences with death had it survived the battle at Homestead. Records reveal an ongoing debate about the nature of the organization and whether it should stick to the bread-and-butter issues of wages, hours, and conditions or broaden into other areas, such as mutual benefits. Local lodges began to offer some benefits in the 1870s and pressured the national leadership to adopt a more universal system that flowed from the national union to the local lodges. The debate persisted for twenty-five years. Locals provided modest, usually $50, death benefits, while the AAISW declined to provide mutual benefits to all members. By the time the national organization adopted such a system in late 1903, their declining membership meant that only a tiny fraction of steelworkers, and nearly none in western Pennsylvania, could count on the AAISW for support. The union had come relatively late to serving its members as a mutual benefit institution, but it was clear that it was finally convinced that death benefits would help maintain current members and attract new ones.[33] By that point, it was largely too little, too late. No one held an official memorial service for the once-mighty AAISW, but in the realm of providing steelworkers with a system of benefits, the union was nearly as impotent as a body in a grave.

As the union's membership and influence plummeted, the power of steel corporations soared. Corporate antiunion efforts coincided with a march toward consolidation in the industry. The process produced the United States Steel Corporation in 1901. Capitalized at $1.4 billion, U.S. Steel became the largest corporation in the world and forever changed the economic landscape of steel production.[34] A 1911 U.S. Senate report found that U.S. Steel dominated half of the industry; six independent firms accounted for most of the rest.[35]

The consolidation of capital provided the power to reshape life on the job and in the community. The large firms' antagonism to unions cast a pall over work and community life. Touring western Pennsylvania as part of the Pittsburgh Survey, John Fitch reported that steelworkers were hesitant to discuss their working conditions, wages, or the power of steel corporations in their communities for fear of losing their jobs. They worried that corporate spies informed on them and could cite examples of mass firings to halt free discussion. In 1895 the Carnegie Steel Company "discharged men by fives and tens for daring to attend a public meeting." Fitch concluded that steelworkers "learned to respect the vigilance and power of their employers, and they have learned the cost of defiance."[36] If they wanted to draw a paycheck, they had to avoid any criticism of their employers and avoid openly advocating unionism. Freedom of speech and freedom of association were two casualties produced by the nonunion era.

The antiunion campaign and the power of monopoly capital shaped workers' lives and their experiences with death in profound ways. "Technological revolution, work reorganization, massive immigration, and the restructuring of urban space," historian Francis Couvares notes, "all occurred simultaneously with the anti-union drive and transformed the character of everyday experience at work, at home, and in the streets of the city."[37] These changes shaped how steelworkers, their wives, and their children experienced death. To be able to decode the meanings of their death rituals, it is important to explore how their lives and the meanings about work, family, and community changed during the industrial era.

The evolving managerial practices of the industrial era reshaped workplaces, but the changes also challenged traditional ideas about the dignity of work and the worth of the individual to an economic enterprise. During the age of iron, skilled workers wielded their knowledge as a tool to carve out spheres of semiautonomy. They exercised the authority to monitor networks of apprenticeships and held powerful bargaining positions when negotiating wage scales. Steel, on the other hand, could be produced with a greater reliance on technology, which had the effects of transferring control of production from workers to managers, eliminating jobs, and creating more semi- and unskilled jobs. At the renovated J. Edgar Thomson works in Braddock—an early 1880s prototype of the coming industrial order—machines replaced five out of every six skilled men in the furnace and rail departments.[38] Between 1884 and 1907, the proportion of unskilled workers rose from 49 to 62 percent, while the number of skilled workers shrank from 37 to just 17 percent of steelworkers.[39] Employment of manual workers for the period 1870 to 1910 increased at a rate of 1,204 percent—a rate of growth second only to the chemical, oil, and rubber industry.[40] These transformations impacted the type of labor workers performed. A man became, in the critical words of the *National Labor Tribune,* "a mere machine tender" rather than a manipulator of raw materials and molten metal.[41]

Changes in the organization of work occurred in conjunction with intense competition between manufacturers that spurred the incessant drive to cut costs in what historian David Brody terms the "impulse for economy" that prevailed in the industry. As discussed in chapter 1, a social and cultural divide grew between the front offices, where men calculated costs, and the mill, where men made the steel. The physical distance also increased between the top echelons of the industry's businessmen and the workers, as steel mills took advantage of economies of scale. Whereas the typical blast furnace employed 71 hands in 1869, the average steel mill employed 412 in 1899.[42] Driven by competition, management increased the size of the works and justified a hierarchical regime of work discipline that featured long hours, low wages, and dire conditions.[43] Late-nineteenth-century steel manufacturers and the growing managerial ranks reduced workers to their labor power and conflated their worth with the equations of efficiency and labor costs.

Evolving organization of work occurred concurrently with a transformation of the people who rolled the nation's steel. In 1870 Pittsburgh's laboring population reflected immigration patterns from Ireland, Germany, and Great Britain. Over the next four decades, Croats, Serbs, Slovenes, Slovaks, Lithuanians, Hungarians, Ruthenians, Bohemians, Romanians, Poles, Ukrainians, Russians, and others arrived to work in the Monongahela Valley's mills. By 1908, according to Immigration Commission data, immigrants from southern and eastern Europe occupied a majority of the unskilled jobs in the industry (see table 1). African Americans constituted between 2 and 4 percent of the workforce before the World War I–era migration brought thousands of black men to work in the area's mills.[44]

New immigrant workers bumped some of the older immigrants into skilled positions or into the ranks of foremen. Some native-born workers and old immigrants, however, chose to leave the mill rather than work with the new-

Table 1. Percentage of foreign-born employees reported from each country of birth

Country of birth	Percentage of foreign born from each country		
	1880[a]	1890[b]	1908[c]
English-speaking countries	70.0	56.5	14.0
British America	5.3	4.2	0.5
England, Scotland, and Wales	24.4	24	8.6
Ireland	40.3	28.3	4.9
Non-English-speaking countries	30.0	43.5	86.0
Austria-Hungary	([d])	4.2	56.0
Germany	22.4	23.5	8.9
Italy	([d])	0.8	5.9
Russia	([d])	1.0	5.5
Sweden and Norway	2.5	5.7	2.4
Other countries	5.1	8.3	7.3

Source: Report on Conditions of Employment in the Iron and Steel Industry in the United States, vol. 3, *Working Conditions and the Relations of Employers and Employees* (Washington, DC: Government Printing Office, 1913), 92.

[a] Tenth Census, 1880, Population, 754, 755.

[b] Eleventh Census, 1890, Population, pt. 2, 488, 489.

[c] Reports of Immigration Commission, 8:33.

[d] Included with "Other countries."

comers, whose inability to speak English, social customs, and predominantly Catholic religion marked them as "other." Immigration initiated changes in steel communities that proved important in shaping how workers experienced death and how others, whether employers, foremen, or native-born skilled workers, interpreted such deaths. It also revealed schisms that operated along lines of ethnicity and race, skill, and social class.

Changes to the organization of work and the introduction of various immigrant groups transferred much of the burden of labor from the brains of native-born and old-immigrant workers to the brawn of the newer immigrants. Wages became dependent on a worker's body withstanding the daily rigors of steel production. Many workers recognized this transformation. Some embraced the physicality of the work and the manliness such strenuous conditions bestowed. "I'm no chicken—feel that arm," one steelworker told a visiting journalist when discussing the physically exhausting labor.[45] Thomas Anshutz's early 1880s painting *Ironworkers' Noontime* captures such a scene in the mill's homosocial environment. It depicts several bare-chested workers, with one grasping his bicep in a pose of manly fortitude. Vincent Bulmanis, an unemployed steelworker in Phillip Bonosky's novel *Burning Valley*, set in the early twentieth century, would have been a proper subject for Anschutz's painting. In a poignant scene, he taps his arm to show the potential labor power he felt when he started work in America. "All I had was my strength," he noted of his first years on the job. "My work. In my arms, my back, in my legs—there it lay: work. With it, I had everything."[46] If steelworkers like Bulmanis lost their strength, they lost their livelihoods as steelworkers.

Steel mills presented myriad threats to workers' bodies and ways to sap their vitality. Visiting Homestead in 1894, Hamlin Garland reported being paralyzed by fear as he stepped into the factory. "I dared not move for fear of flying metal, the swift swing of a crane, or the sudden lurch of a great carrier," he wrote. Garland described the scene as resembling a primeval battle between men and machines. "Everywhere in this pandemoniac shed was the thunder of reversing engines, the crash of falling iron, the rumbling growl of rollers, the howl of horrible saws, the deafening hiss of escaping steam, the wild vague shouts of workmen." The roaring engines and deafening crashes made it hard to hear shouts of warning as cranes passed by or molten metal flew. Donning overalls, Yale alumnus and assistant editor of the *Atlantic Monthly* Charles Rumford Walker took a job in the mill to experience a steelworker's lot firsthand. As he worked, he strained to hear the "Slavic polyglot" the steelworkers had developed as a word of caution. "That word, 'Tchekai!—Watch out!'—even the Americans use it. It's a word that is crying in your ears all night," Walker wrote. "Watch out for the crane that is taking a ladle of hot metal over your head, or a load of scrap, or a bundle of pipes; watch out for the hot cinder coming down the hole from the furnace-doors; watch out for 'me' while I get this wheelbarrow by; and 'Heow! Tchekai!' for the trainload of hot ingots that passes your shoulder."[47] Noise increased the danger and damaged workers' hearing.

Fluctuations of heat and cold also took a toll on laboring bodies. Pouring steel in molds or standing next to hot furnaces sapped their strength. During the summer months, the mills resembled infernos where workers said they were as close to hell as they hoped to get.[48] "It takes grit to stand there in July and August," one man noted.[49] It also took sweat. Journalist James Parton reported that puddlers' helpers worked so strenuously that they had "to stop, now and then, in summer, take off their boots, and pour the perspiration out of them." During the winter, the extremes were more pronounced. One steel pourer at the Homestead Works received frostbitten ears even though he tapped a furnace that recorded a temperature at the tapping hole of 2,930 degrees.[50]

Long hours compounded the inherent dangers of the job. After the union's defeat at Homestead, most steel mills operated two twelve-hour "turns," or shifts.[51] Every two weeks, steelworkers transitioned between shifts by working the "long turn" on Sunday—one twenty-four-hour shift that achieved rotating the workers from the day to the night shift for the succeeding two weeks. A 1913 U.S. Bureau of Labor investigation of working conditions in the steel industry encountered many men who "were on duty continuously for 36 hours, often without an hour's sleep or rest and sometimes without even hot food."[52] In 1910 another investigation concluded that 29 percent of all steelworkers and 88 percent of blast-furnace workers were on the job seven days a week.[53] Such intense labor kept the mills producing steel around the clock. Overtime and long turns increased chances for fatigue-related accidents in an already dangerous work environment.[54]

The combined effect of intense work and long hours took its toll on bodies and family lives. One Homestead worker said of the long hours, "It brutalizes a man. You can't help it. You start in to be a man, but you become more and more a machine, and pleasures are few and far between."[55] The logic of the industry dictated that workers' bodies be used like other materials in the production process and tossed on the industrial scrap heap when their utility had been extracted. John Fitch concluded that working conditions in the steel mills aged men more rapidly than in less strenuous occupations—they hit "old age at 40."[56] Steelworkers did not need an outsider to tell them what the work did to their bodies. Surveying the people laboring in the Homestead Works, one man noted, "You don't notice any old men here. . . . [T]he long hours, the strain, and the sudden changes of temperature use a man up. He quits before he gets fifty."[57] Even if men felt virile enough to continue working, employers often privileged the strength and speed of youth. As early as 1874, "A Toiler" penned a poem lamenting the expendability of older workers.

> And often, when a man grows old,
>   And cannot work so hard—
> They give to him, in accents cold,
>   A very strange reward:
> "We've kept thee, now," to him they say,
>   "As long as e'er we can—
> Therefore we must send thee away,
>   And find a younger man."[58]

By 1900 occupational data from the U.S. Census statistically confirmed the poem's sentiment. Younger workers dominated the iron and steel industry, with ten- to forty-four-year-olds taking more than 80 percent of the jobs. Men older than sixty-five accounted for just 0.7 percent of the workforce.[59]

The stress and fatigue involved in manufacturing steel were a continual battle. "Steel is war," observed Progressive Era reformer William Hard. "When it is finished it brings forth, for the victors, Skibo Castles and Peace Conferences. But while it is in process it is war."[60] Like all wars, manufacturing steel claimed casualties. The full extent of the accidents and deaths that occurred is impossible to know. Steel companies carefully guarded information regarding work accidents, and no federal system of data collection existed. While conducting her study of work accidents in Pittsburgh, Crystal Eastman suggested that steel companies defended their "policy of silence" about the number and character of accidents to prevent "unintelligent hysterical outcry and clamor on the part of the public."[61] Some Chicago-area workers attributed less magnanimous motivations for steel companies' secrecy. Rumors swirled that the Illinois Steel Company prevented a full accounting of accidents because the corporation concealed deaths in the plant by burying "victims secretly in mounds of slag."[62]

The fragmentary sources that do exist—data collected by Progressive Era reformers, Bureau of Labor investigations, and scattered newspaper reports—reveal remarkably dangerous work environments. Men met death or a disfiguring accident in a multitude of ways. They were obliterated by an exploding blast furnace, scalded by steam, singed by flying bits of molten metal, crushed by falls of materials, run over by locomotives or smashed by train cars, asphyxiated by noxious gases, electrocuted, knocked senseless by loaded cranes, or fell from ladders or high walkways (see table 2). Crystal Eastman documented 195 fatalities in Pittsburgh's steel mills during the year June 30, 1906, to July 1, 1907. The Bureau of Labor found that at least 569 steelworkers died as a result of work accidents between June 1908 and June 1910.[63]

Table 2. Men killed in the Allegheny County steel industry, July 1, 1906–June 30, 1907

Nature of accident	Aggregate	Carnegie Steel Company	Jones & Laughlin	National Tube Company	Pressed Steel Car Company	American Steel and Wire Company	Crucible Steel Company of America	Other companies
Operation of cranes	42	19	5	5	8		1	4
Falls	24	11	3	2	2	3		3
Explosions	22	2	19				1	
Operation of railroad in yards	18	9	2	2	4			1
Operation of dinkey trains	13	10	2	1				
Operation of rolls	10	4	2	3		1		
Loading and piling steel and iron products	8	1	5				1	1
Electric shocks	7	3	3					1
Asphyxiation by furnace gas	5	1	3			1		
Miscellaneous	46	13	7	8	2	5	5	6
Total number of men killed	**195**	**73**	**51**	**21**	**16**	**10**	**8**	**16**
Approximate number of men employed		23,337	9,125	16,000	6,000	4,487	4,982	

Source: Crystal Eastman, *Work-Accidents and the Law* (New York: Russell Sage Foundation, 1910), 51.

Accidents did not afflict all ethnic groups equally. At one plant from 1906 to 1910, Polish workers and southeastern Europeans accounted for more than 60 percent of all accidents. Non-English-speaking workers over the same years sustained 3,273 injuries versus 1,213 for English-speaking foreign-born and 761 for American-born workers.[64] A fatality list including surnames at the Homestead Works for 1911 echoed the findings: Chimko, Wynera, Dudash, Guesa, Winchuck, Fustin (Suhi), Seltz, Konkol, Susner, and Matsko. Alois Koukol remarked that he met men maimed by industrial accidents "everywhere in Pittsburgh"—they were "so common as to excite no comment." Work segregated by ethnicity and skill proved most dangerous to Slavs. "In proportion to their numbers the Slavs are the greatest sufferers from accidents in the Pittsburgh region, for to their lot falls the heaviest and most dangerous work," he reported. The Bureau of Labor concluded that the high frequency of accidents suggested that "the two groups of Polish and southeastern Europeans have a racial difference affecting their accident rates."[65] English-speaking workers and others in the community coined the pejorative racial epithet "hunky" to mark the so-called new immigrants as inferior.

As the epithet "hunky" demonstrates, ethnicity and experience combined to shape how foremen and skilled workers interpreted the deaths of laborers. "Oh, that is significant," a superintendent remarked when told that four Slavs were killed by hot metal falling from a crane. "Americans would know enough to keep out from under those loads." Foremen frequently ordered laborers into dangerous situations, sometimes eliciting protests from laborers worried for their safety. Such fear prompted one eighteen-year-old Slavic laborer to refuse orders to work in a certain section of the mill. "But the foreman insisted," according to Crystal Eastman, "telling him with a rough laugh that it did not matter whether he was killed or not." Afraid to lose his job, the young worker started work. Only a few minutes later, a bucket loaded with sixty-nine hundred pounds of material fell and crushed him.[66] Language barriers compounded risks. Immigrants unfamiliar with English could misinterpret or simply not understand instructions.[67]

Skilled native-born workers sometimes shared with the foremen similar attitudes toward responsibility for accidents and the social worth of the deceased. American or native-born men usually performed the skilled work in the mill, such as operating cranes or driving the dinkey trains that transported materials across the plant. When a load fell from a crane or a train car crushed a worker, the casualty normally came from the Slavic or other eastern European ranks. These characteristics of production shaped how skilled native-born workers viewed the deaths of their immigrant coworkers and revealed tension between the two groups. Crane operators blamed the "stupidity and slowness" of the immigrant laborers, while friends of the injured laborer put fault on the operator for not waiting for the proper signal.[68] One train engineer with twenty-five years' experience in the mill confided to John Fitch that he had killed two men while operating his engine and "smashed fingers or hands of so many hook-ons that he had no idea as to the number."[69] Persistent danger seemed to blunt the engineer's sense of responsibility. The ethnicity of his victims likely also played a role in his nonchalant attitude toward the carnage.

These attitudes affected how English-speaking workers and the native-born public interpreted death in the steel industry. Castigating common laborers as "hunkies" facilitated a process of attributing accidents to individual failings within a race of people expected to perform to lower standards than their English-speaking counterparts. One wife of a mill worker found comfort that her husband had a relatively safe job in the mill. Nevertheless, she decided to contribute food to a dinner benefiting a local hospital, "even if most of the injured are Hunkies."[70] In her study on work accidents, Crystal Eastman tried to provoke action by puncturing the "moral comfort" in the idea that immigrants suffered the overwhelming majority of accidents. Her data revealed that 42.5 percent of those killed or injured were American. She implied that once the fatalities were known to be American, they could be counted as fully human. This revelation, she hoped, would fuel the fires for safety reform.[71]

Racial animosity combined with economics to shape how employers interpreted workplace accidents. Dead workers posed little financial burden on steel corporations in the era before workmen's compensation. Eastman argued that companies cared little for the safety of immigrant workers because it was cheaper to kill them than install safety devices. Workers who had no relatives in the United States posed little financial burden on the company. Four killed workers cost one steel company seventy-five dollars for each man's funeral expenses, plus seven dollars for medical expenses.[72] The triumvirate of nineteenth-century tort law—contributory negligence, the fellow-servant rule, and the assumption of risk—placed legal liability almost solely with the workers. Dynamics of wealth and power dissuaded many from initiating a lawsuit. Those who gambled against the odds faced the possibility of intimidation by foremen and superintendents at work—if they were not fired outright—and put their meager financial resources against those of multimillion-dollar corporations.

Corporations also used language differences and presumptions of immigrants' ignorance to their advantage. Allegheny County coroners' files reveal examples where workers and foremen disagreed on the nature of job instructions and the culpability for resulting accidents. After an explosion killed five laborers at the Carnegie Steelworks in Duquesne on September 28, 1902, the coroner's jury returned a verdict that the workers' negligence caused the accident. Testimony from foremen, some of whom did not witness the accident and who claimed the workers disobeyed orders, trumped statements from eyewitnesses who said the workers obeyed their instructions precisely.[73]

Accidents brought workers' deaths to the courts, but working communities felt them more directly in their neighborhoods. Pittsburgh's factories and mills produced more than steel and iron. They were also "widow makers."[74] Census data reveal a higher frequency of widows in neighborhoods around the mills than in more affluent suburbs. In 1880 widows headed more than one-fifth of households in mill neighborhoods, compared to the wealthier areas where widows headed one-tenth of the households. Reflecting the accident rates in the mills, immigrant women were the most likely to lose husbands. In 1900 16 percent of the foreign-born women had lost their spouses, while 15 percent of the black women and 9 percent of native-born white women were widows.[75] Of 526 industrial accidents from June 1906 to June 1907, 258 men left widows, while 129 more of the deceased men had provided support to a family.[76] Reformer William Hard wondered what happened to the widows and children. "They do not evaporate. They do not comfortably disappear. What do the widows and orphans do?"[77]

Pittsburgh's reliance on heavy industry largely excluded women from the paid workforce, which impacted their options in widowhood. The intense labor of the steel mills and gendered notions of women's work severely limited their employment options.[78] In the families of Homestead, Margaret Byington found that "the women almost never go out to work," due to the "simple fact that one industry cannot use the work of women and children."[79] Women's participation in the workforce in Pittsburgh paralleled other industrial cities. The number of women wage earners grew from 16 percent in 1880 to 22 percent in 1900 but was 5 percent below the national average for 1900. Ethnicity played a role in women's workforce participation. Irish, Germans, and black women were more likely to join the paid workforce in Pittsburgh during this period than were native-born white, Italian, or Polish women.[80] Elements of working-class culture that prized the male-breadwinner ideology reinforced labor segmentation and restricted access. "In a properly ordered universe," historian S. J. Kleinberg notes, "men earned the bread, and women baked it."[81] Pittsburgh's sexually segregated workforce and ethnocultural attitudes toward women's work made many of the area's women reliant on males' wages.

These conditions meant that steelworkers' widows found it difficult to conform to the elaborate rules of Victorian mourning etiquette.[82] Instead of worrying about the appropriate color of dress or whose company they kept, the widows oftentimes entered the labor force. Of 132 widows Crystal Eastman tracked during the year after a husband's industrial accident, 55 had joined the wage-earning labor force.[83] Twenty-one percent of widows worked in Pittsburgh in 1900. Almost all found jobs normally coded as women's work. According to census data for 1900, almost 30 percent worked as domestic servants, the single largest category of employment for widows. Others earned wages as sewing workers, laundresses, boardinghouse keepers, nurses, teachers, and a handful of other pursuits.[84] A husband's death "almost invariably means hard work, long hours, poor pay, and in most cases children neglected," Crystal Eastman concluded. "It is the bitter, unequal struggle of one person trying to do the work of two." Even when widows found employment, they often had to move to smaller houses to find cheaper rents and to economize in other areas of life. It was not uncommon for children to leave school early after the death of a father in order to supplement the family income.[85]

Some women coped with a husband's death by remarrying or relying on charity. Yet only a fraction of those widowed by industrial accidents found another husband. Only 16 out of 258 women made widows from industrial accidents in Crystal Eastman's study remarried.[86] Children adversely affected their chances. Only 3 widows with more than 1 child remarried. When not remarrying, some widows drew on the goodwill of their communities and lived, at least for a time, from the proceeds of raffles or collections for their family's benefit. Relying on charity provided a short-term solution for Ellen Silefsky, whose husband died in 1900. She subsisted on the charity of neighbors and the assistance of a local priest, who paid her rent. These arrangements did not last long. Pittsburgh's Department of Charities intervened, calling Mrs. Silefsky demented from malnutrition and alleging that she beat her children when they cried for food. Social workers sent her to a poor farm and placed the children in the care of the Humane Society.[87] Experiences like those of Mrs. Silefsky's substantiated Eastman's claim that widows in Pittsburgh were largely denied the luxury of grief. Grief and mourning had to compete for time against the demands of daily survival.

Work-related deaths that produced a long list of widows and fatherless children represented only part of steelworkers' and their families' relationships with dying. Skilled workers in the industry earned wages that allowed them to purchase homes and feed their families. Yet in an industry dominated by semi- and unskilled work, most workers' wages provided just enough to hover at the poverty line. They concentrated in neighborhoods near work in living arrangements that drew the attention of Progressive Era reformers. In Homestead's Second Ward, between the river and railroad tracks, Margaret Byington inspected twenty-one courtyards surrounded by tenements that provided housing for 239 families—predominantly Slovak, but also Hungarian, Russian, Polish, and "Slavs of other origins." The scene paralleled other conditions of urban life during the period. Overcrowding led families to use kitchens as sleeping quarters, and many families took in boarders. Fifty-one families occupied one-room tenements. Trash, laundry, and other refuse littered common areas. Only three houses had running water inside. Households generally shared a common water source and privy in the court. Byington documented cases where hundreds of people shared one yard hydrant for water. Mill neighborhoods in Pittsburgh, Braddock, and other steel communities shared many of these characteristics.[88]

Unsanitary dwellings harbored disease, and densely concentrated populations facilitated transmission. At the turn of the century, Pittsburgh ranked near the top of the list of deadliest cities for illnesses such as typhoid, diarrhea, pneumonia, bronchitis, and others.[89] "Between public indifference, private selfishness, and political inertia, the germ has pretty well had its own way with Pittsburgh, and the city's annual waste of life from absolutely preventable disease has been a thing to make humanity shudder," Samuel Hopkins Adams wrote in 1909. Like work accidents, wage earners and immigrants suffered higher death rates and incidents of infant mortality than more affluent citizens. One child out of every three died before the age of two in Homestead's Second Ward. Farther up the hill, where "detached and livable" dwellings prevailed, infant mortality registered one death for every seven or eight children. Mill neighborhoods in the city also reflected higher death rates than wealthier neighborhoods. Residents of working-class wards near the river were twice as likely to die of bronchitis and four times as likely to die of typhoid when compared with a recently developed East End neighborhood. Paul Kellogg, editor of the reform-oriented *Survey* magazine, said the data demonstrated that the "dice were loaded in Pittsburgh" against working people's ability to maintain their health. "Our American boast that everybody has an equal chance falls flat before" such statistics, he concluded.[90]

Progressive Era hygiene campaigns balanced critiques of environment with stinging rebukes of immigrant character. From New York to San Francisco, squads of social workers imposed regimes of hygiene and investigated everything from milk to baby washing.[91] Reformers often blurred the lines between behavior and biological inferiority in the midst of such campaigns while reinforcing immigrants' difference.[92] Deaths from disease in Pittsburgh thus entered a much broader debate about public health, the social body, and cultures of industrialization.

Claiming Dignity: Institution Building, Mutual Aid, and Labor Militancy

With death all around and a broader culture dismissive of their suffering, steelworkers and their families responded by maintaining networks of mutual aid and initiating a remarkable period of institution building before World War I. In an era before widespread government social programs, few institutions existed to facilitate coping with life's unpredictability. Dangerous working conditions in the mills made commercial insurance options prohibitively expensive for many.[93] Steelworkers turned to religious and secular fraternal societies as an institutional framework of mutual aid to help care for the sick and bury the dead.

Fraternal societies became important institutions for maintaining ethnic ties while accommodating the new social and economic conditions immigrants met in the urban economies of industrial America. Immigrants transplanted traditions of mutual assistance to allay fears of dying on "foreign soil," in the words of one Slovak, with only "your close family and the undertaker" coming to the funeral.[94] Membership in a fraternal society prevented an anonymous death, took a step toward ensuring a good death, and provided a method of preserving ethnic consciousness.[95] Slovak fraternalists, like other ethnic variants, ensured that the deceased received burials reminiscent of village obsequies, and most organizations stipulated that all members of a lodge or branch accompany the deceased's remains to the cemetery. In 1900 the First Catholic Slovak Union's Branch 50 in Pittsburgh dictated that all members had to attend the funeral of a deceased member, even if it meant missing a day's work. Such mandates guaranteed that a member received a dignified burial reminiscent of traditional Slovak customs.[96]

Immigrants used fraternals to perpetuate customs of the Old Country and to form networks of self-help to accommodate their new environment. The conditions of urban, industrial America compelled action.[97] Croatian immigrants organized the Croatian Fraternal Union in 1894, Stephen Devunich recalled, "because there was no protection. The worker had no protection whatever. They didn't have money or a penny to bury them. They collected among themselves. That's how the fraternal organization was born." In another case, Stefan Fiala sought to persuade Slovaks in southeastern Pittsburgh to form a branch of the National Slovak Society by reminding his audience of the persistent dangers that lurked in the workplace. He argued that workers had a moral duty as male breadwinners to protect their families from utter ruin.[98]

While fraternals could not completely replace a man's wages, fraternal benefits provided a small amount of income in the event of sickness or accident and defrayed the costs of burial. A male member of the St. Stephens Lodge in Homestead received $5 per week in sick benefits, while a member in the Home Guards received $13.60 for sixteen weeks.[99] Margaret Byington found death benefits in Homestead's fraternals ranging from $150 for members of the Home Guards to $1,000 for members of the Modern Woodmen and the Royal Arcanum.[100]

Even if only token amounts in some instances, these benefits played important roles in immigrants' and workers' lives. Membership in such organizations connected an individual or family to a larger network of mutual assistance that facilitated community building and, in some cases, heightened ethnic consciousness. Michael Grasha recalled that the Croatian Fraternal Union was important because "it provided not only economic help, help in the case of dire need such as loss of life or limb. . . . [I]t served as a haven, a home, a common meeting ground for people of common language, heritage, culture."[101]

The desire for community and economic factors combined to cause a remarkable proliferation of ethnic fraternal organizations during the two decades before World War I. The city directory for McKeesport listed sixty beneficial and secret societies in 1895, and Byington noted fifty announcements for fraternal meetings in one day's paper in Homestead.[102] African Americans in Steelton, Pennsylvania, formed the Home Club of Steelton, the Negro Widows and Orphans Committee, the Galilean Fisherman Lodge, and the Union Republic Club and chartered an all-black lodge of the Independent Order of Odd Fellows. Croats and Slovenes joined together in 1893 to form the Slovenian and Croatian Society of St. Nicholas to provide sick and death benefits. Even though Serbs in Steelton "were so poor they joined local fire companies in order to take a shower," historian John Bodnar notes, "they formed the St. Nicholas lodge in 1901 to provide burial services for workmen." Likewise, Slovaks joined together to create the secular National Slovak Society in February 1890 and later two religious fraternals, the First Catholic Slovak Union and the Slovak Evangelical Union. By 1911 Hungarians had formed eight hundred organizations. Slovaks in Pittsburgh could choose between more than thirty different lodges founded by their compatriots by 1915.[103] Taken together, these activities represented a remarkable period of institution building, as African Americans, Bulgarians, Croatians, Hungarians, Italians, Poles, Romanians, Serbians, Slovenes, Slovaks, and others formed networks of self-help to facilitate community responses to death. Workers joined and created fraternal societies to bring a semblance of order to chaotic urban environments.

Many groups followed their organizing of fraternal organizations with the construction of churches. Slavs and Lithuanians owned church property estimated at a value of three-quarters of a million dollars before the outbreak of World War I.[104] The Ukrainian community built twelve churches in the area before World War I and a total of twenty-six between 1891 and 1956.[105] Immigrant churches perpetuated tradition and reaffirmed ties to Old World culture. A U.S. Census Bureau report estimated that nationwide, 2,230 Catholic churches delivered services exclusively in a foreign language in 1916, while 3,846 reported speaking both a foreign language and English.[106] Immigrant churches also provided another link in the chain of migration that allowed immigrant families to reconnect to kin and friends. "In a strange land," historian John Bodnar writes, "it was especially satisfying to listen to the gossip and information of congregations where newcomers knew almost everyone in sight."[107] Immigrant churches erected literal and figurative walls against alienation. They provided a central location for family events such as births, marriages, and deaths.[108] For these reasons, the distinctive architecture of immigrant churches dotted the landscape of western Pennsylvania.

In the midst of a broader society that often castigated them, immigrants created their own institutions to ensure they were treated with respect by people familiar with their past traditions and present lives. Immigrant and African American steelworkers, like working people more generally, feared the ignominy of a pauper's burial or a funeral attended by only an undertaker. They were anxious about having a priest or pastor available who would treat the soul of the departed with due respect.[109]

Although a work of proletarian fiction, Phillip Bonosky's *Burning Valley*, which is set in a Monongahela Valley mill town, captures anxieties that Bonosky probably witnessed growing up in the region during the early twentieth century as the son of a steelworker or during his own stint as a steelworker in the 1940s. In a revealing scene, two Catholic priests argue about the sanctity of steelworkers' bodies and souls. Longtime priest Father Dahr wonders if his potential successor, Father Brumbaugh, a younger priest more accustomed to the refined streets of Boston than the open sewers of the mill town, "will be forced to hold his pale white nose as he goes among these souls already doomed to Purgatory of poverty and labor!" Dahr insinuates that Brumbaugh's bigotry against immigrants and working people will prevent him from being a proper advocate for their souls as they confront the Moloch of the mill. "Let him go to the Mill and throw himself before it," he fumes, and beg it to give back the numberless souls it already has eaten up: the broken bodies on the wheels, the bodies burned to ash, the bodies cracked bone by bone until they lie a soaking heap on the floor. . . . [A]sk him how will he recognize the human being who is handed him on a shovel, scooped up from the furnace floor; or how will he bless the box of ashes with confidence, or pass his blessing hands over the ton of pig-iron in whose heart is fastened the body of some poor human soul sealed forever in this iron prison that not even dynamite but only the flames of Hell could loosen again!"[110]

After Dahr ends his rampage and stalks away, Father Brumbaugh confirms his class and racial bias. "What's so special about these people I'd like to know?" he retorts. "They're all foreigners—and colored! Why, most of them have no education, and you know they hardly know how to speak English! They're just common laborers. . . . All they do is work! Why, my father hires and fires people like them everyday!"[111]

In the burning valleys of western Pennsylvania, immigrant and African American communities built churches and organized fraternal societies to insulate themselves from the haughty condescension of the Father Brumbaughs of the era. Ethnic fraternal societies and churches were neither symbols of alienation nor symbols of assimilation, but examples of accommodation as immigrant communities negotiated new work and social environments.[112] These institutions, although at times beset by factional infighting, "obstructed bourgeois control of American life at every turn," historian David Montgomery notes, and "provided effective leverage over economic and social life."[113] Indeed, they profoundly shaped how many steelworkers memorialized the dead.

Fraternal societies played key roles in the rituals of dying. After the wake, fraternal societies and churches choreographed the next stages in the ritual memorialization of the departed. Fraternal members, often referred to as "lodge brothers," took charge of transporting the body to the church or, if the deceased was not religious, immediately processed to the cemetery. Each fraternal organization developed specific symbols and rituals to impose order to the proceedings. One popular fraternal among steelworkers, the Independent Order of Odd Fellows, organized a funeral procession according to members' ranks in the local lodge. Their manual prescribed the type of funeral regalia to be worn and how to display it. IOOF members wore "a black crape [sic] rosette, having a centre of the color of the highest degree to which the wearer may have attained, to be worn on the left breast; above it a sprig of evergreen, and below it (if the wearer be an elective or past officer) the jewel or jewels which as such he may be entitled to wear." Near the rosette, they wore a "mourning-badge" in memory of the deceased brother.[114]

Once outfitted in their mourning regalia, IOOF members assembled according to a thirteen-point rank system outlined in *The Odd Fellows Manual*. The marshal headed the procession wearing a black scarf and bearing a baton decorated with black crepe. Next came the "Outside Guardian" who bore a red staff and the "Scene Supporters" carrying white wands. The remaining participants fell into rank order wearing particularly colored scarves and some carrying symbolic items. Once fully assembled, the procession incorporated the casket and the family, some of whom might ride in carriages. If the deceased was a member of the Catholic Church, tradition held that a priest arrive at the house, sprinkle the coffin with holy water, and recite Psalm 130.[115]

After church services, the fraternal organization reassembled their ranked formation and transported the body to the cemetery. This task they took seriously. The manual for the Odd Fellows mandated that they were "solemnly bound to commit the mortal remains of a departed brother carefully and lovingly to the tomb, to cherish a lively recollection of his many virtues, and to bury his imperfections with his body beneath the clods of the valley." Some fraternals, including the Odd Fellows, purchased plots in prime sections of cemeteries to inter their members. After the church performed graveside services, the fraternal society closed the burial service with an address specific to their ritual. Odd Fellows joined hands and crowded around the grave in one or more circles to listen to an address, prayer, or both. Just before filling the grave, each member, "from left to right in regular succession, and in such numbers at a time as not to cause confusion," advanced to the grave and tossed the sprig of evergreen—a symbol of everlasting life—from their regalia into it. With this last token of hope, the services ended.[116]

While the rituals and benefits of the Odd Fellows attracted many steelworkers to join their ranks, it is unclear what role women played in funeral processions such as the Odd Fellows'. The organization admitted women into sex-segregated lodges named the "Degree of Rebekah." Given that women had "long been considered among men . . . the best part of our physically developed humanity," it was no wonder that "a fraternity like Odd Fellowship . . . should provide a degree especially for her," according to one Odd Fellow author. The fraternal served as a way to enforce gender relationships in general and marital relationships in particular. Bible stories served as models for women's behavior. Odd Fellows vowed to "watch over and care for" the widows of deceased members and proposed "to the widow to be as an husband to her, and a father to her fatherless children." Odd Fellows treated women as the dependent sex, which supplemented the male-breadwinner ideology of the period. Nationwide, the Odd Fellows provided relief to more

Figure 2. Fraternal organizations on parade

than six thousand widows and buried nearly eighty-five hundred men in 1896. They maintained a relationship of paternalism with women and excluded them from fraternity-style funerals. Fraternal societies reserved the honor of highly ritualized funerals for men.[117]

Although most fraternal societies organized across class lines, steelworkers in western Pennsylvania tended to concentrate in a few organizations. Many immigrant workers preferred to join fraternals organized by their fellow countrymen. In such organizations, rituals and regalia assumed additional significance as extensions of Old World customs (figure 2). Native-born and more established immigrant steelworkers joined fraternals such as the Odd Fellows because of modest dues and relatively generous benefits. Margaret Byington found the Odd Fellows to be "probably the most influential organization in Homestead."[118] Excluded from most white organizations, African Americans formed segregated branches or organized their own fraternal societies.[119]

By their existence, fraternal societies offered an implicit critique of individualism and an economic system that cast citizens to the industrial scrap heap. "An important difference between a brotherhood and an insurance company lies in the fact that the latter, when called on, will perform no more than its stipulated duty, while the former will do more," a Czech American newspaper observed. "These are certainly remarkable instances which reflect true sentiment and effective help on the part of our brotherhoods. Capitalistic insurance companies cannot match them."[120] Fraternal societies served as networks of solidarity at death and provided the ritual commemoration of workers' lives. Such societies ensured that steelworkers would not simply be shrugged off as the spent materials of industrial society.

The Limits of Politicized Death: McKees Rocks, 1909

Although steelworkers increasingly turned to ethnic, fraternal, and religious networks to commemorate the dead during the nonunion era, violent strikes such as at McKees Rocks in 1909 demonstrated workers' continued insistence that their lives had meaning. In many ways, McKees Rocks, situated on the south bank of the Ohio River just below Pittsburgh, represented a microcosm of the broader conditions characterizing the steel industry. The Pressed Steel Car Company had opened a plant there in 1899 and attracted a diverse workforce. In 1910 the city had a population of 14,702, of which a majority, more than 10,000 people, were either foreign born or native born of foreign parents. As many as seventeen nationalities worked at Pressed Steel, and the surrounding landscape reflected a clear spatial segregation based on skill and ethnicity. Skilled American workers generally lived across the river in North Side Pittsburgh. The immigrant workers—Austrians, Hungarians, Slovenians, Serbs, and others—collected pay in the ranks of the semi- and unskilled. Many lived in the "Bottoms" along the river in densely packed houses with wooden balconies and fluttering clotheslines. Others lived just on the edge of the plant in a company town variously referred to as Presston, Schoenville, "Hunkytown," or "Hunkeyville."[121]

Inside the plant, workers labored under a system inspired by principles of scientific management and assembly-line production. Electric cranes hoisted car frames along a track divided into twelve work stations. Gangs of workers assembled the railcar piece by piece from one station to the next until it reached the end of the line and was ready to roll on the nation's railroads.

As financial panic gripped the country in 1907, demand for steel railcars declined. President Frank N. Hoffstot used the lean times to change management tactics. When orders rebounded again early in 1909, workers confronted a similar assembly-line process, but Hoffstot had overhauled the pay scale. Rather than paying an hourly or piece-rate wage, Pressed Steel devised a pooling system of wages for each gang on the line. This plan distributed wages by the output of the entire assembly line rather than by the work of an individual. Therefore, if one section of the assembly line held up production, or if a mechanical failure or other problem slowed production, the entire line bore the costs rather than the company. The company refused to reveal the pay rates, so workers labored without knowing what to expect when they opened their pay envelopes. Payday brought frustration. Workers who had earned $3, $4, and $5 a day in 1907 unsealed envelopes in 1909 that held $1.25 for five days' work. One worker reported receiving 20 cents for two ten-hour days and another 90 cents for four days' work.[122]

As the mercury spiked in thermometers across western Pennsylvania in the summer of 1909, tempers flared at the Pressed Steel plant. On July 13, six hundred foreign-born workers walked out to protest the pooling system and secret wage scale. The strike spread, as the American workers joined the immigrants. On July 14, five thousand workers had quit work. They searched streetcars for potential strikebreakers and prevented a ferry, the *Steel Queen*, from transporting workers across the Ohio River to the plant in a scene reminiscent of the Homestead strikers' clash with Pinkertons seventeen years earlier. In both cases, the strikers wanted to prevent business as usual at the plant.

The workers' stand inspired a violent clash with the state police, the notorious Coal and Iron Police, and local deputy sheriffs. Troopers fired their carbines in the air to disperse crowds. When the gunfire did not produce the desired results, they spurred their mounts to full speed and charged crowds of men, women, and children, leaving in their wake many bruised and injured.[123] The sight of the mounted troopers brought unpleasant memories to the minds of the eastern European immigrants. They had fled the "Cossacks" to come to the United States. Now, the Cossacks rode again, brandishing riot maces three feet long to disperse crowds.[124] Troopers also sought to arrest strike leaders. Wives and women sympathizers resisted the authorities, "with a babe in one arm and bricks or slag in their free hand." One trooper countered such resistance by driving his horse through the front door of the home of a striker, arresting him, and galloping off to place the man in a boxcar transformed into a makeshift prison to house strikers.[125] After the first day of conflict, calm settled over McKees Rocks, as law enforcement ruled the district with an air of martial law.[126]

The uprising startled onlookers, just as it has historians since. Steelmakers had worked hard to prevent just such a protest from occurring. A labor force divided by skill, nationality, and nativity should have been rendered nearly powerless, as differences obscured opportunities for solidarity. "It was not a question of a trade union; it was not a question of general industrial unrest," Rufus Smith wrote in the *Survey*. "It was simply a united claim on the part of unskilled, ignorant 'Hunkies' for justice, and the Americans stood with them."[127] Smith's tone of slight surprise regarding the strike and clear condescension toward immigrant workers reveal broader assumptions about foreign-born and unskilled steelworkers, shared by many American-born workers, the American Federation of Labor, and employers. They did not think immigrants had the intelligence to mount such resistance. They were wrong.

Notions of a respectable life and dignified death swirled around McKees Rocks. The strike showed workers during the nonunion era rebelling against notions that they were ignorant, expendable cogs in the industrial machine. This episode of militancy provided a glimpse of what the industrial solidarity of the future might look like. Before the strike, American workers earned higher wages from their skill and derived psychological wages from their status as native born. They generally steered clear of the immigrant workers. Or, as Paul Kellogg noted, "They had never mixed with the Hunkies before." But once the strike started, the Americans "were with the Slavs." C. A. Wise, the American-born chairman of the strike committee, explained the American workers' actions by saying, "We are trying to be men among men."[128]

Workers used the calm that followed the initial clashes with law enforcement to begin organizing. Thousands gathered at mass meetings held at the historic Indian Mound, a ridge overlooking the Ohio River about a mile from the plant. Speakers reiterated the necessity for conducting a peaceful protest and refraining from violence. A strike committee known as the Big Six because it included six workers—four Americans and two foreigners—wanted the newspaper headlines to announce their grievances rather than sensationalize violence. Although the Big Six officially represented the strikers, a second committee, referred to as the Unknown Committee, worked behind the scenes to establish a picket network and a watch system to sound the alarm if strikebreakers were headed to the plant. With these committees in place, the strikers remained peaceful but vigilant for the rest of July. Attention could therefore be focused on their grievances against Pressed Steel.

The pooling system provided the spark necessary to ignite the strike and set ablaze passions that had been smoldering for months. In addition to the pooling system and complaints about wages, Pressed Steel workers alleged that a system of graft determined who was awarded jobs and who could keep them. Payments ranging from ten to fifty dollars ensured a place in the works in some cases; one worker reported that a keg of beer was the price of his job. Such fees did not provide job security, however. Workers reported that foremen would fire workers after a few weeks so that they could hire new men and collect a new fee for the privilege of working at Pressed Steel.[129] After making an inspection of the plants and talking with the men, the Reverend Father A. F. Toner of the St. Mary's Roman Catholic Church at McKees Rocks suggested that graft extended to human trafficking as well. The men were "driven lower than the degradation of slaves and compelled to sacrifice their wives and daughters to the villainous foremen and little bosses to be allowed to work."[130]

Toner's investigation also revealed dangerous working conditions that added injury to the insult of the graft system. "A man is given less consideration than a dog," he said, "and dead bodies are simply kicked aside while the men are literally driven to their death." Although Toner was surely exaggerating, Pressed Steel workers' experiences validated the sentiment. They reported that the assembly line created "rushed-to-death conditions" that presented "continuous danger."[131] They named one of the mill buildings the "Slaughter House" due to the high number of fatal accidents that occurred there, and they called another "Last Chance" because "if a man ever worked in this mill he has no chance on earth outside."[132] Joseph G. Armstrong, who had served as coroner of Allegheny County, corroborated the unsafe working conditions. He asserted that "deaths averaged about one each day." A closer inspection of the evidence suggests that Armstrong inflated the numbers, but the plant still produced many fatalities. In seven years preceding the strike, forty-three workers met their demise.[133] In some cases, the company contributed to the funeral expenses of the deceased in amounts that ranged up to three hundred dollars or more in some cases; in others, the county bore the burial expenses if relatives did not claim the body.[134] This body count did not include injuries sustained in the works, but the evidence substantiates Paul Kellogg's claim that "the company . . . has a general reputation for consideration of Hunkie-life, very much in keeping with the contempt it accords its employes [sic] industrially—as machine tenders, rather than men."[135] Therefore, the workers struck at McKees Rocks in 1909 for more than wages. They challenged the degradation inherent in the pooling system, the system of graft, dangerous working conditions, and exploitation in company-owned houses.

As the workers aired their grievances in the first days of the strike, President Hoffstot launched a public relations counteroffensive. He bluntly stated in a press release, "There is no strike." Instead, he suggested that the six hundred men who walked out had merely intimidated the rest of the workforce. Therefore, the conflict was limited to a few troublemakers rather than representing widespread discontent. He defended the pooling system as providing an opportunity for workers to earn higher wages and said that allegations of graft and exorbitant fees for company houses were false. As for working conditions, Hoffstot insisted that the forty-three fatalities did not make the plant a slaughterhouse. He refused to acknowledge the workers' grievances, declined to meet with the Big Six, and clung to the notion that the only right a worker had was the right to quit.[136]

The situation settled into a standoff. Strikers' pickets watched for strikebreakers, guards protected the plant, and the public waited for a resolution to the conflict. Both the workers and the public hoped peace would prevail. Hoffstot wanted his plant operating again.

Hoffstot's strategy to break the strike centered on evictions and replacement workers, with law enforcement serving the notices and protecting the strikebreakers. Altercations between workers and troopers flared during late July and early August, with a fatal altercation occurring on August 12, the day Sheriff Gumbert began evicting tenants from company houses. Steve Horvath, an Austrian, was on picket duty when he challenged Major Smith, a black man, to prove he was not a strikebreaker. Smith withdrew his automatic Colt pistol, shot, and killed Horvath.

Horvath became a martyr, in the words of the strikers, and they treated him as such. Five thousand people flocked to a meeting at the Indian Mound to cheer Horvath's sacrifice.[137] Several thousand marched seven miles in his funeral possession to St. Nicholas' Croatian Catholic Church, after which Horvath was interred in a nearby "Bohemian" cemetery.[138]

The funeral march served as an extension of the ongoing debate about the nature of the strike. To win public opinion, the Big Six and speakers at the Indian Mound had continually spoken against violence and urged workers to abstain from alcohol. They wanted to present a united front dedicated to an orderly demand for justice. If the strikers remained peaceful, the public would focus on their grievances. This strategy bore fruit in the first days of the strike. Even conservative papers like the *Gazette Times* echoed the tone of more sympathetic Pittsburgh dailies such as the *Leader* by training most of their editorial criticism on Hoffstot rather than blaming the workers.[139] The strikers even garnered financial support from the First English Evangelical Church in the early stages of the conflict. Horvath's violent death jeopardized public support. Indeed, the *Gazette Times* editorialized soon after the shooting that it "was not a good sign." Horvath's altercation with Smith was "evidence that the strikers are not impressed that it is a serious matter to resort to violence and makes it clear that the peace authorities of the state and county need to redouble their vigilance to guard against further attacks

Figure 3. Steve Horvath's funeral procession

upon persons."[140] This view did not favor the strikers, and there seemed a fine line between support and opposition in the press.[141]

Horvath's funeral procession therefore allowed the strikers to stage an orderly and peaceful march of thousands as one small effort to counteract the depiction of the workers as a group in a downward spiral toward lawless disorder. Pennsylvanians witnessed the procession either along the route or by viewing photographs taken to memorialize the occasion. One photo, reprinted in several periodicals, captured the organization and magnitude of the procession (figure 3).[142] Row upon row of men and at least one row of women led an ornate white casket that gleamed in the August sun. Other carriages followed the casket, and a solid mass of marchers stretched as far as the camera's lens could capture. The first several rows of men posed for the camera, smirking, smiling, or wearing an inscrutable facial expression that was likely intended to be a mask of determination. Such a scene was intended to connect with an audience. The procession commemorated Horvath's death with an orderly ritual.

The funeral march interacted with other discussions that circulated around the strike, especially regarding the nature of immigrant workers. The immigrant community had been segregated into different neighborhoods, the so-called Hunkeyville at Schoenville primarily, and occupied the lower rungs of the occupational ladder. Americans had a difficult time avoiding using the word *ignorant* as an adjective to modify the pejorative noun *Hunky*. The social, political, and cultural commentary en vogue during the early twentieth century placed eastern Europeans on a lower, less evolved, branch of the family tree of humanity. The growing call for immigration restriction hoped to exclude such people from coming to the United States.

It was against hostile and degrading attitudes such as these that a funeral procession like Horvath's could be particularly effective. The funeral march featured participants dressed in their Sunday best. Some of the men sported dashing straw hats to shield themselves against the heat, and women wore vibrant, but modest, white dresses cinched at the waist with black belts.[143] The lead row of men carried a large American flag, and at least four additional flags appeared at intervals down the length of the column of marchers. With every step on the route to the cemetery, the workers challenged degrading and dehumanizing stereotypes. Could ignorant, barbarian hordes celebrate their dead in such an honorable fashion? While the prejudices that existed in the United States in 1909 were too entrenched to be countered by one funeral procession, the march clearly had meaning. After Horvath's death, the Unknown Committee informed the state constabulary that "for every man you kill of us, we will kill one of you."[144] The strikers would not consent to being merely the victims of violence, as if their lives could be held with such low regard. They implied that the life of every striker was just as important as the life of a man who wore a trooper's uniform. More than wages were at stake at McKees Rocks.

The sight of nearly 7,000 people marching to remember Steven Horvath did not sway Hoffstot's resolve to stand firm against the workers. Indeed, as the strikers buried Horvath, Pressed Steel was busy. The company had contracted the services of the New York agency of Pearl Bergoff to import strikebreakers. Shielded by a heavy fog that hung over the Ohio River valley on August 13, 450 men ferried across the river to the plant. To deter an attack on the ferry, the company installed a machine gun on its deck.[145] Reinforcements arrived on the side of the strikers, too. Industrial Workers of the World organizer William Trautmann addressed a mass meeting of 8,000 on August 15. Neither side was ready to abandon the fight.

Each side's resolve was on display for the next week, as the company imported strikebreakers and strikers searched for effective means to keep the plant idle. Rumors swirled of threats to company property. Women hurled stones and insults at state troopers. Strikers continued to search the streetcars to deter strikebreakers from entering the plant and reportedly shot at windows and a searchlight the company had erected to help protect the perimeter of the company's property at night.¹⁴⁶ The temporary boxcar prison was kept busy, as troopers arrested Albert H. Carr, a member of the Big Six strikers committee, on the charge of disorderly conduct. Other immigrant workers landed in the car next to him as a result of throwing stones at troopers.¹⁴⁷ Pressed Steel's problems mounted when some of the replacement workers claimed that they had been recruited under false pretenses and then forced by sheriff's deputies to remain at the plant under threat of bodily harm. Their working conditions amounted to forced labor, or peonage, they claimed, and the U.S. Justice Department eventually investigated the allegations.¹⁴⁸

The charged atmosphere in McKees Rocks exploded in violence on Sunday, August 22. As strikers monitored streetcars for potential strikebreakers, they encountered Harry Exley, a deputy sheriff "notorious for strikebreaking." When they ordered him to leave the car, Exley "denounced the strikers in vile language, pulled a gun and fired at the strikers."¹⁴⁹ The men returned fire, killing Exley and sparking a series of skirmishes. State troopers rushed to the scene and exchanged fire with the retreating strikers. At least twelve people died from the gun battles—estimates range to as high as twenty-six total fatalities. The list included two troopers, two strikebreakers, and at least eight strikers and sympathizers. Between forty and fifty people sustained wounds. Troopers imposed order through virtual martial law. They filled the boxcar prison with strikers, raided houses in search of leaders, and dispersed all meetings. Troopers dragged some of the injured to jail with wounds still streaming blood. They searched houses in Schoenville, confiscating guns, knives, and other weapons on the authority of a state law that "prohibited possession of weapons by aliens." The labor and Socialist press labeled the day's events "Bloody Sunday," and headlines roared that the conditions were "Worse than Russia."¹⁵⁰ The *Gazette Times* placed blame squarely on the shoulders of the strikers. "There must be no more going about of marauding bands of armed and desperate foreigners defiant of the laws of the land and ignorant of the usages of civilized and orderly communities," the paper editorialized.¹⁵¹ These varying sentiments framed the violence at McKees Rocks. For the second time in ten days, the strikers mobilized around funeral rites to express their condolences for the deceased.

The funerals for the victims of the Bloody Sunday violence were more subdued than that for Steve Horvath. Strikers had been out of work and without pay for more than a month. The atmosphere in McKees Rocks had changed remarkably in the preceding days. As tensions rose with the importation of replacement workers, each side accused the other of participating in little less than a reign of terror. Strikers hoped to intimidate potential replacement workers in order to keep the mill idle and force the company to negotiate. Pressed Steel hoped to outlast the strikers' relief fund and use the threat of homelessness by eviction notice to gain the upper hand. Troopers and deputy sheriffs used whatever means necessary to preserve the peace. They even ordered the bells of the Catholic cathedral in McKees Rocks, which had begun tolling for the dead at noon on August 23, silenced. The troopers feared that the bells would only agitate the strikers.[152]

While the troopers could silence the bells, they could not halt the funeral processions. On August 24, long lines of strikers and their sympathizers viewed the bodies that lay in state in the Catholic church and then, led by an eight-member band, proceeded to the cemetery just outside of Schoenville.[153] The strike committee paid the expenses for three of the deceased.[154]

These scenes produced competing interpretations among observers. One wire reporter connected the rituals to the discourse of the "ignorant foreigner." The article, appearing in the pages of the *Chicago Tribune*, described the strikers and their families as presenting "an air of deep grief" as they marched, "dressed in their finery." The author called the strikers "pitiful in their attempt at proper decorum," as if the immigrant families might be able to perform the script of the ritual but lacked the qualities necessary to fully appreciate the gravity of the rites. In death, just as in life, some observers stigmatized the foreigners as merely pretenders to American proprieties.[155]

The Reverend Lyman Edwyn Davis, pastor of Grace Church in Pittsburgh, agreed, in part. Writing in the *Independent*, Davis viewed the strikers as a "vast ignorant but innocent throng" who suffered from "the frenzy of their native temperament." Although sharing some of the similar rhetoric, he parted ways with other onlookers by situating the funeral rituals in the broader drama of immigration to America. He saw in the faces of the marchers the same thing he had witnessed earlier in the summer aboard the *President Lincoln* as it crossed the Atlantic with immigrants aboard and in the medical lines at the immigration station in New York. "I saw viciousness in not a single face, either of the throng in Pittsburgh or of the strong multitude on shipboard," Davis recalled. "But this I saw; the despair of the Old World in every single face lighted up by the awakening hope of the New World." He viewed the strike at McKees Rocks, as made clear by the long and winding funeral procession, as evidence that immigrants' dreams were being crushed under the weight of exploitation. "They may be treated often as brutes rather than men," Davis wrote. "But, they know very clearly the supreme object of their immigration to America. They have come not alone for liberty, but especially liberty to seek prosperity." Liberty and prosperity fueled the workers' passion. The Pressed Steel Car Company's labor relations and conduct during the strike allowed despair to creep in again, "where hope had come to shine." For Davis, the funeral procession represented the life and death of the American dream.[156]

While Davis complicated the narrative of the ignorant foreigner, Socialists and Wobblies rejected it entirely. Eugene Debs addressed the strikers on August 25, suggesting that they were participating in an important struggle that revealed the ills of capitalism. Writing in the *International Socialist Review*, Louis Duchez suggested that the immigrant workers were neither helpless nor ignorant. A number of men had been involved in the trade union movement in Europe and had strike experience from Hungary, Russia, and Germany. Others had been members of Socialist Parties in Europe. They brought these credentials to the class struggle in the United States and were therefore to be valued rather than scorned.[157] The IWW saw the McKees Rocks conflict as an opportune moment to "bring its program of direct action and its principles of industrial unionism" to the steel industry.[158]

The themes of death and dignity continued to define the strike as the calendar pages turned through the end of August into early September. The allegations of peonage and tales of abuse inflicted on imported workers emboldened the claims against the company. A report circulated on August 29 that three of the strikebreakers had died as a result of harsh treatment and poor food. Rumors alleged that the company cremated the bodies in a furnace to destroy the evidence rather than having a proper funeral.[159] Variations of the rumor suggested that the three men had been thrown alive into the furnace. True or false, the accusations continued to frame the Pressed Steel Car Company in a negative light. Nearly one hundred pages of testimony collected as part of the Justice Department's peonage investigations suggested the workers were taking a proper stand against degrading conditions. "Conditions in the Pressed Steel Car plant at Schoenville are a disgrace," the *Gazette Times* editorialized. The "system which obtains there is un-American and shameful and is bringing Pennsylvania and Pittsburgh into disgrace and disrepute."[160]

With Pressed Steel under investigation and the immigrant strikers still reeling from the "Bloody Sunday" violence, the time was ripe for settlement. Pressured by Charles P. Neill, U.S. commissioner of labor, Pressed Steel discussed terms with C. A. Wise of the Big Six. On September 7, Wise called the strikers to the Indian Mound and presented the company's proposal. Sunday work would be abolished, and Saturdays would be half-days. The company refused to reinstate the 1907 wage scale, but promised a 10 to 15 percent raise in sixty to ninety days. Although the company's proposed terms said nothing about the pooling system, graft, improved safety, or company housing, Wise declared a formal vote would be held the following day. The strikers accepted the company's terms, with only a handful of no votes cast. Wise and many others declared a victory for the workers.

Relief at a settlement was short lived for the immigrant workers. The company soon released a statement that said it had not agreed to any pay raises and would not abandon the pooling system. They vowed not to tolerate graft, which was hardly a concession since they had denied the practice from the beginning of the strike. "The immigrants and Wobblies," historian Melvyn Dubofsky notes, realized at this point that they "had been had."[161] Wise and the American workers, who were skilled workers not impacted by the pooling system, had pushed a settlement on the majority foreign-born workforce that merely reverted to the status quo ante. More than four thousand foreign workers responded by once again putting down their tools and walking out. By September 16, nearly forty-five hundred workers were out. The strike was on again.

At this stage, Pressed Steel did not need to contract Pearl Bergoff for more strikebreakers. The skilled Americans broke the strike. On September 16, Wise organized around two thousand men to challenge the pickets. Mobilized behind a huge American flag, at least five hundred Americans in the group armed themselves. A violent confrontation did not ensue, however. The thirty-five hundred men who had formed a picket at the company's gates parted to make way for the procession. The first few weeks of the strike had been effective due to the unity between American and foreign workers. That solidarity had now been shattered. The demoralized strikers abandoned their protest and returned to work.[162]

What, then, had the strike accomplished? How did it shape or reflect workers' experiences with death? What does it reveal about steelworkers' experiences with death? Judged by bread-and-butter issues of wages, conditions, and the pooling system, the strike had been a failure. More was at stake. The McKees Rocks strike was part of "new patterns of labor conflict," according to historian Shelton Stromquist, that featured some level of significant violence and surging class conflict.[163] Workers across the country between 1908 and 1914 were fighting back against an industrial system that sought to make them expendable. The alleged corporate philosophy at Pressed Steel was "A human life is worth less than a rivet. Rivets cost money."[164]

Steelworkers had been trying to claim their dignity through death rituals throughout the period after Homestead, but the McKees Rocks struggle suggests two things. First, the workers at Pressed Steel sought a showdown to counter the degrading conditions established in the works. The widespread publicity of the strike provided a broader platform from which to challenge prevailing attitudes toward immigrants and unskilled workers than the more localized rituals associated with fraternal societies and church burials. Second, but closely related, the McKees Rocks strikes show a persistent tendency for steelworkers to respond, even in the nonunion era, with militancy. This point connects the battle of Homestead in 1892 and McKees Rocks in 1909 to future violent confrontations in 1919 and the 1930s.

More immediately, the strike forced observers to reassess their notions of unskilled, immigrant labor. As the strike waned, the conservative *Pittsburgh Gazette Times* editorialized on this point. "'Hunkey' labor" was workmen coming "from southern Europe to dig, delve, fetch and carry and generally to perform the kind of hard labor which . . . Americans and the more adept of our foreign-born population will not do." Such workers had been commonly viewed "as a being entitled to scant courtesy and small consideration, something lower than a man and yet little above an animal." This was an injustice, according to the editorial. Immigrants served valuable roles in the community. Such ostracism made foreign workers ripe for exploitation by "unwise counselors" who encouraged them to defy the law, which was certainly a veiled reference to the IWW. To prevent future upheaval, immigrants "should [not] be relegated to a position outside the pale as one beneath society's notice."[165] The *Gazette Times* was not the only newspaper reassessing views on immigrant labor. Near the end of the strike, a correspondent for the *Pittsburgh Sun* wrote, "The foreigner takes on a new, higher aspect after this demonstration of good qualities."[166] These sentiments referred to the workers' pursuit for fair treatment in the face of a clearly more powerful, intractable foe backed by U.S. Steel, the largest corporation in the world. They referred to their insistence on nonviolence until the goads of strikebreakers and evictions were too much to bear.

Yet it would be a mistake to infer too much from McKees Rocks. The key components that constituted the nonunion era were left intact. Despite the public relations lumps the Pressed Steel Company took, it and other subsidiaries of U.S. Steel still held the upper hand in labor relations and in community politics. The labor force continued to be divided along the lines of skill, nationality, and race, even though the McKees Rocks strike showed that these factors did not create an insurmountable obstacle to solidarity. Indeed, similar scenes would recur in western Pennsylvania and other sectors of the steel industry in the nationwide strike of 1919. Then, too, violence would occur. Then, too, steelworkers would need to bury their dead.

Conclusion: The Life and Times of Joe Magarac, Steelman

The themes of life and death became more than everyday worries. They became legend. Writing in *Scribner's* magazine in 1931, Owen Francis reported a folk story he claimed to have heard while working in the steel mills of the Monongahela Valley. It told the tale of Joe Magarac, steelman. "He is to the Hunkie," Francis explained, "what Paul Bunyan is to the woodsman and

Old Stormalong is to the men of the sea." In the tale, Magarac appears in "Hunkietown," astonishing a crowd with his rugged handsomeness and a feat of strength. When the awestruck audience asks, "What kind of mans are you?" the stranger replies, "My name is Joe Magarac, what you think of dat, eh?" The crowd laughs because "*magarac* in Hunkie means jackass donkey." "Sure! Magarac, Joe. Dats me," the hero elaborates. "All I do is eatit and workit same lak jackass donkey. Me, I be only steelmans in whole world, ya damn right." The story details Magarac's superhuman work ethic and concludes with the hero melting himself into steel as a sacrifice to build a new mill.[167]

Although scholars rightly question the authenticity of the folktale, the Magarac story offers striking parallels to experiences in turn-of-the-century mills.[168] Immigrants testified that work dominated their lives; they too felt like donkeys driven to perform hard labor, allowed brief rest, and then compelled to repeat the cycle. They could have read Magarac's heroism as symbolic of their daily battles in the heat of the mill. And, like Magarac, thousands of workers died producing the steel that made many features of the industrial economy possible.

Magarac's act of dying punctuated the folktale. A steelworker's death in the late nineteenth and early twentieth centuries provided more of a transition in the drama rather than an end point. The next act unfolded in the rituals of burial. Remembering the dead proved an important feature of working people's lives. Caring for the body and commemorating the deceased reflected the dynamic work and community experiences of the living. Funeral practices allowed, as at Homestead in 1892, a commentary on the wage earners' position in the Republic. Death on the job revealed fractious politics and illustrated how xenophobia and racism fueled desires for dignified burials. Well-attended funerals signified that a worker's life carried importance, regardless of broader discourses of difference and inferiority.

Steelworkers' experiences in the 1890s and 1900s connected to a broader working-class project. Their rituals conveyed meanings about work and life in the industrial era that stretched back to the labor struggles of the 1870s and 1880s. They interacted with similar trends that had motivated Illinois coal miners in the 1890s to venerate their dead with such passion. In their own way, steelworkers added several threads to the rich tapestry that workers across the country were weaving. The product was a belief in the dignity of workers and a set of ritual practices meant to convey respect for common people.

In a wonderfully evocative phrase near the end of *Out of This Furnace*, Thomas Bell reflects on the varied meanings and lived experiences that life in the Monongahela Valley produced: "*Out of this furnace, this metal.*"[169] The travails steelworkers endured at work and in the community produced, Bell suggests, hardened citizens who held firm to ideas of political and economic freedom. Surveying steelworkers' rituals of dying during part of the nonunion era suggests that death provided a key place where they nurtured spirits of resistance. Labor upheavals in 1919 and again during the 1930s testify to their strength. Out of these experiences came this resolve.

Conclusion

(Un)Freedom of the Grave

When Samuel Gompers, a leader of growing importance in the young American Federation of Labor, addressed the International Labor Congress in 1893, he chose the theme "What Does Labor Want?" In laying out his program, Gompers excoriated the wage system as one that put workers "in a position involving a degradation of mind and body." Amid traditional calls for shorter hours and increased wages, Gompers paid special attention to asserting workers' human worth. In an era when political economists treated workers' labor power as nothing more than a commodity to be bought and sold, Gompers reminded his audience that workers had hearts and brains like the rest of humanity. He proclaimed that a critical demand of labor should be that "the lives and limbs of the wage-workers shall be regarded as sacred as those of all others of our fellow human beings." Gompers asserted the sacredness of workers' bodies at a time when many sectors of society acted as though workers were merely disposable tools of production, to be used and discarded when their utility had been exhausted. This was perhaps the defining problem of the era. The reckless and inhuman "waste of labor" threatened the very "continuance of civilization."[1]

Gompers's comments reflected the broader debate unleashed by the Civil War, emancipation, and industrialization about the proper social ordering of the United States. Contested meanings of human and social worth became an undercurrent of U.S. history from 1865 to 1920. Broad transformations in the economy pushed farmers away from the land and pulled millions of immigrants to labor in the nation's industrial cities. Once-sturdy icons of American success, the yeomen farmer and the independent producer increasingly became symbols of a bygone era misfit for the industrial age. Americans clung to beliefs that a sound work ethic led to economic independence, but rags-to-riches stories became more properly the plots of dime novels than accurate reflections of social mobility. Even the most optimistic commentators bemoaned the "labor problem" and worried about the formation of an industrial working class.

Working people felt these changes on their bodies. Industrial workplaces devoured lives and mangled bodies with incredible efficiency. Disease, spawned by crowded tenements, the breathing of dust and noxious fumes, and myriad other causes, ravaged their constitutions. Hunger gnawed at stomachs during the depressingly regular intervals of economic downturns, when modern workplaces worked too well and flooded the market or when millionaire moguls decided to play with stock markets. Absorbing these changes in a corporeal way spawned a battle for dignity in which working people sometimes claimed solace in a well-attended funeral and accommodated the changes swirling around them. At other times, workers responded to indignities suffered by filling the streets in protest and making the halls of state government and courthouses reverberate with their condemnation. Exhuming working people's experiences with death adds emotional depth to the industrial era. For many, the circumstances of death represented the dynamics of power in the United States. If workers became peripheral to the social and economic functioning of the country, then the grave had the power to reinscribe conditions of dependence, exploitation, racism, and sexism.

Working people developed a variety of ways to escape such an ignominious end. Class-based repertoires of ritual developed as an undercurrent of industrialization from the end of the Civil War to the close of the Progressive Era. Working communities infused their funerals, processions, and memorials with meanings and invented traditions that became customs by which wageworkers could measure the dignity and respect paid to the deceased. A "good death" for an American worker by 1920 had come to signify something that had accrued additional layers of meaning because of the economic and political development of the country. Parts of the *Ars moriendi* tradition persisted in claiming a good death. A worker approaching the end of life still preferred to know of death's approach, hoped to be able to take appropriate steps to prepare for the afterlife (spiritual or practical), and preferred to die in the company of family with the hope that a respectful burial would follow.

However, the evolution of industrialization after the Civil War threatened to disrupt traditions of dying, just as the war itself had. Soldiers and loved ones struggled to maintain a sense of normalcy in deathways during the crisis of the war. Workers and their families engaged in a similar project, as the Industrial Revolution continued to destabilize their lives and traditions after 1865. In the midst of war and economic transformation, Americans attempted to develop innovative techniques to preserve access to a good death, even in the face of daunting challenges such as bodies littering a battlefield hundreds of miles from home or bodies being trapped in coal mines with families oceans away. Workers created networks of solidarity, demanded dignity for the dead, and connected the deceased to the living in ways that would allow the community to heal and press on for brighter futures.

Whereas the Civil War caused massive human losses and disrupted traditional rituals, the Industrial Revolution did that and more. Meeting death in a soldier's uniform or on the field of battle often carried honor and respect. A dying soldier might reasonably expect that his death would have a lasting place in the nation's memory. Meeting death on the job, during a strike, or in a working-class neighborhood came to be defined through the developing cultures of industrialization. Meanings attached to dead workers were fluid, to be sure, but some of the prevailing trends questioned the human worth and dignity of an individual who earned a wage. Therefore, while the Civil War motivated Americans to develop embalming, industrialization inspired workers to develop traditions to ensure the deceased would be respected. The decades after the Civil War produced moments of ritual creation and consolidation where, by the early twentieth century, workers had established a set of practices that became routine when they met death in any number of ways but especially mass tragedy and labor violence. They created rituals that allowed them to explore the politics of death in the industrial age to lay claim to the dignity of labor and the human value of the laborer. A working-class *Ars moriendi* had developed that fused the individual act of dying with the community act of remembering.

This historical development unfolded from the 1860s to the 1910s. These decades produced a number of venues for the articulation and performance of the new rituals. Focusing on particular moments and places shows the ebbs and flows of the ideas associated with work and social class. Workers learned lessons from the upheavals of the 1870s and the hangman's nooses that came after the Haymarket Affair. Class-based rituals developed in areas of the country where unions grew powerful, such as the coalfields of central Illinois. They also proliferated in areas where unions were not as strong, such as in the steel communities of western Pennsylvania, where workers blended strategies to combat the alienation of urban, industrial life in ways that both paralleled and diverged from the practices of other social classes. The space of death also reflected social relationships defined by gender, ethnicity, and religion. Rituals of dying and the acts of commemorating the dead could challenge and confirm prevailing beliefs, could cement the bonds of solidarity or expose fissures that widened to fragment the working classes. Native-born white workers sought distance from "new" immigrant or black workers in life as well as in death. Immigrant and black workers turned to institution building to combat degrading treatment and negative stereotypes. The culture privileged the lives and deaths of men over women in many, but certainly not all, circumstances.

These trends interact with broader practices of death and dying across time and cultures. Scholars have noted that death rituals have served in various societies to convey ideologies and maintain authority. Anthropologist Robert Hertz, a student of Émile Durkheim, suggested that death rituals expressed three relationships: first, body-soul; second, individual-community; and third, community of the living–community of the dead.[2] Of the three relationships, the available sources most clearly allow an exploration of workers' experiences with death as illustrative of the individual-community relationship.

In this nexus, death became a contested terrain of political authority and ideology that contained elements of class, gender, ethnicity, race, and religion. Anthropologists have long studied death rituals' relationships to social order. In some cultures, especially certain hunter-gatherer societies, "the handling of death is not put to work as a device for the creation of ideology and political domination."[3] Stated in slightly different terms, the dead in hunter-gatherer societies received little attention when there was no political authority to be maintained or differences of wealth or status to be emphasized.[4]

This comparison suggests why workers' deaths, especially violent deaths or deaths caused by workplace accidents, became such politicized spectacles during the nineteenth century. The industrialization of the United States after the Civil War had transformed the country in such ways that class and status became more entrenched. Death rituals provide evidence. Elaborate Victorian-era funerals reflected complicated struggles for social, economic, and political power in the United States. The level of attention that dead workers received, and the elaborate strategies working people developed to memorialize the dead, suggests that the individual-community bond and the struggles over authority were defining features of life between 1865 and 1920.

Studying the body-soul relationship or the role religion played in shaping the working-class subculture of death and dying is more difficult. Workers left few sources to reveal their innermost feelings and attitudes about whether religious faith provided comfort or answered some of the mysteries of dying. Two things are relatively clear, however. First, many of the funerals examined in this study incorporated elements of the Christian ritual, whether Protestant or Catholic. Mourners flocked to churches and huddled in pews to hear ministers and priests read the liturgy and deliver funeral orations.

Second, the meanings Christians attached to the grave did not prove entirely satisfactory for many working people. If Christians broadly interpreted the grave as a gateway to freedom into a better world in the hereafter, the evidence indicates that the matter was much more complicated for workers. Many refused to accept that accidents or more common deaths were providential acts of God. They situated their deaths within broader social and economic relationships. They sought worldly explanations as well as heavenly.

While the role of religion remains murky, workers had clearly developed rituals and attitudes by the early twentieth century that shaped their responses to workplace tragedies. Mass deaths in the ten years between 1907 and 1917, a period that began with a rash of industrial disasters and ended with the U.S. declaration of war against Germany, produced responses that were decades in the making. In December 1907, an explosion in Monongah, West Virginia, claimed the lives of 362 men and boys. Less than two years later, the Cherry Mine fire in Cherry, Illinois, claimed the lives of 259 miners. Then, in 1911, disaster struck the Triangle Shirtwaist Factory in New York City, where 146, mainly immigrant, women perished. At Cherry the community sought to reclaim the bodies to provide dignified burial. They formed a charitable organization to care for widows and children left without husbands and fathers. Organized labor used the event to demand safer working conditions, and the UMWA erected a handsome monument in Cherry's cemetery to memorialize the dead miners.[5] After the Triangle fire, workers took to the streets of New York City to memorialize the dead through massive processions and to fight for the living by reforming safety regulations and arguing for compensation.[6] Tragedies such as these demonstrated that working people had been creating rituals over the previous decades that could guide their actions during times of devastating loss. The memorials bore witness to continuities with other rituals that stretched back in time and across oceans to immigrant homelands. The mourners inserted class-based arguments about life and death into Progressive Era America.

Labor conflict also produced an array of funerary tableaus in the years leading to American participation in World War I. Death was a recurring theme in the Lawrence Textile Strike (1912), the Paint Creek and Cabin Creek Mine Strikes (1912), the Ludlow Massacre (1914), and others. During the Paterson Silk Strike (1913), death was on display both in the confrontation with employers that led to the death of Valentino Modestino and during a pageant the workers performed to raise funds to support strikers. More than a thousand workers re-created elements of their struggle before a crowd at Madison Square Garden in New York City. Scene 3 of the pageant re-created the mass funeral of Modestino, a striker who had been shot and killed by a detective hired to protect the plant. Singing the "Funeral March of the Workers," the participants carried a coffin down the middle aisle as strike leaders and a parade of workers followed.[7] These episodes from Lawrence to Ludlow combined with the persistence of workplace accidents to prove that the meanings attached to dead workers' bodies continued to be contested and that working people used their repertoires of ritual to situate themselves within the broader social body.

These rituals were part of the Progressive Era that presented different paths toward improving workers' lives and respecting their contributions to society. Middle-class progressives mobilized representations of workers as victims to press for legislative reforms. In 1910 select states began paying mothers' pensions, and twenty-one northern states established workmen's compensation systems between 1911 and 1913. These reforms began blunting the harsher edges of industrial society. They "gave birth to an infant welfare state."[8]

Working people had an ambivalent relationship with Progressive reforms. Labor leaders such as Samuel Gompers bristled at the paternalism exhibited by some middle-class efforts. He believed working people could represent themselves if provided a level playing field. The AFL spent the years leading up to World War I lobbying for legal protections for workers' rights to organize and strike and for federal legislation to improve working conditions. Such efforts rejected the notion that workers should be viewed as victims of industrialization or dependents of paternalist state programs. Working people wanted to be considered equal partners in the Republic.

Pursuing legislative reform and protections for basic human rights provided a strategy to reject the victimization theme middle-class reformers created. Successes such as the Clayton Act (1914) and the Adamson Act (1916) demonstrated the competing paths reform could take and showed dueling meanings mapped to workers' bodies: dependent victims versus independent citizens with political power. Workers continued to prize independence, and the AFL pursued tactics of "pure and simple politics" to achieve what they could through voluntarism and by pressuring the government to assist when necessary.[9] They were reluctant to empower the state or to create state or federal bureaucracies to compete with labor unions to provide services. Radical groups such as the Industrial Workers of the World and revolutionary Socialists rejected the AFL's strategy. They argued that respect for workers' lives and dignity on the job could be achieved only through a fundamental reordering of society. These competing strategies and visions produced a variety of ideas about what it meant to live and die as a wageworker in the United States.

Events abroad refocused the debates about life and death during the Progressive Era. Americans watched as Europe went to war in 1914, protected by the broad expanse of the Atlantic and a long history of isolationist policy. They soon discovered that the Great War would be one of horrific casualties—a "mechanized war with industrial might behind it," in the apt characterization of historian Mark Meigs. The jagged line of the western front scarred Europe, stretching from the English Channel to the Swiss Alps. Battles along this front produced rivers of blood but largely failed to move the positions of the great armies. The pattern of attrition claimed between 3,000 and 4,000 dead a day and was punctuated by months-long battles.[10] The five-month siege of Verdun that began in February 1916 produced staggering fatalities of 350,000 Frenchmen and 330,000 Germans. The British campaign in the Somme River valley that same year produced more than 1 million dead. Between the outbreak of the war and the early months of 1917, 5 million dead had failed to appreciably shift the battle lines.[11] The optimistic nationalism with which soldiers had buoyantly marched to war had been swallowed in the mud and blood of trench warfare.

President Woodrow Wilson's official proclamation of neutrality in 1914 kept Americans safe from the carnage. Most Americans preferred it that way, and middle-class progressives worked to keep Americans from the trenches. Paul Kellogg and Florence Kelley formed the American Union against Militarism, while Jane Addams worked with like-minded women to form the Woman's Peace Party. Progressives worried that the war would stall the momentum for social progress and reform.[12] These efforts combined with widespread attitudes that the war in Europe was a war that need not concern the United States or claim the lives of American soldiers.

To these general arguments for neutrality, groups such as the IWW and the antiwar faction of the Socialist Party infused class-based opposition to involvement. They used the war to reflect on the relationship between industrial society, war, and workers' bodies. For them, the war would be another instrument of capitalist exploitation of the working classes. The workers would pay the ultimate price on the battlefields, while the elite shared the spoils. The best way to benefit workers and to safeguard their lives was to oppose American involvement and argue for international class solidarity.[13]

Gompers offered a different strategy for increasing workers' role in the Republic. He cloaked himself in nationalism and worked to make labor unions equal partners in preparedness efforts. Speaking at the annual meeting of the National Civic Federation in 1916, Gompers said that the "stupendous horror" of the war had compelled all men to think deeply about the "principles underlying our institutions and the spirit that makes for human progress and liberty." Men, if they were true men, would fight "even for a 'scrap of paper' when that paper represents the ideals of human justice and freedom." Wage earners had a duty to fight, Gompers declared, and no one could question their willingness to bear arms for the "cause of liberty, freedom and justice."[14]

Gompers's approach in 1916 may seem contradictory to his 1893 address when he argued that the labor movement's key goal was to convince the rest of America that the lives and limbs of wageworkers should be regarded as sacred. While Haywood and Debs would have ridiculed his logic, Gompers believed that the war provided a path to greater participation for workers in the mechanisms of power. He was willing to commit workers' bodies to a war effort in order to secure a more equal relationship between business leaders, the labor movement, and political power brokers.

Although Gompers had clearly added his voice to the minority preparedness lobby and nationalist conservatives such as Theodore Roosevelt who barked for war, American neutrality held through 1916. Americans continued to prefer that position. The president of the United Mine Workers of America criticized preparedness as an attempt to make the United States an "armed camp" for the purpose of extending "commercialism abroad and exploit[ing] labor at home." President Wilson capitalized on the spirit of neutrality by using the slogan "He kept us out of war" to achieve victory in the 1916 election. Shortly thereafter, he critically reflected on the evolution of warfare that had produced the bloody stalemate in Europe. "War, before this one," he wrote privately as he prepared a final attempt to negotiate a peace settlement, "used to be a sort of national excursion ... with brilliant battles lost and won, national heroes decorated, and all sharing in the glory accruing to the state." The current war was little more than "a gruesome contest of systematized destruction" that produced "unprecedented human waste and suffering." Wilson wondered, "Where is any longer the glory commensurate with the sacrifice of the millions of men required in modern war to carry and defend Verdun?"[15] Meaningless sacrifice did not appeal to Wilson late in 1916, nor did it appeal to Americans.

In the space of a few brief months, Wilson abandoned neutrality. After failing to negotiate a peace settlement, he appealed to Congress to declare war against Germany on April 2, 1917. As he addressed Congress, he redefined the war from one producing senseless slaughter to a conflict that the United States should join to defend the ideals Americans had always carried nearest to their hearts—"for democracy, for the right of those who submit to authority to have a voice in their own governments, for the rights and liberties of small nations, for a universal dominion of right by such a concert of free peoples as shall bring peace and safety to all nations and make the world itself at last free."¹⁶ Congress agreed with Wilson, and the United States went to war.

The abandonment of neutrality meant that Americans would be putting their bodies in harm's way. Most Americans rallied to the cause and felt the mission a noble way to serve their country and fight for democracy. Wobblies and Socialists did not. They maintained their criticism of the war. A poem appeared in the *Industrial Worker* in April that made plain the harmful effects the war could have on workers' bodies. The anonymous author wrote:

> I love my flag, I do, I do,
> Which floats upon the breeze
> I also love my arms and legs,
> And neck, and nose, and knees.
> One little shell might spoil them all
> Or give them such a twist,
> They would be of no use to me;
>   I guess I won't enlist.¹⁷

Eugene Debs, the key spokesmen for the antiwar Socialists, offered a withering critique of a war for the sake of democracy in a speech he delivered at Canton, Ohio, in 1918. "They have always taught and trained you to believe it to be your patriotic duty to go to war and to have yourselves slaughtered at their command," Debs thundered at the audience. "And here let me emphasize the fact—and it cannot be repeated too often—that the working class who fight all the battles, the working class who freely shed their blood and furnish the corpses, have never yet had a voice in either declaring war or making peace. It is the ruling class that invariably does both."¹⁸ These words earned Debs a prison sentence for violating the Espionage Act.

Once the country was at war, however, public opinion shifted rapidly from favoring neutrality to supporting the American war effort. Intense nationalism helps explain the shift. Where love of country failed to change hearts and minds, a series of coercive measures—ranging from vigilantism and 100 percent Americanism to the Espionage and Sedition Acts—emerged to silence dissent. The Wobblies became one of the favored targets of intimidation. Nevertheless, "nine out of ten draft-eligible Wobblies registered for the Selective Service, and most of those reported for duty when called," which was a similar rate as AFL members, who had been more receptive to government policies.¹⁹

As it concerned workers' relationship with death, the war provided a different answer to the question of what workers had been dying *for*. Before the war, working people had been interpreting their deaths in a variety of ways that often overlapped. Some died due to the will of God. Others succumbed to the simple misfortunes of accident or disease, or they passed at the end of a long life. Still others interpreted their deaths as part of the growing class struggle that had characterized industrialization in the United States. Capitalist greed caused workplace fatalities and led to the epic confrontations of the era that usually produced dead bodies for the cause of unionization and for the defenders of capital. These interpretations created a calculus of us versus them that pitted workers against bosses and wealth. The war changed those dynamics. It provided an opportunity to blend ideas of citizenship and nationalism. "The men and women who helped fight the Great War were products of a society whose cultural and religious landscape was shaped by a particular understanding of faith, citizenship, and manhood in which all three converged in the realm of strenuous action," religious studies scholar Jonathan Ebel suggests. "Struggle, strain, and sacrifice demonstrated and enhanced physical and spiritual vigor, vitalized American culture, and gave life to the American nation."[20] Workers wanted to be closer to the center of this project rather than on the periphery. The war provided an opportunity for workers to join with other Americans in a crusade for democracy.

What democracy would mean, or how workers might be recognized as full citizens in the Republic, was not entirely clear. Men called to service were supposed to fight abroad for American principles. Those men and women who remained on the home front were encouraged to support the war effort by working diligently at their jobs, buying war bonds, and silencing their dissent. The motivating themes that President Wilson had sounded in his war message and later in his "Fourteen Points" address echoed the issues that had caused contentious labor relations since the Civil War. Workers had been fighting to bring democracy to their workplaces and struggled to preserve self-determination in the face of new technologies and management regimes. For this truly to be a war for democracy, and a war to end all war, workers argued that it would have to be a two-front conflict: a war to defeat the kaiser abroad and a war to "de-kaiser" industry at home.[21]

To fight on the European front, the United States formed the American Expeditionary Force, an army that reflected some of the fissures of prewar American society. Officers often hailed from the social elite, while the platoons and companies they commanded bore witness to the diversity of the country. Immigrants and African Americans suffered similar suspicions during their military service as they had in civilian life. Early in the war, the army deemed some foreign-born soldiers unfit for combat and assigned them to "depot brigades" to perform the hard labor of modern warfare. Later, immigrants became targets of Americanization campaigns, where the war became an expedient to teach the English language and U.S. history. African Americans negotiated a military riddled with Jim Crow prejudices that shaped training and constrained possibilities for advancement. They were even more likely than immigrants to be organized into what one General Staff report termed "reserve labor battalions." As others fought, African Americans worked as stevedores, common laborers, and grave diggers.[22]

Despite these divisions, those who fought in Europe confronted the same specter of death. As they fought and died, as some sixty thousand Americans did, the fate of their remains became a matter of consequence and shaped the meanings of the conflict. Where would the war dead find their last resting place? How would the nation commemorate their sacrifice? These questions inspired contentious debate between relatives of the deceased and the various civilian and military bureaucracies tasked with caring for the dead. Widows and mothers strongly favored the repatriation of their loved ones' remains. The U.S. funeral industry agreed. A trade group that named itself the Purple Cross lobbied the government to allow it to return the dead's remains. They claimed that advances in the "mortuary sciences" would allow them to return the bodies to their families "in a sanitary and recognizable condition" even if a number of years had passed.[23] A formidable group composed of former presidents, military officers, labor leaders, chaplains, and others took the opposing view and argued that the war dead should remain in Europe in "Fields of Honor" that would serve as a lasting reminder of America's role in the war. After the war, General Pershing cabled the War Department, supporting permanent cemeteries. "Could these soldiers speak for themselves, they would wish to be left undisturbed, where with their comrades, they had fought their last fight. . . . The graves of our soldiers constitute, if they are allowed to remain, a perpetual reminder to our allies of the liberty and ideals upon which the greatness of America rests."[24] In the end, the voices for repatriation prevailed, and the War Department authorized the return of more than 70 percent of the American war dead to the United States.[25]

The contours of this debate strongly echoed some of the key themes in working people's experiences with death in the previous decades. They had developed rituals to bring honor to their deceased, which required bodily remains. Bodies of their loved ones had become the focal points of relationships of power, just as the bodies of Civil War fatalities had been and those of Great War veterans were in the debate over repatriation. Working communities had viewed death as a form of sacrifice when the deaths occurred from labor conflict and for the principle of unionization. The determination of the last resting place of the Great War dead connected the threads of control, sacrifice, and honor. Those who argued for permanent cemeteries in Europe suggested that the deaths should be viewed as sacrifices for the glory of the nation, which would bestow the greatest honor. The families who chose repatriation wanted to reclaim their loved ones for purposes other than nationalist pride. The fate of the war dead connected the battles in Europe to the United States in more ways than burying remains.

On the home front, workers dug trenches of their own, in the form of picket lines and strikes, to articulate what democracy meant for them. "The year 1917 brought unprecedented labor turmoil to the United States," historian Joseph McCartin writes. "An astounding 458 strikes took place during the first full month after the United States went to war. And during the first six months of the war, 6,285,519 workdays were lost to nearly 3,000 strikes." Workers' passions did not abate with the Armistice in November 1918. In 1919 workers from Seattle to Boston unleashed a strike wave of unprecedented size. Four million workers participated in work stoppages that affected all parts of the economy and included nationwide strikes in steel and coal.[26]

These years of turbulence were fueled by an array of factors. Workers felt squeezed by wartime inflation during the war and spiraling prices immediately afterward. They were insulted by employers' adherence to open-shop tactics that contradicted the rationale for fighting a war abroad. As David Montgomery notes, "The desire for a new way of living nurtured by the war had produced a fusion of immediate demands with grandiose social and political goals."[27] Workers demanded adequate wages and rallied around the ideas of "industrial democracy." In the midst of the 1919 steel strike, a Polish steelworker shared at a union meeting what had inspired him to take a stand:

> Mr. Chairman—just like horse and wagon. Put horse in wagon, work all day. Take horse out of wagon—put in stable. Take horse out of stable, put in wagon. Same way like mills. Work all day. Come home—go sleep. Get up—go work in mills—come home. Wife say, "John, children sick. You help with children." You say, "Oh, go to hell"—go sleep. Wife say, "John, you go town." You say, "No"—go sleep. No know what the hell you do. For why this war? For why we buy Liberty bonds? For mills? No, for freedom and America—for everybody. No more horse and wagon. For eight-hour day.[28]

This steelworker's lament and hope for a better future characterized the passions that animated the wartime and 1919 labor upheavals. The questions linked life with death. Why did soldiers sacrifice their lives on the battlefield? Why did workers labor in dangerous conditions that threatened to dehumanize them? How could austere management regimes be reconciled with citizenship rights? Worker protests and the rituals that accompanied the workers' bodies who died during the conflicts represented bold claims on democracy and citizenship.

The death of Fannie Sellins, a union organizer, powerfully captures the tensions of the 1919 strike wave and the broader themes of workers' death between the Civil War and World War I. Sellins had been an effective organizer for the United Mine Workers in western Pennsylvania and began working in 1919 to organize the steel industry. "More than any other individual," chief architect of the steel-organizing campaign William Z. Foster later reflected, Sellins "was responsible for the unionization of the big United States Steel Corporation mills at Vandergrift, Leechburgh and New Kensington, as well as those of the so-called independent Allegheny and West Penn Steel Companies at Brackenridge." Her organizing success attracted the "undying hatred" of the employers, according to Foster, and "open threats were made to 'get' her."[29]

On August 26, 1919, Sellins intervened in an altercation between deputy sheriffs and striking workers at the Allegheny Coal and Coke Company in Brackenridge. The deputies had charged the pickets, shooting and clubbing the strikers. Sellins first rushed to remove a group of children from danger and returned to implore the deputies to stop clubbing Joseph Starzelski, a worker who had been mortally wounded in the initial charge. Sellins's intercession attracted the wrath of a mine official and the deputies. According to the *New Majority*, the mine official "snatched a club and felled [Sellins] to the ground." As Sellins tried to rise and drag herself from harm's way, the official ordered the deputies to kill her. "Three shots were fired, each taking effect," the *New Majority* reported. Sellins "fell to the ground, and [the mine official] cried: 'Give her another!'" After the shooting, Sellins's body was dragged by the heels to a waiting truck. Before removing the body from the scene, "a deputy took a cudgel and crushed in her skull before the eyes of the throng of men, women and children, who stood in powerless silence before the armed men." In remembering Sellins, Foster drew a direct connection between her life and the Great War. "Thus perished the noble Fannie Sellins: shot in the back by so-called peace officers. And she 49 years old, a grandmother, and mother of a boy killed in France, fighting to make the world safe for democracy."[30]

The inherent contradictions of Wilson's claims with the conditions of their daily lives inspired workers in western Pennsylvania and elsewhere to take action. An estimated 10,000 marched in Sellins's funeral procession, and in 1920 the United Mine Workers erected an impressive monument at her grave.[31] The inscription read, "In memory to Fannie Sellins and Joseph Starzelski, killed by the enemies of organized labor." Not long after Sellins's death, nearly 350,000 steelworkers participated in an industry-wide strike to achieve the broad goals of industrial democracy. For employers and most government officials, the strike was yet another example of a Bolshevik plot to foment revolution in the United States.

The fate of democracy for U.S. workers was largely settled on the home front rather than the battlefields of Europe. A powerful Red Scare backlash in 1919 and 1920 united public opinion against the striking workers. Arrests, intimidation, and martial law ensured that modest wartime gains workers had won would not endure. Dreams of industrial democracy were not entirely snuffed by the employer offensives of the 1920s. They would rekindle during the 1930s, when issues of life and death would once again galvanize workers.

These glimpses into workers' experiences with death and dying suggest that the years between the Civil War and World War I wrought great changes in the ways Americans thought about death. A class divide emerged in the rituals of dying, and the politics of death became contested terrain on which debates about the meaning of life during the industrial era were waged. The upper and middle classes had begun to embrace rituals of dying that privileged the professional, the private, and the intimate. Ostentatious displays of the Victorian era gave way to a minimalist modernism. By World War I, they were well on their way to crafting a culture that denied death.

Many working people in America took a different path. Through the ritual performance of last rites, they displayed the polyvalent identities that structured their lives in the late nineteenth and early twentieth centuries. As workers they reclaimed bodies from the time discipline of the factory and shielded bodies from the perpetual gaze of foremen and managers. As families they brought dead bodies again into their homes to, however briefly, reconnect the dead relative with his or her kin network. Spiritually, common people sought to save deceased members from perishing in a hell that, to them, so closely resembled certain work sites across the country. They might reconnect the dead bodies with their spiritual coworker Jesus Christ. Or they might frame the body in a more worldly way by connecting it to the doctrines of trade unionism, which had commandments as simple as a word—Solidarity!—or as communal as the Knights of Labor axiom, "An injury to one is an injury to all." Finally, working people reclaimed their loved ones for the nation at large. Through their ritual practices, they made powerful arguments that the country's industrial present and economic future were being built on the backs of millions of workers.

Their sweat, their tears, and finally their blood fueled the United States' industrial engine. And when that engine turned into the human-crushing monstrous beast William D. Howells briefly glimpsed when gazing at the Corliss engine in 1876, many working communities were there to pick up the bodies. Throughout these experiences, they balanced the imperatives of two legends in the struggle for workers' rights in the United States. One was Joe Hill, the IWW bard who famously instructed workers, "Don't mourn, organize." The other was Mother Jones, who commanded, "Pray for the dead, and fight like hell for the living." Workers in the United States certainly gave meaning to these words, as the rituals of dying and the politics of death powerfully shaped their lives and gave hope for better futures.

Notes

Introduction. In Search of John Henry's Body

1. Scott Reynolds Nelson, *Steel Drivin' Man*, 92.
2. Brands, *American Colossus*, 19.
3. Stiles, *First Tycoon*, 560–66.
4. Scott, "Experience."
5. Faust, *This Republic of Suffering*, xi.
6. Koslofsky, *Reformation of the Dead*, 155.
7. On the colonial and early republic periods, see Stannard, *Puritan Way of Death*; Charles O. Jackson, "Death in American Life"; and Seeman, *Death in the New World*.
8. Pleck, *Celebrating the Family*, 186.
9. On Victorians and death, see Ariès, *Western Attitudes toward Death*, 67–68; Halttunen, *Confidence Men and Painted Women*, 124–97; Pleck, *Celebrating the Family*, 184–206; and Schlereth, *Victorian America*, 287–93.
10. On Americans' attitudes toward death and their framing of the war, see Schantz, *Awaiting the Heavenly Country*.
11. Faust, *This Republic of Suffering*, 268; Laderman, *Sacred Remains*.
12. Farrell, *Inventing the American Way of Death*, 5; Laderman, *Rest in Peace*.
13. Gorer, "The Pornography of Death"; Mitford, *American Way of Death*.
14. Ariès, "Forbidden Death," 148; Mellor, "Death in High Modernity," 11; Seale, *Constructing Death*.
15. Montgomery, *Workers' Control in America*; Peiss, *Cheap Amusements*; Denning, *Cultural Front*; Enstad, *Ladies of Labor, Girls of Adventure*.
16. For examples of historians examining death and the working class in the United States, see Kleinberg, "Death and the Working Class"; Corbin, *Life, Work, and Rebellion*, 166–67; and DiGirolamo, "Newsboy Funerals." The literature on occupational disease and work accidents is far more voluminous. See, for example, Cherniak, *Hawk's Nest Incident*; Barbara Ellen Smith, *Digging Our Own Graves*; Rosner and Markowitz, *Dying for Work*; Sellers, *Hazards of the Job*; and Rogers, *Making Capitalism Safe*.

Chapter 1. The Marks of Capital

1. Haywood quoted in Lukas, *Big Trouble*, 223. He would only add more. His later affiliation with the Industrial Workers of the World and the Socialist Party left marks on his body and soul and ultimately led to self-imposed exile in the Soviet Union to avoid prison. Haywood, *Bill Haywood's Book*; Dubofsky, *"Big Bill" Haywood*.

2. "The Death Roll in Industry"; Hoffman, "Industrial Accidents" and "Industrial Accidents in the United States." See also "'Casualty List' of American Industries"; and Mark, "The Industrial Scrap Heap."

3. "Museum of Safety Devices," *Chicago Tribune*, April 5, 1908. It is unclear whether the figures include the Caribbean and Pacific theaters in the Spanish-American-Filipino War. Statistical estimates vary widely because no centralized data collection agency existed. Although Congress created the federal Bureau of Labor in 1884, it relied on voluntary accident reporting from state bureaus and individual corporations. Only three states participated in the program before World War I, a number that inched up to fourteen by 1970 and the founding of the Occupational Safety and Health Administration. Drudi, "Century-Long Quest." See also Goldberg and Moye, *First Hundred Years of the Bureau of Labor Statistics*.

4. "Risks and Diseases of Toil," 154.

5. "Safety of American Mines"; Witt, *Accidental Republic*.

6. The three constituent parts of "the body" as a category of analysis are most clearly explained in Baron and Boris, "'The Body' as a Useful Category"; and Esyllt Jones, "Politicizing the Laboring Body." For examples of other examinations of "the body" and discourses mapped to them, see, for example, Foucault, *The History of Sexuality*, vol. 1, *An Introduction*; Duden, *Woman beneath the Skin*; Canning, "Body as Method?"

7. Baron and Boris, "'The Body' as a Useful Category," 29; Bourdieu, *Distinction*.

8. Licht, *Industrializing America*, 102; Bensel, *Political Economy of American Industrialization*, 1–100; Engerman and Sokoloff, "Technology and Industrialization."

9. Burton, *The Age of Lincoln*, 329; Porter, "Industrialization and the Rise of Big Business," 5.

10. Saxton, *Rise and Fall of the White Republic*; Roediger, *Wages of Whiteness*; Eric Foner, *Free Soil, Free Labor, Free Men*; Wilentz, *Rise of American Democracy*; Dana D. Nelson, *National Manhood*; Lause, *Young America*.

11. Hicks, *Populist Revolt*, 84; McMath, *American Populism*, 46–47.

12. Burton, *The Age of Lincoln*, 329.

13. In 1914 Florence Kelley suggested that the ideal of agricultural producer still held a privileged place in the American cultural lexicon, even though she viewed it as out of date. The "morality of agricultural individualism is [still] our accepted morality. This affords no adequate guidance in the intricate relations of our rapidly changing life; and its insufficiency becomes from year to year more obvious with the evolution of industry. Between that obsolete morality which remains embodied in our laws, and our human needs in modern daily life, the contradiction has become intolerable" (*Modern Industry in Relation to the Family*, 117–18).

14. Chandler, *Visible Hand*, 249.

15. Wright quoted in Jacoby, *Employing Bureaucracy*, 11.

16. Gutman, "Labor Policies of the Large Corporation," 214–15.

17. Daniel Nelson, *Managers and Workers*, 4. For the relationship between the size of the firm and managerial style, see Licht, "Studying Work."

18. Manufacturers, Daniel Nelson observes, "gradually substituted managerial direction and controls for the informal, ad hoc methods of the past, particularly those that relied on the judgment of the supervisor and worker" (ibid., 9). See also Ramirez, *When Workers Fight*, 87–103.

19. Ozanne, *Century of Labor-Management Relations*, 20.

20. David M. Gordon, Edwards, and Reich, *Segmented Work, Divided Workers*, 101. Roethlisberger and Dickson more generally described the relationship between worker and supervisor during the period. The production worker, they wrote in the gendered language of the 1930s, occupied "the bottom level of a highly stratified organization," where "established routines of work, his cultural traditions of craftsmanship, his personal interrelations" were all "at the mercy of technical specialists" (*Management and the Worker*, 16–17).

21. Barrett, *Work and Community in the Jungle*.

22. Daniel Nelson coined the wonderfully evocative phrase "congeries of workshops" in *Managers and Workers*, 4. Montgomery, in *Workers' Control in America*, has persuasively shown how workers' knowledge provided a source both of power and of conflict during the late nineteenth century.

23. David M. Gordon, Edwards, and Reich, *Segmented Work, Divided Workers*, 135. See also Chandler, *Visible Hand*; Montgomery, "White Shirts and Superior Intelligence," in *Fall of the House of Labor*, 214–56; and Richard Edwards, *Contested Terrain*.

24. Daniel Nelson, *Managers and Workers*, 35–55.

25. Fritz quoted in Chandler, *Visible Hand*, 266; F. W. Taylor, *Principles of Scientific Management*, 43–48; Elspeth H. Brown, *Corporate Eye*.

26. David A. Wells, "Economic Disturbances since 1873," 588.

27. U.S. Senate, Committee on Education and Labor, *Relations between Labor and Capital*, 1:743.

28. Campbell, *Prisoners of Poverty*, 34.

29. Stanley, *From Bondage to Contract*; Montgomery, *Citizen Worker*, 8–9.

30. Steward quoted in McNeill, "The Hours of Labor," in *Labor Movement*, 481.

31. U.S. Senate, Committee on Education and Labor, *Relations between Labor and Capital*, 1:682.

32. Campbell, *Prisoners of Poverty*, 33. For a slightly different use of "cheaper than shingles," see Garland, *Prairie Radical*, 111.

33. Temin, "Manufacturing," 447 (emphasis in the original).

34. Zunz, *Making America Corporate*, 1.

35. Trachtenberg, *Incorporation of America*, 42.

36. Hunter, *History of Industrial Power*, 296–98.

37. W. D. Howells quoted in Dee Brown, *Year of the Century*, 130.

38. Howells, "Sennight of the Centennial."

39. Laurie, *Artisans into Workers*, 115.

40. Carroll D. Wright, "Factory System as an Element of Civilization," 117. Brooks echoes these sentiments. He points to symbols of industrialization—machines, railroads,

and streetcars—as implements that "make for better manners as well as for temperance, promptness, and accuracy" (*Social Unrest*, 173).

41. "Modern Improvements and the Workingmen."
42. "Conference of Labor and Capital." On Flint's career during the Gilded Age, see Cashman, *America in the Gilded Age*, 57.
43. "Address of Welcome to Manufacturers."
44. *Labor Problem in the United States*, 26.
45. Carnegie, "Wealth," 655; Nasaw, *Andrew Carnegie*, 345–54.
46. Sumner, *What Social Classes Owe to Each Other*; Hofstadter, *Social Darwinism in American Thought*; Bannister, *Social Darwinism*; Hawkins, *Social Darwinism in European and American Thought*; Claeys, "'Survival of the Fittest.'"
47. Quoted in Brody, *Steelworkers in America*, 27.
48. Hoganson, *Fighting for American Manhood*, 15–42.
49. Bederman, *Manliness and Civilization*, 77–120, 170–215; Deloria, *Playing Indian*, 95–127.
50. Roosevelt, "Value of an Athletic Training."
51. Roosevelt quoted in Murphy, *Political Manhood*, 1.
52. Kimmel, *Manhood in America*, 83–87; Murphy, *Political Manhood*; Bederman, *Manliness and Civilization*, 17.
53. James, "What Makes a Life Significant," 275. See also Trachtenberg, *Incorporation of America*, 140–44.
54. Early in his life, Taylor took an apprenticeship at a Philadelphia pump works. Taylor had been plagued by extreme headaches and troubling eye strain. A 1906 biographical account suggested that he took the apprenticeship to "develop his physical strength until his eyesight should become sufficiently restored to resume his studies" (Kanigel, *One Best Way*, 100–101).
55. Higbie, "Retelling Life Stories: Floating Labor and the Terrain of Progressive Era Social Investigation," in *Indispensable Outcasts*, 66–97; Pittenger, "World of Difference"; Vapnek, *Breadwinners*, 55–65.
56. This type of logic echoes, perhaps faintly, cultural associations with nation and manhood of the earlier frontier eras. See Slotkin, *Regeneration through Violence* and *Fatal Environment*.
57. Witt, *Accidental Republic*; Rogers, *Making Capitalism Safe*, 11–30; Bergstrom, *Courting Danger*, 58–68; Asher, "Failure and Fulfillment." On child labor accidents and the law, see Schmidt, *Industrial Violence*, 121–63.
58. This is not to say that ideas about negligence and liability were frozen in time. Rather, as Witt and others point out, the nineteenth century produced a spike in personal injury litigation that forced the legal system to reevaluate prevailing legal doctrines. Individual states began modifying assumption of risk statutes as early 1856. By 1911 the federal government had passed the Federal Employer's Liability Act, and twenty-five states had "enacted legislation variously abolishing the fellow servant rule, modifying the contributory negligence doctrine, and limiting the assumption of risk rule" (Witt, *Accidental Republic*, 67). See also Welke, *Recasting American Liberty*; and Karsten, *Heart versus Head*.
59. Hard, "Law of the Killed and Wounded," 363.

60. Alger, *Moral Overstrain*, 163, 166.

61. McNeill criticizes this prevailing assumption in "The Hours of Labor," in *Labor Movement*, 479.

62. Taillon, "'What We Want Is Good, Sober Men,'" 325. See also Kaster, "Labour's True Man."

63. Sellers, *Hazards of the Job*, 22.

64. Woods, "Accidents in Factories and Elsewhere," 312.

65. Peck, "Manly Gambles"; Glickman, *Living Wage*, 43; Rotundo, *American Manhood*, 176.

66. The cultural symbolism attached to victims of accidents and their disabled bodies reinforced the cult of physicality around work, but meanings associated with missing limbs and broken bodies changed toward the end of the nineteenth century. See Williams-Searle, "Courting Risk" and "Cold Charity," 165, 171; and Sarah F. Rose, "'Crippled' Hands."

67. O'Donnell, "Women as Bread Winners," 187.

68. Kessler-Harris, *In Pursuit of Equity*, 19–63.

69. Flanagan, *America Reformed*, 63; Stromquist, *Reinventing "the People,"* 121–23.

70. Smith quoted in Stromquist, *Reinventing "the People,"* 123.

71. See, for example, Eastman, *Work-Accidents and the Law*, 13.

72. Benjamin Franklin, *Observations Concerning the Natural Increase of Mankind* (1751), quoted in Schama, *American History*, 240–41.

73. Knobel, *Paddy and the Republic*. On Samuel Morse, see Kenneth C. Davis, *Nation Rising*, 203–5.

74. Daniels, *Coming to America*, 136–37; Roediger, *Wages of Whiteness*, 133–63.

75. Almaguer, *Racial Fault Lines*, 162–64.

76. Spickard, *Almost All Aliens*, 163.

77. Takaki, *Different Mirror*, 188; Almaguer, *Racial Fault Lines*, 157.

78. Lee, *At America's Gates*, 27; *Report of the Joint Special Committee to Investigate Chinese Immigration*, 34, vi.

79. Takaki, *Different Mirror*, 189.

80. Stuart Creighton Miller, *Unwelcome Immigrant*; Jacobson, *Barbarian Virtues*, 78–80.

81. Lee, *At America's Gates*, 20–22 (quote on 22).

82. Lodge, "The Restriction of Immigration," 32–33.

83. Roediger, *How Race Survived History*, 136–37.

84. Francis A. Walker, "Immigration and Degradation."

85. Francis A. Walker, "Restriction of Immigration," 828. On Roosevelt and race suicide, see Dyer, *Roosevelt and the Idea of Race*, 14–15, 123–67; Bederman, *Manliness and Civilization*, 200–206; and Roediger, *How Race Survived History*, 136–37.

86. Lodge, "The Restriction of Immigration," 35; *Extracts from the Report of the Commissioner-General of Immigration, for the Year Ending June 30, 1903*, in "An American Time Capsule: Three Centuries of Broadsides and Other Printed Ephemera," Library of Congress, http://hdl.loc.gov/loc.rbc/rbpe.07902100 (accessed June 3, 2010). See also Zeidel, *Immigrants, Progressives, and Exclusion Politics*.

87. Jacobson, *Whiteness of a Different Color*, 80, 84; Ngai, *Impossible Subjects*, 22–24.

88. Schrag, *Not Fit for Our Society*, 108–25; Zolberg, *Nation by Design*, 258–62; Ngai, *Impossible Subjects*, 21–55.

89. Richard White, *Railroaded*, 29–30.
90. Saxton, *Indispensable Enemy*, 62.
91. Takaki, *Different Mirror*, 181.
92. Saxton, *Indispensable Enemy*, 63; Esch and Roediger, "One Symptom of Originality," 16.
93. Saxton, *Indispensable Enemy*, 65.
94. Schmidt, *Industrial Violence*, 14–15.
95. Blackmon, *Slavery by Another Name*; Shapiro, *New South Rebellion*.
96. Esch and Roediger, "One Symptom of Originality," 35.
97. Roediger, *How Race Survived History*, 148, 153.
98. Ross, *Old World in the New*, 291. For a chart titled "Racial Adaptability to Various Types of Plant Work" from Pittsburgh's Central Tube Company, see Bodnar, Simon, and Weber, *Lives of Their Own*, 240.
99. Graebner, *Coal-Mining Safety*, 117. To economist Frank Julian Warne, the least-valuable members were clearly the "Slavs" ("Effect of Unionism," 34). See also Warne, *Slav Invasion*.
100. Fitch, *The Steel Workers*, 12.
101. Attaway, *Blood on the Forge*, 44.
102. See, for example, Coroner's Case Files, Allegheny County, File Number 190506-493, Box 118; 190506-495, Box 118; and 190701-192, Box 139.
103. Roediger, *Working toward Whiteness*, 43–44.
104. Feldman, *Racial Factors in American Industry*, 148, quoted in ibid., 44.
105. Ross, *Old World in the New*; Frank Julian Warne, *The Immigrant Invasion*; Grant, *Passing of the Great Race*.
106. Jacobson, *Barbarian Virtues*, 96.
107. Strong, "Our Industrial Juggernaut," 1032 (emphasis in the original); "The Death Roll in Industry."
108. Asher, "Failure and Fulfillment"; Witt, *Accidental Republic*, 146–47; Bellamy, *History of Workmen's Compensation*.
109. Mink, *Old Labor and New Immigrants*, 185–97, 248–57; Philip Foner, *History of the Labor Movement*, 3:75; Greene, *Pure and Simple Politics*.
110. Aldrich, *Safety First*, 91–92; Rogers, *Making Capitalism Safe*, 52–53; Wiebe, *Businessmen and Reform*, 166–67, 197–98.
111. Filene, "Obituary for 'the Progressive Movement'"; Rodgers, "In Search of Progressivism"; Gilmore, *Who Were the Progressives?*
112. Mary Rankin Cranston, "What Is the American Institute of Social Service," *New York Times*, May 20, 1906; Cranston, "A Social Clearing-House."
113. "Safety and Security"; "Hold Life Too Cheap," *Washington Post*, January 29, 1907; "'Casualty List' of American Industries"; "A Safety Devices Exhibition"; "Worker's Life Held Cheap; Safety Devices on Exposition," *Chicago Daily Tribune*, February 24, 1907.
114. The transatlantic exchange of ideas and rivalry was as important to the issue of workplace safety as to other issues of the Progressive Era. Rodgers, *Atlantic Crossings*, 209–66.
115. "Exposition of Safety Devices and Industrial Hygiene."
116. Slavishak, *Bodies of Work*; Rabinbach, *Human Motor*. The late-nineteenth- and early-twentieth-century literature on fatigue is voluminous. See, for example, Goldmark, *Fatigue and Efficiency*.

117. Quoted in Storrs, *Civilizing Capitalism*, 13. On Kelley's early career, see Sklar, *Florence Kelley*.

118. Flanagan, *America Reformed*, 60; Nancy Woloch, "Muller v. Oregon," 9; Storrs, *Civilizing Capitalism*, 41–46.

119. Quoted in Woloch, "Muller v. Oregon," 10, 9.

120. Sklar, "Two Political Cultures," 51.

121. Kessler-Harris, *In Pursuit of Equity*, 29.

122. People v. Williams 189 N.Y. 131 (1907); Kessler-Harris, *In Pursuit of Equity*, 29–30.

123. Goldmark quoted in Woloch, "Muller v. Oregon," 13.

124. For interpretations of *Lochner v. New York*, see, for example, Kens, "*Lochner v. New York*"; and Gillman, *Constitution Besieged*.

125. Brandeis, *Women in Industry*, 30, 47.

126. Muller v. Oregon, 208 U.S. 412 (1908).

127. Rodgers, *Atlantic Crossings*, 238; Storrs, *Civilizing Capitalism*, 45. On the broader impact of *Muller v. Oregon* on women's rights, see Kessler-Harris, *In Pursuit of Equity*, 31.

128. Eastman, *Work-Accidents and the Law*, 13, 5, 165.

129. Ibid., 166, 207–20.

130. Ibid., 13, 136.

131. See especially the photos *An Arm Gone at Twenty*, *The Wounds of Work*, and *One Arm and Four Children* (ibid., 144, 153).

132. Stromquist, *Reinventing "the People*," 165–90; "They Don't Suit the 'Intellectuals,'" 132.

133. Brooks, *Social Unrest*, 171.

134. "Declaration of Independence, July 4, 1886, by an American Socialist," in *Labor Movement in America*, by Richard T. Ely, 372.

135. "Manifesto of the International Working People's Association," in ibid., 360.

136. Montgomery, *Workers' Control in America*; English, "'I Have . . . a Lot of Work to Do.'"

137. Quoted in Montgomery, *Fall of the House of Labor*, 90.

138. U.S. Senate, Committee on Education and Labor, *Relations between Labor and Capital*, 745–46.

139. Rosenzweig, *Eight Hours for What We Will*, 35–64; Barrett, *Work and Community in the Jungle*, 81–85; Taillon, "'What We Want Is Good, Sober Men.'"

140. Roediger and Foner, *Our Own Time*, 101–208.

141. On the Knights of Labor, see Ware, *Labor Movement in the United States*; Fink, *Workingmen's Democracy*; and Weir, *Beyond Labor's Veil*.

142. McNeill, "The Problem of To-Day," in *Labor Movement*, 466.

Chapter 2. The Power of the Dead's Place

1. Spinney, *City of Big Shoulders*; Donald L. Miller, *City of the Century*. Chicago also earned less glamorous reputations during the period that stemmed from moral crusaders like William T. Stead and muckraking journalists such as Lincoln Steffens and Upton Sinclair. Stead, *If Christ Came to Chicago!*; Steffens, "Chicago"; Sinclair, *The Jungle*. See also Adler, *First in Violence, Deepest in Dirt*.

2. Hard, "Making Steel and Killing Men," 590–91. See also "Injured Gaze on Coffins," *Chicago Tribune*, June 20, 1907.

3. Sandburg, *Chicago Race Riots*, 4.

4. Harvey, *Condition of Postmodernity*, 233; Hayden, *Power of Place*, 9, 11. See also Ryan, *Civic Wars*.

5. Schlereth, *Victorian America*, 290–91; Stannard, *Puritan Way of Death*; Isenberg and Burstein, *Mortal Remains*.

6. Blaney, "The Modern Park Cemetery," 219.

7. Harris, "The Cemetery Beautiful," 103; "City Built on Graves," *Chicago Tribune*, August 8, 1897.

8. French, "Cemetery as Cultural Institution," 74.

9. Sclair, "Ethnic Cemeteries: Underground Rites," 620–21.

10. Pattison, "Land for the Dead of Chicago," 40. Concerns about the proximity of the dead to the living persisted throughout the nineteenth century. See Windmuller, "Graveyards as a Menace"; and "Writes of Burial: Louis Windmuller Discusses Graveyards and Health," *Chicago Tribune*, July 31, 1898.

11. French, "Cemetery as Cultural Institution," 73.

12. Harris, "The Cemetery Beautiful," 104.

13. French, "Cemetery as Cultural Institution," 78.

14. Bender, "'Rural' Cemetery Movement"; Connors, "Romantic Landscape." Cemeteries established after Mount Auburn that reflected principles associated with the rural cemetery movement include Laurel Hill Cemetery (1836) in Philadelphia, Pennsylvania; Mount Hope at Rochester, New York; Greenmount at Baltimore, Maryland; and Worcester Rural Cemetery at Worcester, Massachusetts, all opened in 1838; Allegheny Cemetery (1844) at Pittsburgh, Pennsylvania; Spring Grove (1845) at Cincinnati, Ohio; Cave Hill (1848) at Louisville, Kentucky; Hollywood (1849) at Richmond, Virginia; and Magnolia (1850) at Charleston, South Carolina. See French, "Cemetery as Cultural Institution," 85.

15. Kenneth T. Jackson and Vergara, *Silent Cities*, 5.

16. Sloane, *Last Great Necessity*, 56.

17. Although the number of cemeteries outside city limits has changed with each territorial annexation, William Pattison estimated that three-fourths of the cemeteries that served Chicago lay outside of the city in 1952. Nevertheless, these were "Chicago institutions" and an extension of urban land use, politics, and social dynamics. Pattison, "Land for the Dead in Chicago," 2.

18. Bourke, *Fear: A Cultural History*, 28.

19. Sandburg, "The Right to Grief," in *Chicago Poems*, 25.

20. Addams, "Why the Ward Boss Rules."

21. Kephart, "Status after Death," 643. See also Kenneth T. Jackson and Vergara, "Potter's Fields," in *Silent Cities*, 36–37.

22. Bourke, *Fear: A Cultural History*, 28.

23. Statistics on pauper burials in Chicago are hard to determine. "For the city of Chicago the pauper burial returns are of doubtful value, since there is apparently a lack of uniformity in the statistical practice and some confusion in the official statements," statistician Frederick Hoffman commented in 1919. He estimated that the city buried 711 people in 1918, or 27.4 pauper burials per 100,000 of population. Hoffman, "Pauper Burials," 16.

24. Donald L. Miller, *City of the Century*, 50.

25. Simon, *Chicago: The Garden City*, 119. Simon reports that land prices in Chicago's cemeteries were on par with those of the East. Prices in leading cemeteries of New York, Philadelphia, and Boston ranged from $1.50 to $5 per square foot.

26. Yalom, *American Resting Place*, 178–79; Hucke and Bielski, *Graveyards of Chicago*, 25–27.

27. "Beautiful Cemeteries," *Chicago Tribune*, February 7, 1909.

28. Sandburg, "Graceland," in *Chicago Poems*, 23.

29. Gilbert, *Perfect Cities*, 144–45.

30. Salvatore, *Eugene V. Debs*, 126–38.

31. James Green, *Death in the Haymarket*, 296.

32. Donald L. Miller, *City of the Century*, 546; Gilbert, *Perfect Cities*, 165; Yalom, *American Resting Place*, 179.

33. George Schilling, "The Lessons of the Homestead Troubles," in *The Sunset Club Yearbook, 1892–1893*, 15, quoted in Donald L. Miller, *City of the Century*, 482.

34. Simon, *Chicago: The Garden City*, 119.

35. "Mr. Wentworth Is Dead," *Chicago Tribune*, October 17, 1888; "The Great Wentworth Monolith," *Chicago Tribune*, December 20, 1888; Simon, *Chicago: The Garden City*, 128; Donald L. Miller, *City of the Century*, 78; Windel, "John Wentworth."

36. Simon, *Chicago: The Garden City*, 144, 119. Simon ultimately did not mind this state of affairs. He argued that the well-appointed lots added value to the smaller lots.

37. Kenneth T. Jackson and Vergara, *Silent Cities*, 5.

38. Pattison, "Cemeteries of Chicago," 250.

39. Yalom, *American Resting Place*, 170.

40. See Pattison, "Cemeteries of Chicago," 252; and Yalom, *American Resting Place*, 170.

41. Funchion, "Irish Chicago," 61–62; Barrett and Roediger, "Irish and the 'Americanization' of the 'New Immigrants,'" 17–25. For a broader view of Irish influence in the Catholic Church, see Barrett, *Irish Way*, 62–66.

42. Sclair, "Ethnic Cemeteries: Underground Rites," 622; Hucke and Bielski, *Graveyards of Chicago*, 34; Simon, *Chicago: The Garden City*, 140.

43. Vojan, *Semi-centennial Jubilee*, 7–8.

44. Bruce C. Nelson, "Revival and Upheaval," 239–40; Simon, *Chicago: The Garden City*, 175; Vojan, *Semi-centennial Jubilee*, 4. See also "The Old Catholic Religion among Bohemians," *Svornost*, September 14, 1898, Reel 1, Chicago Foreign Language Press Survey, hereafter cited as CFLPS; and "Churches on Decline," *Svornost*, March 29, 1899, Reel 1, CFLPS.

45. Simon, *Chicago: The Garden City*, 179.

46. Vojan, *Semi-centennial Jubilee*, 32, 60, 68.

47. *Chicago Tribune*, June 25, 1879, Reel 1, CFLPS. See also "How the Americans Care for Chicago's Bohemians: We Are Infamous Heathens According to an American Missionary Society," *Svornost*, September 16, 1884, Reel 1, CFLPS; "Insulting the Bohemians," *Svornost*, January 29, 1885, Reel 1, CFLPS.

48. "Manners and Customs of the Bohemian Portion of the City's Population," *Chicago Tribune*, March 7, 1886, Reel 1, CFLPS.

49. "Laborer Question: Bohemian Workers and the Foreign Press," *Svornost*, March 19, 1896, Reel 1, CFLPS. See also "Attitude of Germans toward Bohemians," *Denni Hlasatel*, January 7, 1909, Reel 1, CFLPS.

50. "Yesterday's Proletarian Riot," *Chicago Tribune*, May 9, 1876, Reel 1, CFLPS; "Laborer Question: Bohemian Workers and the Foreign Press," *Svornost*, March 19, 1896, Reel 1, CFLPS.

51. "Decoration Day," *Denni Hlasatel*, May 31, 1906, Reel 7, CFLPS.

52. "Bohemian National Undertakings of Chicago," *Denni Hlasatel*, June 15, 1911, Reel 5, CFLPS; Vojan, *Semi-centennial Jubilee*, 5–6.

53. Ibid., 35–36. On annual celebrations, see 24, 30, 52.

54. Blight, *Race and Reunion*; Blair, *Cities of the Dead*.

55. "To Honor Loyalty," *Chicago Tribune*, May 30, 1890.

56. "Unveiling Ceremonies at the Bohemian National Cemetery: Grand Bohemian-American Manifestation," *Svornost*, May 30, 1892, Reel 7, CFLPS. See also "Inauguration of the First Bohemian Soldier Monument," *Illinois Staats-Zeitung*, May 30, 1892, Reel 7, CFLPS.

57. "To the Memory of the Dead: Celebration at the Cesky Narodni Hrbitov," *Denni Hlasatel*, May 31, 1914, Reel 7, CFLPS.

58. Vojan, *Semi-centennial Jubilee*, 67.

59. "Decoration of Graves: Impressive Speech of Leo Palda at the Bohemian National Cemetery," *Denni Hlasatel*, May 31, 1902, Reel 7, CFLPS; "Decoration Day," *Denni Hlasatel*, May 31, 1906, Reel 7, CFLPS; "Decoration Day: Dignified Ceremonies Held on All Chicago Cemeteries: Those Held on the Bohemian Cemeteries Were Most Beautiful," *Denni Hlasatel*, May 31, 1911, Reel 7, CFLPS; "Decoration Day Ceremonies at the Bohemian National Cemetery," *Denni Hlasatel*, May 31, 1912, Reel 7, CFLPS; "Decoration Day Celebrations: Cesky Narodni Hrbitov," *Denni Hlasatel*, May 31, 1913, Reel 7, CFLPS.

60. "Decoration Day: Dignified Ceremonies."

61. Reed, *Black Chicago's First Century*; Grossman, *Land of Hope*.

62. Grossman, "African-American Migration to Chicago," 319.

63. Chicago Commission on Race Relations, *Negro in Chicago*, 107–8.

64. Reed, *Black Chicago's First Century*, 241–56, 391–95; Spear, *Black Chicago*, 29–49; Elizabeth Dale, "'Social Equality Does Not Exist.'"

65. Sclair, "Ethnic Cemeteries: Underground Rites," 630.

66. "No Civil Rights at the Grave," *Chicago Tribune*, January 14, 1890.

67. "Rambling about Chicago," *Chicago Defender*, March 4, 1910.

68. Reed, *Black Chicago's First Century*, 436.

69. Sclair, "Ethnic Cemeteries: Underground Rites," 627; Hucke and Bielski, *Graveyards of Chicago*, 169, 188.

70. Spear, *Black Chicago*, 42–43.

71. Ida B. Wells, *Crusade for Justice*, 309.

72. "Representative Greene's [sic] Amendment Passes First Reading of House," *Chicago Defender*, March 18, 1911; "Representative Ed Green Passes Cemetery Bill," *Chicago Defender*, April 15, 1911; "Hon. Ed D. Green Fights for His City," *Chicago Defender*, April 22, 1911; "Batch of Bills Passed," *Chicago Tribune*, May 5, 1911.

73. *People v. The Forest Home Cemetery* 258 Ill. 36 (1913).

74. Tuttle, *Race Riot*, 161 (quote), 108–22; Barrett, *Work and Community in the Jungle*, 172–74; Ida B. Wells, *Crusade for Justice*, 309–20; Spear, *Black Chicago*, 47–48.

75. *People v. The Forest Home Cemetery*.

Notes to Chapter 2

76. "Cemetery Rights," *Chicago Defender*, May 17, 1913.
77. Pattison, "Cemeteries of Chicago," 246; Hirsch, *Making the Second Ghetto*.
78. For an excellent account of the bombing, trial, and execution, see James Green, *Death in the Haymarket*, 175–273. For a detailed account of the state's case, see Messer-Kruse, *Trial of the Haymarket Anarchists*.
79. "Waldheim," *Chicago Tribune*, August 18, 1873.
80. David, *History of the Haymarket Affair*, 464–65; Ashbaugh, *Lucy Parsons: American Revolutionary*, 139–40; Avrich, *The Haymarket Tragedy*, 395–96.
81. "Police Restrictions," *Chicago Tribune*, November 13, 1887.
82. Buchanan, *Story of a Labor Agitator*, 422–23; Mary Harris Jones, *Autobiography of Mother Jones*, 22.
83. Rebecca Nell Hill, "Men, Mobs, and Law," 151.
84. "Speeches at the Grave," *Chicago Tribune*, November 14, 1887; James Green, *Death in the Haymarket*, 276; David, *History of the Haymarket Affair*, 465.
85. Simon, *Chicago: The Garden City*, 167.
86. "Will Not Permit a Demonstration," *Chicago Tribune*, November 13, 1887. After the eventual burial of Spies, Parsons, Engel, Lingg, and Fischer, the cemetery association voted to prohibit the burial of executed men and women unless they had purchased a lot prior to conviction. See "Lingg's Weak Excuse for His Crimes," *Chicago Tribune*, November 18, 1887.
87. "An Anarchist Burying-Ground," *Chicago Tribune*, November 23, 1887.
88. "Beer or No Beer, Which?," *Chicago Tribune*, December 6, 1887.
89. "They Bury Their Dead," *Chicago Tribune*, December 19, 1887. On religious analogies in anarchist rhetoric and memorial speeches, see McKinley, "'Religion of the New Time.'"
90. *Alarm*, November 17, 1888, quoted in Dabakis, *Visualizing Labor in American Sculpture*, 60.
91. "Exercises at Waldheim," *Chicago Tribune*, November 12, 1888; "They Will Celebrate," *Chicago Tribune*, October 24, 1888; "Reds at Waldheim," *Chicago Tribune*, November 11, 1889; "Go on with the Fight," *Chicago Tribune*, November 10, 1890; de Cleyre, *First May Day*.
92. See "At the Grave in Waldheim" and "Light upon Waldheim," in *Selected Works of Voltairine de Cleyre*, 33–34, 66.
93. McKinley, "'Religion of the New Time,'" 392.
94. Avrich, *The Haymarket Tragedy*, 412.
95. Ibid.
96. "Reds at Waldheim," *Chicago Tribune*, November 11, 1889; "Go on with the Fight," *Chicago Tribune*, November 10, 1890.
97. Graham Taylor, *Pioneering on Social Fronts*, 132. Taylor further recalled that Lucy Parsons provoked such treatment "whenever and wherever she had attempted to speak since the riot." Parsons's biographer Carolyn Ashbaugh concluded that the Chicago police feared Parsons more than male anarchists such as Johann Most, whom they allowed to speak in 1896 after leading Lucy to the police station (*Lucy Parsons: American Revolutionary*, 197–98).
98. "Our Chicago Letter," *Alarm*, November 24, 1888, quoted in Dabakis, *Visualizing Labor in American Sculpture*, 50. Using a cemetery as a meeting place would not have

been extraordinary in the late nineteenth century. Resembling parks, landscape-lawn cemeteries were inviting spaces that people often made their end destination during leisure-time excursions. Anarchists may have also hoped that the hallowed ground of a cemetery might provide a protected space in which to meet free from police surveillance.

99. McLean, *Rise and Fall of Anarchy in America*, 264–65.

100. See Dabakis, *Visualizing Labor in American Sculpture*, 49; and William J. Adelman, "The True Story behind the Haymarket Police Statue," in *Haymarket Scrapbook*, edited by Roediger and Rosemont, 167–68.

101. "Unveil the Statue," *Chicago Tribune*, June 26, 1893; James Green, *Death in the Haymarket*, 290–91; Dabakis, *Visualizing Labor in American Sculpture*, 35–37, 52–53; Avrich, *The Haymarket Tragedy*, 413; Ashbaugh, *Lucy Parsons: American Revolutionary*, 188; David, *History of the Haymarket Affair*, 491.

102. Lloyd Lewis and Smith, *Chicago*, 166, quoted in Avrich, *The Haymarket Tragedy*, 414.

103. Lang, *Tomorrow Is Beautiful*, 27; Dabakis, *Visualizing Labor in American Sculpture*, 61; Avrich, *The Haymarket Tragedy*, 414.

104. James Green, *Death in the Haymarket*, 291; Dabakis, *Visualizing Labor in American Sculpture*, 4–5; David, *History of the Haymarket Affair*, 467.

105. Schilling quoted in Ashbaugh, *Lucy Parsons: American Revolutionary*, 191.

106. Mary Harris Jones, *Autobiography of Mother Jones*, 22–23.

107. Avrich, *American Anarchist*, 49.

108. "An Anarchist Buried at Waldheim," *Chicago Tribune*, November 25, 1888; James R. Barrett, introduction to *The Spirit of Labor*, by Hutchins Hapgood, xl; Barrett, *William Z. Foster*, 272.

109. James Green, *Death in the Haymarket*, 299.

110. Bachin, *Building the South Side*, 6.

111. See, for example, McGerr, *Fierce Discontent*; and Stromquist, *Reinventing "the People."*

112. Kenneth T. Jackson and Vergara, *Silent Cities*, 6.

Chapter 3. Every New Grave Brought a Thousand Members

1. Crawford, *Poet Scout*, 63–64. See also Archie Green, *Only a Miner*.

2. "Taking Out the Dead," *St. Louis Globe-Democrat*, January 10, 1883; "The Coulterville Mine Explosion, Whereby Ten Persons Were Killed," *Chicago Tribune*, January 10, 1883; "A Holocaust," *St. Louis Post-Dispatch*, January 9, 1883.

3. "Horror's Climax," *Wilmington (IL) Advocate*, February [no date on microfilm], 1883.

4. "About Our Neighbors," *Wilmington (IL) Herald*, February 23, 1883.

5. "The Black Year," *Chicago Tribune*, February 17, 1883.

6. Ibid.; "The Braidwood Tragedy," *New York Times*, February 18, 1883.

7. Illinois Bureau of Labor Statistics, *Statistics of Coal Production in Illinois, 1883*, 99.

8. "The Braidwood Tragedy."

9. "Braidwood," *Chicago Tribune*, February 19, 1883.

10. Faust, *This Republic of Suffering*, 6–17; Kellehear, *Social History of Dying*, 86, 92; Ariès, *Western Attitudes toward Death*, 33–39.

11. Neuberger, *Dying Well*, 63.
12. Kellehear, *Social History of Dying*, 94.
13. Faust, *This Republic of Suffering*.
14. On death rituals during the nineteenth century, see Halttunen, "Mourning the Dead: A Study in Sentimental Ritual," in *Confidence Men and Painted Women*, 124–52; Charles O. Jackson, "Death in American Life"; Robert W. Habenstein and William H. Lamers, "The Pattern of Late Nineteenth-Century Funerals," in ibid., 91–102; and Schlereth, *Victorian America*, 287–93.
15. Scholars have written extensively about the role of fear and guilt in death rituals. For an excellent overview, see Kellehear, *Social History of Dying*, 106–9.
16. *Journal of the House of Representatives of the Thirty-Third General Assembly*, 249.
17. "The Braidwood Calamity," *Chicago Tribune*, February 26, 1883; "The Flooded Mine," *Chicago Tribune*, February 25, 1883.
18. "The Braidwood Calamity."
19. Faust, *This Republic of Suffering*, 92–94.
20. "The Braidwood Mine," *Chicago Tribune*, March 11, 1883; "Illinois: The Braidwood Mine," *Chicago Tribune*, March 21, 1883. Quote from "A Sad Search," *Chicago Tribune*, March 23, 1883.
21. "Mournful Miners," *Chicago Tribune*, March 13, 1883; "Illinois: The Braidwood Mine."
22. "A Sad Search"; "Corridors of Death," *Chicago Tribune*, March 24, 1883; "The Flooded Mine."
23. "Disgraceful Quarrel," *Chicago Tribune*, March 20, 1883.
24. "Two of the Dead," *Chicago Tribune*, March 25, 1883.
25. "An Awful Search," *Chicago Tribune*, March 26, 1883. The crowd estimate of four thousand appeared in "Two of the Dead." "An Awful Search" estimated fifteen hundred people surrounded the mine, waiting for the first bodies to appear.
26. "An Awful Search"; "Claiming the Dead," *Chicago Tribune*, March 27, 1883.
27. "Claiming the Dead."
28. Ibid.
29. "The Diamond Mine Disaster," *Wilmington (IL) Advocate*, March 30, 1883; "Claiming the Dead."
30. "The Diamond Mine Disaster."
31. "Claiming the Dead"; "The Diamond Mine Horror," *Los Angeles Times*, March 27, 1883.
32. "More Bodies," *Chicago Tribune*, March 31, 1883; "A Dangerous Task," *Chicago Tribune*, March 30, 1883; Dan, "From Braidwood," *National Labor Tribune*, April 14, 1883.
33. Illinois Bureau of Labor Statistics, *Statistics of Coal Production in Illinois, 1883*, 105.
34. Hockey, "Changing Death Rituals," 187; Pleck, *Celebrating the Family*, 188–89.
35. Evidence from women's everyday lives in coal communities suggests, however, that they rarely behaved in a manner that warranted patronizing labels of weakness. See Long, *Where the Sun Never Shines*, 42–43, 87; Corbin, *Life, Work, and Rebellion*, 92–93; Gorn, *Mother Jones*, 71; and Merithew, "'We Were Not Ladies.'"
36. *Frank Leslie's Illustrated Newspaper*, April 7, 1883, 109. For earlier examples of Leslie's pictorial portrayals of workers, see Joshua Brown, "Great Uprising and Pictorial Order."
37. *National Labor Tribune*, February 24, 1883.

38. Amy Zahl Gottlieb, "Influence of British Trade Unionists."

39. "About Our Neighbors"; John McLaughlan, "From Illinois," *National Labor Tribune*, March 3, 1883.

40. McLaughlan, "From Illinois."

41. R. McKinnon, "Moving in the Right Direction," *National Labor Tribune*, March 10, 1883.

42. Illinois Bureau of Labor Statistics, *Third Biennial Report*, 417–19, quote on 417; Roy, *History of the Coal Miners*, 142–43; Beckner, *History of Labor Legislation in Illinois*, 315.

43. Government reports defined disasters and "exceptional accidents" as those that resulted in the death of five or more workers. See Fay, *Coal Mine Fatalities in the United States*, 65–73.

44. Illinois Bureau of Labor Statistics, *Eighteenth Annual Coal Report, 1899*, ix.

45. Frederick W. Horton, *Coal-Mine Accidents in the United States and Foreign Countries*, 87. See also Frederick L. Hoffman, "Fatal Accidents in Coal Mining"; and Frederick W. Horton, *Coal-Mine Accidents in the United States, 1896–1912, with Monthly Statistics for 1912*. Historian Alan Derickson suggests that metal and coal mining were the most hazardous occupations in the United States. "A hardrock worker was," he notes, "more than ten times more likely to be killed by an accident on the job in 1910 than a worker in manufacturing" (*Workers' Health, Workers' Democracy*, 37).

46. Illinois Bureau of Labor Statistics, *Coal in Illinois, 1894*, xvii; Department of Mines and Minerals, *Thirty-Sixth Annual Coal Report of Illinois*, 4, 99–100; Fay, *Coal Mine Fatalities in the United States*, 69–73.

47. Illinois Bureau of Labor Statistics, *Coal in Illinois, 1898*, 157, 158.

48. Illinois Bureau of Labor Statistics, *Statistics of Coal in Illinois, 1891*, 165.

49. For more on dead work, see Long, *Where the Sun Never Shines*, 38, 269; Aldrich, *Safety First*, 43–45; Goodrich, *Miner's Freedom*, 32, 37–39, 91; and Wallace, *St. Clair*, 187.

50. Illinois Bureau of Labor Statistics, *Coal in Illinois, 1898*, 223.

51. Illinois Bureau of Labor Statistics, *Coal in Illinois, 1894*, 7.

52. Receiving payment for dead work became a key union demand at the turn of the century. For a case where the employer failed to provide ample timber so a miner could properly brace the roof, see The Kellyville Coal Company v. Desire Strine 217 Ill. 516; 75 N.E. 375 (1905). The court awarded the miner two thousand dollars; the employer appealed the decision to the Illinois Supreme Court.

53. State Mining Board, *Thirteenth Annual Coal Report of Illinois*, 167.

54. *Statistics of Coal in Illinois, 1891*, 106.

55. Illinois Bureau of Labor Statistics, *Coal in Illinois, 1894*, 58.

56. Illinois Bureau of Labor Statistics, *Coal in Illinois, 1893*, 86.

57. State Mining Board, *Coal in Illinois, 1911*, 167.

58. These attitudes were present in Great Britain and the United States. See Laslett, *Colliers across the Sea*, 52.

59. Illinois Bureau of Labor Statistics, *Fourth Biennial Report*, 543–44.

60. Beckner, *History of Labor Legislation in Illinois*, 289.

61. On hiring inexperienced workers in the mining industry, see Illinois Bureau of Labor Statistics, *Coal in Illinois, 1894*, xlvii; *Minutes of the Sixteenth Annual Convention*, 29; and Mitchell, "Report of President Mitchell to the Sixteenth Annual Convention of the United Mine Workers of America," *United Mine Workers Journal*, January 19, 1905.

62. Illinois Bureau of Labor Statistics, *Coal in Illinois, 1894*, xlvii.

63. Goodrich, *Miner's Freedom*; Haring, "Three Classes of Labor to Avoid." On miners' attitudes toward risk, see Lantz, *People of Coal Town*, 49, 130; Wallace, *St. Clair*, 253, 258–26; Peck, "Manly Gambles"; and Aldrich, *Safety First*, 50–52.

64. "Mine Accidents," *National Labor Tribune*, February 24, 1883; *Report of the Industrial Commission on the Relations and Conditions of Capital and Labor*, 56; Watchorn, "Cost of Coal in Human Life," 171.

65. Jack Battuello memoir (1974), Coal Mining and Union Activities, 12–13. Likewise, one Pennsylvania miner went so far as to suggest that the mules he worked with had it better than the miners. Mules were guaranteed food and shelter, he said, while miners had no such security. "A Miner's Story," *Independent* 54 (June 12, 1902): 1407–10, reprinted in *Plain Folk*, edited by Katzman and Tuttle, 141–47.

66. U.S. Immigration Commission, *Immigrants in Industries*, 581–91; Graebner, *Coal-Mining Safety*, 117; Warne, "Effect of Unionism," 34.

67. Graebner, *Coal-Mining Safety*, 117.

68. Merithew and Barrett, "'We Are Brothers in the Face of Starvation,'" 128–29; Jensen, *Winning of the Midwest*, 252–53.

69. See, for example, Zelizer, "Human Values and the Market"; Jason Kaufman, *For the Common Good?*; and Webb and Webb, *Industrial Democracy*, 152–54. See also Hayhurst, "Health of Illinois Coal Miners"; Sartorius von Waltershausen, *Workers' Movement in the United States*; Lankton, *Cradle to Grave*, 188; Derickson, *Workers' Health, Workers' Democracy*, 57–85; and Beatrix Hoffman, *Wages of Sickness*.

70. United Mine Workers of America, *Minutes of the Twelfth Annual Convention*, 87. In an oral interview recounting his experiences during the late 1930s in Illinois, miner Duke Allison explained that as soon as he identified himself as a miner, insurance companies would say, "Oh, boy, let's back up here. It's going to cost you a little more." Duke Allison memoir (1986), Coal Mining and Union Activities, 13–14.

71. Beito, *From Mutual Aid to Welfare State*, 44, 45.

72. Miners creatively filled the void for death benefits by enrolling in various institutions that offered funeral benefits. Upon coal miner Ben Rieken's death, his family collected two thousand dollars from the Knights of Ladies of Honor and funds from the German sick society, the local fire department, and Local Union No. 728 of the United Mine Workers of America. "Ben Rieken's Sudden Death," *Mount Olive (IL) Herald*, July 15, 1899. Likewise, UMWA treasurer Duncan McDonald belonged to at least three fraternal organizations: Odd Fellows, Masons, and Shriners (McDonald Papers, Box 1, Folder 2).

73. Quoted in McNeill, "Coal Miners," 244–45. Weaver represented a broader influence of Scottish and Welsh miners in Illinois who had a history of advocating social and labor reform. See Amy Zahl Gottlieb, "British Coal Miners."

74. Wieck, *American Miners' Association*, 93. The AMA did not discriminate based on nationality and sought to organize all workers in the mine, two positions that resembled later industrial unions.

75. Quoted in McNeill, "Coal Miners," 246. On the spirit of mutuality in northern Illinois coalfields in the late 1860s, see Gutman, "Labor in the Land of Lincoln," 130–31.

76. Wieck, *American Miners' Association*, 75.

77. Roy, *History of the Coal Miners*, 71–72, 142–44.

78. Corn, "Protective Legislation for Coal Miners," 77.

79. Quoted in Roy, *History of the Coal Miners*, 254.

80. *Constitution and Laws of the United Mine Workers of America*, 2.

81. Warne, *Coal-Mine Workers*, 8–10.

82. Although the UMWA hewed to a line of nondiscrimination in principle, organizing and community life in particular localities often displayed exceptions to the rule. For a debate about the UMWA and racial tolerance, see Gutman, "The Negro and the United Mine Workers of America: The Career and Letters of Richard L. Davis and Something of Their Meaning," in *Work, Culture, and Society*, 119–208; Herbert Hill, "Myth-Making as Labor History." On the UMWA and immigrants, see Wynn, "Trade Unions and the 'New' Immigration"; Waldron, "'Great Spirit of Solidarity,'" esp. 192–243; and Merithew and Barrett, "'We Are Brothers in the Face of Starvation,'" 121–54. For the descriptions of the nearly fifty occupational classifications in coal mines, see Warne, *Coal-Mine Workers*, 32–33.

83. Sub-District No. 6, *Constitution of Sub-District No. 6*, 8.

84. See, for example, *By-Laws Local Union No. 605*, 4; *Report of the Industrial Commission on the Relations and Conditions of Capital and Labor*, 31, 90. By the time war erupted in Europe, funeral benefits had increased to $250 and to $350 by 1924. See United Mine Workers of America, *Constitution of the Twelfth District of the United Mine Workers of America*, 40–42; and Hayhurst, "Health of Illinois Coal Miners," 387.

85. "Illinois Miners in Session," *Chicago Tribune*, February 28, 1899.

86. In his classic study *Work, Culture, and Society*, Gutman found that common rituals such as Macclesfield and Ashton wakes, celebrating saints' days, and staging festivals cemented immigrant working-class communities while preserving Old World customs (43).

87. See, for example, "Honored the Dead: Fitting Memorial Services at the Grave of Ernst Long," *Mount Olive (IL) Herald*, October 20, 1900; "Inquest Commenced: On the Remains of Miners Killed in Wednesday's Accident at Auburn Town," *Illinois State Register*, February 27, 1903.

88. "Secretaries Are Urged by Mine Workers of Mount Olive, Ills., to Furnish Correspondence for Journal," *United Mine Workers Journal*, September 29, 1898.

89. "Four Dead at Herrin," *Carbondale (IL) Daily Free Press*, May 12, 1904; "Local News," *Carbondale (IL) Daily Free Press*, May 13, 1904.

90. United Mine Workers of America, *Constitution of the Twelfth District (Illinois) of the United Mine Workers of America*, 14–16.

91. McNeill, "Coal Miners," 241.

92. John McLaughlan, "From Illinois," *National Labor Tribune*, April 28, 1883.

93. For UMWA membership in 1897, see W. C. Pearce's testimony in *Report of the Industrial Commission on the Relations and Conditions of Capital and Labor*, 90. For the number of miners working in 1897, see Department of Mines and Minerals, *Thirty-Sixth Annual Coal Report of Illinois*, 4, 99–100. Nationally, UMWA records list 9,731 members in 1897 (*Minutes of the Sixteenth Annual Convention*, 45).

94. *United Mine Workers Journal*, July 22, 1897, quoted in John E. George, "Coal Miners' Strike of 1897," 191.

95. "The Coal Miners' Strike of 1897," in *Daily News Almanac and Political Register for 1898*, edited by Plumbe, 242.

96. John E. George, "Coal Miners' Strike of 1897," 207–8.

Notes to Chapter 3

97. John E. George, "Settlement in the Coal-Mining Industry," 451.

98. Between 1881 and 1900, miners waged 2,515 strikes, making coal and coke the second-most strike-prone industry in the United States, according to government statistics (*Sixteenth Annual Report of the Commissioner of Labor*, 352).

99. Phelan, *Divided Loyalties*, 33.

100. John E. George, "Settlement in the Coal-Mining Industry," 451.

101. Hicken, "Virden and Pana Mine Wars of 1898," 265–68.

102. "Watched by Sentries," *Illinois State Register*, October 11, 1898. See also "More Miners to Virden," *Illinois State Register*, October 11, 1898.

103. "Watched by Sentries."

104. Hoganson, *Fighting for American Manhood*, 1–132; Bederman, "Theodore Roosevelt: Manhood, Nation, and 'Civilization,'" in *Manliness and Civilization*, 170–215.

105. "Labor's Voice Raised," *Illinois State Register*, October 12, 1898.

106. Ibid.

107. Ibid.

108. Keiser, "Black Strikebreakers and Racism in Illinois"; Arnesen, "Specter of the Black Strikebreaker"; Whatley, "African-American Strikebreaking"; Ronald L. Lewis, *Black Coal Miners in America*, 82–84; Philip Foner, *Organized Labor and the Black Worker*, 77–79.

109. Hicken, "Virden and Pana Mine Wars of 1898," 274.

110. Coroner's Inquests; "Terrible Riot and Bloodshed: Eleven Men Killed and over Thirty Wounded at Virden," *Illinois State Register*, October 13, 1898; Carl Weinberg, "Hotter than San Juan Hill," Illinois Labor History Society, http://www.illinoislaborhistory.org/virden-massacre.html (accessed May 17, 2011).

111. "Bagwill, of Murphysboro Ill Speaks of the Lessons Taught and the Purchase Made with the Lives of the Fallen at Virden's Battle Decoration Day and Its Observance," *United Mine Workers Journal*, November 10, 1898.

112. "Negro Miners Return to Virden," *Illinois State Register*, October 14, 1898; "The Battle at Virden," 471–72; "The Heroines of Virden," *United Mine Workers Journal*, October 27, 1898; "A Day Not to Be Forgotten," *Illinois State Register*, October 15, 1898.

113. Illinois Bureau of Labor Statistics, *Coal in Illinois, 1898*, 6.

114. Evans, *History of United Mine Workers of America*, 608.

115. Henry Cartwright, "Miners Called to Funeral," *Illinois State Register*, October 13,1898.

116. "Two Thousand in Line: Impressive Was the Funeral of Edward Welch," *Illinois State Register*, October 15, 1898.

117. On Lincoln's funeral, see Laderman, *Sacred Remains*, 157–63.

118. Nick Walraven, "From Coffeen Illinois as Told by Nick Walraven," *United Mine Workers Journal*, October 27, 1898; "Short Local News," *Mount Olive (IL) Herald*, October 22, 1898.

119. "The Funeral at Mt. Olive," *United Mine Workers Journal*, October 27, 1898; J. D. Orcutt and Family, "Card of Thanks," *Mount Olive (IL) Herald*, October 22, 1898; Wm. Long and Children, "Card of Thanks," *Mount Olive (IL) Herald*, October 22, 1898.

120. "In Memory of Our Martyred Brothers at Virden," *United Mine Workers Journal*, November 3, 1898; United Mine Workers of America, *Official Report of the Tenth Annual Convention of District 12*, 5.

121. "Anent the Virden Affair," *United Mine Workers Journal*, November 3, 1898.

122. "Editorial Jottings," *United Mine Workers Journal*, October 20, 1898. The *UMW Journal*'s prophecy was fulfilled through folklore, song, and public memorialization of the October 12 battle. Folklorist George Korson included a chapter titled "Remember Virden" in *Coal Dust on the Fiddle*. The Illinois Humanities Council funded the centennial publication in 1998 of *Remember Virden, 1898*, edited by Rosemary Feurer. Bucky Halker and the Complete Unknowns recorded a track titled "Remember Virden" on their 2002 compact disc *Welcome to Labor Land*. Activists in central Illinois dedicated a monument on October 28, 2006, commemorating the event.

123. *United Mine Workers Journal*, November 10, 1898.

124. "For the Widow and Orphan," *United Mine Workers Journal*, November 3, 1898.

125. "They Will Be Cared For," *Mount Olive (IL) Herald*, September 2, 1899.

126. Fink, *Workingmen's Democracy*, 11–12; Levine, *Labor's True Woman*, 129–53; Clawson, *Constructing Brotherhood*, 173–75. This is not to say that women in Illinois coal communities passively accepted gender inequality or ideologies of domesticity. See Waldron, "'Great Spirit of Solidarity,'" 138–91. On the status of widows and maternalist politics, see Kleinberg, *Widows and Orphans First*; Linda Gordon, *Pitied but Not Entitled*; and Skocpol, *Protecting Soldiers and Mothers*, 311–524.

127. "Miners Win at Virden: A Settlement Reached by Which the Chicago-Virden Coal Co. Concedes to All Demands Asked," *Mount Olive (IL) Herald*, November 19, 1898.

128. Keiser, "Black Strikebreakers and Racism in Illinois," 322–23; Philip Foner, *Organized Labor and the Black Worker*, 78.

129. "Five Negroes Killed: Blacks Open Fire upon White Union Miners at Carterville and Were Riddled with Bullets," *Mount Olive (IL) Herald*, September 23, 1899.

130. Genovese, *Roll, Jordan, Roll*, 194–202; Roediger, "And Die in Dixie"; Stuckey, *Slave Culture*, 39–43, 108–9.

131. Rabinowitz, *Race Relations in the Urban South*, 140–42; Hughes and Bontemps, *Book of Negro Folklore*, 105–13, 589–90.

132. Zion Cemetery Project, "Zion Cemetery History"; Roberta Hughes Wright and Hughes, *Lay Down Body*, 143; Suzanne E. Smith, *To Serve the Living*. On black benevolent associations in Memphis during the post–Civil War era, see Page, "Local Matters," 107–63.

133. "Monument to Their Memory," *Mount Olive (IL) Herald*, June 24, 1899.

134. Keiser, "Union Miners Cemetery at Mt. Olive, Illinois," 232.

135. Ibid.; Leonard, "Union Miners Cemetery."

136. James Green, *Death in the Haymarket*, 290–91.

137. "Memorial Day: Held Thursday in Memory of the Four Mt. Olive Victims of the Virden Battle October 12, 1898," *Mount Olive (IL) Herald*, October 14, 1899; "They Footed the Bills," *Mount Olive (IL) Herald*, October 21, 1899. Due to a shipping delay, the monument did not arrive in time for the October 12 dedication. Miners and community members reassembled to dedicate the monument Thanksgiving Day, November 30, 1899. "Unveiled: The Monument Erected to the Memory of the Four Mt. Olive Victims of the Memorable Virden Battle Dedicated to Them," *Mount Olive (IL) Herald*, December 2, 1899.

138. "In Memoriam: The Second Annual Memorial Demonstration Held in This City Yesterday," *Mount Olive (IL) Herald*, October 13, 1900; "Memorial Demonstration," *Mount Olive (IL) Herald*, October 12, 1901; "To Honor the Dead," *Mount Olive (IL) Herald*, October 10, 1903, 1; "Honored the Dead," *Mount Olive (IL) Herald*, October 15, 1904.

139. Gorn, *Mother Jones*, 289–90.

140. On the 1930s mine wars in Illinois, see Carl D. Oblinger, *Divided Kingdom*.

141. United Mine Workers of America, *Minutes of the Twelfth Annual Convention*, 61; John Mitchell, "Report of President Mitchell to the Sixteenth Annual Convention of the United Mine Workers of America," *United Mine Workers Journal*, January 19, 1905; Warne, *Coal-Mine Workers*, viii; Laslett, *Colliers across the Sea*, 151.

142. Crawford, *Poet Scout*, 63.

143. *Report of the Industrial Commission on the Relations and Conditions of Capital and Labor*, 90; Woody Guthrie, *Struggle*, Smithsonian/Folkways (CD), 1992.

Chapter 4. As Close to Hell as They Hoped to Get

1. Eastman, *Work-Accidents and the Law*, 223.

2. Barrett and Roediger, "Inbetween Peoples," 3–42. For a counterargument to the "inbetween peoples" thesis, see Guglielmo, *White on Arrival*.

3. Saposs, "The Mind of Immigrant Communities in the Pittsburgh District," in *Public Opinion and the Steel Strike*, by Interchurch World Movement (New York, 1921), 239, quoted in Roediger, *Working toward Whiteness*, 89; Higham, *Strangers in the Land*, 173.

4. Montgomery, "Nationalism, American Patriotism, and Class Consciousness," 346. See also David Saposs, "Interview with Mike Stephan," Box 26, Folder 9, Saposs Papers; "Chat on the Street with Polish Worker, South Chicago," Box 26, Folder 7, Saposs Papers.

5. Krause, *Battle for Homestead*, 6.

6. "Minutes of the Carnegie Steel Company Limited from June 28 1892 to February 5, 1900," Folder 7, Carnegie Steel Co.—Minutes—1892–1900, Records of the Carnegie Steel Corporation. On Carnegie profits, see Bridge, *Inside History of the Carnegie Steel Company*, 256, 294–95; and Wall, *Andrew Carnegie*, 535–36. See also Nasaw, *Andrew Carnegie*, 405–27.

7. Couvares, *Remaking of Pittsburgh*, 86; Fitch, *The Steel Workers*, 102.

8. "An Address to the Public," *National Labor Tribune*, July 30, 1892, as quoted in Krause, *Battle for Homestead*, 347.

9. For detailed accounts of the July 6 battle, see Burgoyne, *Homestead*; Stowell, *"Fort Frick"*; and Krause, *Battle for Homestead*, 12–46.

10. Burgoyne, *Homestead*, 84–85 (quote on 84); "A Truce, but under Arms," *New York Times*, July 8, 1892.

11. Burgoyne, *Homestead*, 85.

12. Ibid., 93; "In the Houses of Mourning: Burial of the Victims of the Pinkerton Bullets at Homestead," *New York World*, July 8, 1892, reprinted in *River Ran Red*, edited by Demarest, 106–8 (quote on 106). See also "Rest for the Dead: Funeral Services Held over the Bodies of the Victims," *Chicago Tribune*, July 8,1892.

13. There were six graves, not seven, because George Rutter lay in the hospital. He died later.

14. "Quiet Day at Homestead," *New York Times*, July 8, 1892.

15. "Over the Bier: Funerals of Three of the Dead Homestead Mill Men," *Pittsburgh (PA) Commercial Gazette*, July 8, 1892, reprinted in *River Ran Red*, edited by Demarest, 109, 112.

16. "Burial of the Dead," *New York World*, July 9, 1892, reprinted in *River Ran Red*, edited by Demarest, 117; Stowell, *"Fort Frick,"* 95–96.

17. "Burial of the Dead," 117; "Dead Laid to Rest," *Chicago Tribune*, July 9, 1892; Stowell, "Fort Frick," 97.

18. Krause, *Battle for Homestead*, 19, 20–23.

19. It is possible that Sotak and Fares held memberships in Slovak fraternal societies such as the Homestead Lodge No. 26 of the First Catholic Slovak Union or the First Hungarian Sick Benefit Society of Saint Michael the Archangel. Newspaper articles do not reference either of these in relation to Sotak's funeral. Father Wider urged those assembled around Fares's grave to remain loyal to the "Church Society of Saint Michael" and the "Workingmen's Association." By the latter, Wider may have been referring to the Sick Benefit Society, but he could have just as plausibly been referring to the Amalgamated Association. On Wider's oration, see "In the Houses of Mourning," 108; and Krause, *Battle for Homestead*, 321. On the Slovak community's fraternal activity, see Krause, *Battle for Homestead*, 223–24.

20. Burgoyne, *Homestead*, 93.

21. "Rest for the Dead."

22. Burgoyne, *Homestead*, 93.

23. "In the Houses of Mourning," 107.

24. On gender tensions in the labor movement, see Kessler-Harris, "Treating the Male as 'Other'"; Enstad, *Ladies of Labor, Girls of Adventure*; and DeVault, *United Apart*.

25. "Dead Laid to Rest," *Chicago Tribune*, July 9, 1892; Stowell, "Fort Frick," 97. On Senator Palmer's speech, see Krause, *Battle for Homestead*, 340–41.

26. "Troops Ordered to Homestead by Governor Pattison," *New York Herald*, July 11, 1892, excerpted in *River Ran Red*, edited by Demarest, 129.

27. Krause, *Battle for Homestead*, 347.

28. William W. Delaney, "Father Was Killed by Pinkerton Men," excerpted in Meltzer, *Bread—and Roses*, 146–47. See also Archie Green, *Wobblies, Pile Butts, and Other Heroes*, 238–41.

29. For an illustration of this principle, see Frederick Winslow Taylor's conversation with "Schmidt," in *Principles of Scientific Management*, 5–8, 39–45. See also Montgomery, *Workers' Control in America*.

30. Eckardt, "Death in the Judaic and Christian Traditions."

31. Serrin, *Homestead*, 13.

32. Holt, "Trade Unionism," 10; Robinson, *Amalgamated Association of Iron, Steel and Tin Workers*, 9–10, 19.

33. Robinson, *Amalgamated Association of Iron, Steel and Tin Workers*, 73, 74. Puddlers represented a conservative faction within the Amalgamated and broke with the union in 1907 to form an independent union, the Sons of Vulcan. They had protested the extension of benefit features and excluded them from their new organization. *Report on Conditions of Employment in the Iron and Steel Industry*, 3:129.

34. Brands, *American Colossus*, 540; Nasaw, *Andrew Carnegie*, 580–88.

35. *Report on Conditions of Employment in the Iron and Steel Industry*, 3:110–11.

36. Fitch, *The Steel Workers*, 217.

37. Couvares, *Remaking of Pittsburgh*, 83.

38. Ibid., 86; Brody, *Steelworkers in America*, 27–49.

39. Jacoby, *Employing Bureaucracy*, 72; Stone, "Origins of Job Structures."

40. Montgomery, *Fall of the House of Labor*, 54.

41. *National Labor Tribune*, July 9, 1887, quoted in Couvares, *Remaking of Pittsburgh*, 83. See also Brody, *Steelworkers in America*, 31.

42. Kleinberg, *Shadow of the Mills*, 7.

43. Brody, *Steelworkers in America*, 2, 17.

44. R. R. Wright Jr., "One Hundred Negro Steel Workers"; Dickerson, *Out of the Crucible*, 3, 21, 24; Peter Gottlieb, *Making Their Own Way*.

45. Garland, "Homestead and Its Perilous Trades," 8.

46. Bonosky, *Burning Valley*, 147. Bonosky's father went to work in the mills at the turn of the twentieth century, and Bonosky himself was a steelworker in the 1940s. See Hapke, "Phillip Bonosky's *Burning Valley*."

47. Garland, "Homestead and Its Perilous Trades," 5; Charles Rumford Walker, *Steel*, 50–51.

48. Serrin, *Homestead*, 55.

49. Garland, "Homestead and Its Perilous Trades," 5.

50. Serrin, *Homestead*, 60 (Parton quote), 10.

51. Fitch, *The Steel Workers*, 166–81.

52. *Report on Conditions of Employment in the Iron and Steel Industry*, 3:160.

53. Quoted in Fitch, "Labor Policies of Unrestricted Capital."

54. A Department of Labor investigation for the year ending June 30, 1910, found that "there was a distinct excess" of accidents during the night versus the day shifts. There were 11.6 percent more accidents at night. In some areas of the plant, accident rates soared. Workers sustained accidents at a rate 118 percent higher in mechanical occupations and 127.6 percent in the yards if they worked at night (*Report on Conditions of Employment in the Iron and Steel Industry*, 4:15, 154). See also U.S. Department of Labor, Bureau of Labor Statistics, *Accidents and Accident Prevention in Machine Building*, 12.

55. Garland, "Homestead and Its Perilous Trades," 19.

56. Fitch, "Old Age at 40."

57. Garland, "Homestead and Its Perilous Trades," 16.

58. "God Bless the Workingman," *National Labor Tribune*, April 18, 1874, quoted in Kleinberg, *Shadow of the Mills*, 238. See also Wood, "Problem of the Old Man" and "'Beyond the Age of Earning.'"

59. U.S. Census, Twelfth Census 1900, vol. 2, *Population*, pt. 2, pp. 679–81, cited in Kleinberg, *Shadow of the Mills*, 239.

60. Hard, "Making Steel and Killing Men," 588.

61. Eastman, *Work-Accidents and the Law*, 72–73.

62. Hard, "Making Steel and Killing Men," 590–91.

63. Eastman, *Work-Accidents and the Law*, 49–70; *Report on Conditions of Employment in the Iron and Steel Industry*, 4:87. Extrapolating from a Homestead Works document that details fatal and nonfatal accidents after 1911, it is likely that between eight hundred and one thousand workers died at that plant during its years of operation (Fatality Records for the Homestead Works of United States Steel Company).

64. *Report on Conditions of Employment in the Iron and Steel Industry*, 4:167.

65. Fatality Records for the Homestead Works of United States Steel Company; Koukol, "A Slav's a Man for A' That," 73. Ultimately, however, the report cited lack of experience

rather than "racial qualities of the men" as the key factor in causing the high accident rates (*Report on Conditions of Employment in the Iron and Steel Industry*, 4:164–65, 167). See also Feldman, *Racial Factors in American Industry*, 148, quoted in Roediger, *Working toward Whiteness*, 44.

66. Eastman, *Work-Accidents and the Law*, 64–65.

67. *Report on Conditions of Employment in the Iron and Steel Industry*, 4:167; Byington, *Homestead*, 134.

68. Eastman, *Work-Accidents and the Law*, 64.

69. Fitch, *The Steel Workers*, 68.

70. Byington, *Homestead*, 115.

71. Eastman, *Work-Accidents and the Law*, 13–15.

72. Ibid., 65.

73. Coroner's Case File 190212-088–190212-091. Some workers perished by blatantly disobeying orders and taking risks. Some men died, for example, while attempting to board a moving train to save the walk to the other side of the mill.

74. See Thomas Bell, *Out of This Furnace*, 35, 71, 75; and Kleinberg, *Widows and Orphans First*, 13.

75. Kleinberg, *Shadow of the Mills*, 240.

76. Eastman, *Work-Accidents and the Law*, 119–20.

77. Hard, "Making Steel and Killing Men," 590.

78. Kessler-Harris, *In Pursuit of Equity*, 19–63.

79. Byington, *Homestead*, 107.

80. Kleinberg, *Shadow of the Mills*, 19, 25, 144; Pleck, "Mother's Wages"; Yans-McLaughlin, *Family and Community*; Bodnar, Simon, and Weber, *Lives of Their Own*, 99, 101, 247; Kessler-Harris, *Out to Work*, 108–79.

81. Kleinberg, *Shadow of the Mills*, 159–60.

82. Daphne Dale, *Our Manners and Social Customs*, 254–55; Sangster, *Good Manners for All Occasions*, 205–6; Lou Taylor, *Mourning Dress*; Halttunen, "Mourning the Dead: A Study in Sentimental Ritual," in *Confidence Men and Painted Women*, 124–52; Pleck, *Celebrating the Family*, 184–206.

83. Eastman, *Work-Accidents and the Law*, 135.

84. Kleinberg, *Shadow of the Mills*, 241.

85. Eastman, *Work-Accidents and the Law*, 136. In Eastman's study, 22 children joined the labor force as a result of an industrial accident out of more than 470 left fatherless during the course of the year.

86. Eastman, *Work-Accidents and the Law*, 135. Historian S. J. Kleinberg's examination of marriage records for three years shows that only 2 percent of women remarried in Pittsburgh near the turn of the century, whereas about 10 percent of the widowers remarried (*Shadow of the Mills*, 259).

87. Kleinberg, *Shadow of the Mills*, 243. On orphans and their treatment during the era, see Marilyn Irvin Holt, *The Orphan Trains*; Linda S. Gordon, *Great Arizona Orphan Abduction*; Stephen O'Connor, *Orphan Trains*; and Rebecca Edwards, *New Spirits*, 107–8.

88. Byington, *Homestead*, 135–37.

89. Kellogg, "Community and Workshop," 14, 17; Frank E. Wing, "Thirty-Five Years of Typhoid."

90. Adams, "Pittsburgh's Foregone Asset, the Public Health"; Kellogg, "Community and Workshop," 23; Byington, *Homestead*, 145–47.

91. See, for example, Fairchild, *Science at the Borders*; Curry, *Modern Mothers in the Heartland*; and Leavitt, *Healthiest City*.

92. Ross, *Old World in the New*, 291. For an example of this regarding the Chinese in San Francisco, see Shah, *Contagious Divides*, 20–22.

93. Byington, *Homestead*, 96.

94. Quoted in Alexander, *Immigrant Church and Community*, 19.

95. In an interview recorded in 1975, Angela Silvioni Baccelli discussed Italians' creation of the Lega Toscana fraternal society near the turn of the twentieth century "to keep the Tuscan people more close together" (Baccelli interview, December 1, 1975, Box 1, Ethnic Fraternal Organizations Oral History Project).

96. Alexander, *Immigrant Church and Community*, 25.

97. Bodnar, *Transplanted*, 120–22.

98. Stephen Devunich interview, November 4, 1975, Box 2, Ethnic Fraternal Organizations Oral History Project; Alexander, *Immigrant Church and Community*, 21.

99. Consistent with the gendered ideas of work and wage earning, most organizations did not extend sick benefits to women. If they allowed women to affiliate at all, organizations segregated women into auxiliary branches. See Clawson, *Constructing Brotherhood*, 178–210.

100. Byington, *Homestead*, 96–97, 154. In 1931 Lodge 529 of the Independent Order of Odd Fellows in Braddock provided a one-hundred-dollar death benefit (Constitution and By-Laws, Reel 1, Series 1, Records of the Independent Order of Odd Fellows). Historian John Bodnar found "a $1,000 death benefit was the norm" in the early twentieth century (*Transplanted*, 126).

101. Michael Grasha interview, September 22, 1975, Box 2, Ethnic Fraternal Organizations Oral History Project.

102. *Bell Publishing Co.'s City Directory*, 6–8; Byington, *Homestead*, 113. Homestead's 1902 directory lists sixty-six societies and organizations (*Directory of Homestead Borough*, 11). The *Pittsburgh and Allegheny Directory* for 1900 listed well over one hundred fraternal societies (106–12).

103. Bodnar, *Immigration and Industrialization*, 103, 108; Alexander, *Immigrant Church and Community*, 16, 21.

104. Roberts, "Immigrant Wage-Earners," 58.

105. *Centennial of Ukrainian Settlement in Pittsburgh* (1982), unpaginated, Western Pennsylvania Historical Society, Pittsburgh.

106. U.S. Bureau of the Census, *Religious Bodies, 1916*, 81. See also Linkh, *American Catholicism and European Immigrants*, 108–9.

107. Bodnar, *Transplanted*, 148.

108. On the connections between class, immigration, and religion, see Orsi, *Madonna of 115th Street*; Alexander, *Immigrant Church and Community*; McGreevy, *Parish Boundaries*, 7–54; and Tentler, *Seasons of Grace*. On working-class religiosity, see E. P. Thompson, "The Transforming Power of the Cross," in *Making of the English Working Class*, 350–400; Gutman, "Protestantism and the American Labor Movement"; Hobsbawm, "Religion and the Rise of Socialism," in *Workers: Worlds of Labor*, 33–48; and McLeod, *Piety and Poverty*.

109. Linkh, *American Catholicism and European Immigrants*, 87–89, 103–17.
110. Bonosky, *Burning Valley*, 168–69.
111. Ibid., 170–71.
112. Alexander, *Immigrant Church and Community*, xviii–xix.
113. Montgomery, *Citizen Worker*, 5–6.
114. Grosh, *The Odd Fellows Manual*, 377.
115. Rutherford, *Death of a Christian*, 96–97; Thurston, "Christian Burial."
116. Grosh, *The Odd Fellows Manual*, 102, 380. The Knights of Pythias performed similar rituals as those of the Odd Fellows. They wore specific funeral regalia, formed ranked processions, and read prepared funeral services at the grave. Also, like the Odd Fellows, the Knights deposited an evergreen into the grave at the close of the funeral. Van Valkenburg, *Knights of Pythias*, 234–36.
117. Beharrell, *New I.O.O.F. Monitor and Guide*, 13, 25, 15. Some wage-earning women formed mutual-aid societies of their own that provided death benefits. See Davidge, "Working-Girl's Clubs."
118. Byington, *Homestead*, 115.
119. Dickerson, *Out of the Crucible*, 72–74. See also Du Bois, *Philadelphia Negro*, 221–29; "The Bury League," "Urban Burying Leagues," and "Lodge Sisters at a Funeral" in *Book of Negro Folklore*, edited by Hughes and Bontemps, 105–13, 589–90, 594–95; Spencer, "Black Benevolent Societies"; and Ortiz, *Emancipation Betrayed*, 101–27.
120. "The Essence of the True and Active Spirit of Brotherhood," *Denni Hlasatel*, February 3, 1918, Reel 5, Chicago Foreign Language Press Survey.
121. Kellogg, "The McKee's Rocks Strike," 657; Ingham, "Strike in the Progressive Era," 353–54.
122. "Strike of Pressed Steel Car Workers Brings Fierce Rioting at M'Kees Rocks," *Pittsburgh (PA) Gazette Times*, July 15, 1909; "Court Refuses to Interfere in Strike," *Pittsburgh (PA) Gazette Times*, July 21, 1909; Philip Foner, *History of the Labor Movement in the United States*, 4:282–84.
123. "Strike of Pressed Steel Car Workers Brings Fierce Rioting at M'Kees Rocks."
124. "Martial Law in Force," *Washington Post*, July 17, 1909; William E. Trautmann, unpublished autobiography, Trautmann Collection, 209.
125. "Martial Law in Force."
126. "State Troops Charge Crowds Gathered in M'Kees Rocks Streets," *Pittsburgh (PA) Gazette Times*, July 16, 1909; "Foreigners Searched: Weapons and Bottles of Whisky Confiscated by Police," *Pittsburgh (PA) Gazette Times*, July 18, 1909.
127. Rufus D. Smith, "Some Phases of the McKee's Rocks Strike," 38.
128. Kellogg, "The McKee's Rocks Strike," 665.
129. "Court Refused to Interfere in Strike," *Pittsburgh (PA) Gazette Times*, July 21, 1909; "4,000 Strikers in a Dozen Battles," *New York Times*, July 16, 1909.
130. Quoted in Philip Foner, *History of the Labor Movement in the United States*, 4:284.
131. Ibid.; "M'Kees Rocks Workman Tells of Conditions," *Pittsburgh (PA) Gazette Times*, July 17, 1909.
132. Quoted in Philip Foner, *History of the Labor Movement in the United States*, 4:283.
133. "How Car Workers Met Their Deaths," *Pittsburgh (PA) Gazette Times*, July 18, 1909.
134. "Says Death Toll Was One Daily at Car Plant," *Pittsburgh (PA) Gazette Times*, July 17, 1909.

135. Kellogg, "The McKee's Rocks Strike," 664.

136. "Small Percentage of Men Want Strike: Pooling System of Pay Benefit to Workers, Says President Hoffstot," *Pittsburgh (PA) Gazette Times*, July 16, 1909; "Arbitration Is Declined by the Highest Official of the Schoenville Plant," *Pittsburgh (PA) Gazette Times*, July 17, 1909.

137. "First Fatality in Car Strike," *Pittsburgh (PA) Gazette Times*, August 13, 1909; "The Killing at Schoenville," *Pittsburgh (PA) Gazette Times*, August 13, 1909.

138. "Steel Car Plant Running Again," *Pittsburgh (PA) Gazette Times*, August 14, 1909; "Machine Gun on Deck of Ferry," *Pittsburgh (PA) Gazette Times*, August 15, 1909.

139. See, for example, "The Public's Interest," *Pittsburgh (PA) Gazette Times*, July 16, 1909; "The Risk and a Right," *Pittsburgh (PA) Gazette Times*, July 17, 1909.

140. "The Killing at Schoenville."

141. Smith, "Some Phases of the McKee's Rocks Strike," 38.

142. Duchez, "Victory at McKees Rocks," 292; Smith, "Some Phases of the McKee's Rocks Strike," 39.

143. Black and white were common colors on display during funerals and periods of mourning. See, for example, Hillerman, "Chrysallis of Gloom."

144. Duchez, "Victory at McKees Rocks," 292; U.S. Commission on Industrial Relations, *Industrial Relations*, 10573.

145. "Steel Car Plant Running Again," *Pittsburgh (PA) Gazette Times*, August 14, 1909; "Machine Gun on Deck of Ferry"; Ingham, "Strike in the Progressive Era," 363.

146. "Incendiary Fire Destroys Blankets at M'Kees Rocks," *Pittsburgh (PA) Gazette Times*, August 18, 1909; "Much Disorder in Strike Zone," *Pittsburgh (PA) Gazette Times*, August 19, 1909.

147. "Much Disorder in Strike Zone."

148. "Sheriff Denies Strikers' Charge," *Pittsburgh (PA) Gazette Times*, August 20, 1909; U.S. House of Representatives, *Peonage in Western Pennsylvania*.

149. Philip Foner, *History of the Labor Movement in the United States*, 4:290.

150. "Challenge Answered by Deputy's Bullets and He Quickly Dies," *Pittsburgh (PA) Gazette Times*, August 23, 1909; "Killing of Exley Described," *Pittsburgh (PA) Gazette Times*, August 23, 1909; "Another Detachment of State Police En Route to M'Kees Rocks," *Pittsburgh (PA) Gazette Times*, August 24, 1909; "Five Killed in Strike Riot," *New York Times*, August 23, 1909; "No Cars after Riots," *Washington Post*, August 24, 1909; "Blood Fails to Win Fight for Strikers," *Atlanta Constitution*, August 24, 1909; Duchez, "Victory at McKees Rocks," 294; Ingham, "Strike in the Progressive Era," 366; Dubofsky, *We Shall Be All*, 205.

151. "Put an End to Anarchy," *Pittsburgh (PA) Gazette Times*, August 24, 1909.

152. "No Cars after Riots."

153. Ibid.; "Blood Fails to Win Fight for Strikers"; "Strikers Bury Victims of Riot," *Chicago Tribune*, August 25, 1909.

154. Smith, "Some Phases of the McKee's Rocks Strike," 41.

155. "Strikers Bury Victims of Riot."

156. Lyman Edwyn Davis, "Strike-Riot in Pennsylvania," 536–37.

157. "Debs Sympathizes with the Strikers," *Pittsburgh (PA) Gazette Times*, August 25, 1909; "Quiet Prevails in Strike Zone," *Pittsburgh (PA) Gazette Times*, August 26, 1909; Duchez, "Victory at McKees Rocks," 294–95.

158. Dubofsky, *We Shall Be All*, 199.
159. Duchez, "Victory at McKees Rocks," 292–93.
160. Quoted in Ingham, "Strike in the Progressive Era," 367.
161. Dubofsky, *We Shall Be All*, 207.
162. M. T. C. Wing, "Flag at McKee's Rocks"; Ingham, "Strike in the Progressive Era," 371; Dubofsky, *We Shall Be All*, 207.
163. Stromquist, *Reinventing "the People,"* 168.
164. Dubofsky, *We Shall Be All*, 201.
165. "The Hunkey," *Pittsburgh (PA) Gazette Times*, August 30, 1909.
166. Quoted in Brody, *Steelworkers in America*, 139.
167. Francis, "Saga of Joe Magarac."
168. Archie Green, *Wobblies, Pile Butts, and Other Heroes*, 355; Gilley and Burnett, "Deconstructing and Reconstructing Pittsburgh's Man of Steel." It seems possible, as Philip Bonosky's rendering of the story suggests in *Burning Valley* (134–38), that workers could have used the Magarac tale as a subversive form of hidden resistance to lampoon the racist work atmosphere and joke at the native-born foremen's and workers' expense.
169. Bell, *Out of This Furnace*, 412 (emphasis in the original).

Conclusion. (Un)Freedom of the Grave

1. Gompers, "What Does Labor Want?," 4, 7, 5.
2. Hertz, "A Contribution to the Study of the Collective Representation of Death," in *Death and the Right Hand*, 27–86; Koslofsky, *Reformation of the Dead*, 7.
3. Bloch and Perry, "Introduction," 42.
4. Woodburn, "Social Dimensions of Death"; Koslofsky, *Reformation of the Dead*, 9.
5. Stout, "Tragedy in November."
6. Stein, *The Triangle Fire*; Orleck, *Common Sense and a Little Fire*; Von Drehle, *Triangle*; Greenwald, *Triangle Fire*.
7. Flynn, *Rebel Girl*, 168–69; Golin, *Fragile Bridge*, 157–78.
8. Dawley, *Struggles for Justice*, 103–4.
9. Greene, *Pure and Simple Politics*, 80–81.
10. Meigs, *Optimism at Armageddon*, 154, 157.
11. Kennedy, *Over Here*, 3.
12. Dawley, *Struggles for Justice*, 174.
13. See, for example, "The Deadly Parallel," *Solidarity* (March 24, 1917), in *Rebel Voices*, edited by Kornbluh, 331.
14. Gompers, "Address to the Annual Meeting," 2:853.
15. Quoted in Dawley, *Struggles for Justice*, 174–75; Woodrow Wilson, "An Unpublished Prolegomenon to a Peace Note," in *Papers of Wilson*, edited by Link, 40:67–68, 69–70.
16. Woodrow Wilson, "An Address to a Joint Session of Congress," in ibid., 41:526–27.
17. "I Love My Flag," *Industrial Worker*, April 14, 1917, in *Rebel Voices*, edited by Kornbluh, 331.
18. Eugene V. Debs, "The Canton, Ohio, Speech," in *Eugene V. Debs Speaks*, edited by Tussey, 260–61.
19. Dray, *There Is Power in a Union*, 353.

20. Ebel, *Faith in the Fight*, 2.

21. McCartin, *Labor's Great War*, 94–119.

22. Kennedy, *Over Here*, 158–59, 162; Slotkin, *Lost Battalions*, 8; Meigs, *Optimism at Armageddon*, 178.

23. Piehler, "War Dead and the Gold Star," 179.

24. Quoted in Laderman, *Rest in Peace*, 50.

25. Piehler, "War Dead and the Gold Star," 174.

26. McCartin, *Labor's Great War*, 39; Murray, *Red Scare*.

27. Montgomery, *Fall of the House of Labor*, 388.

28. Fitch, "The Closed Shop."

29. Foster, *The Great Steel Strike*, 146–47.

30. Ibid., 147–48. The autopsy report listed Sellins as fifty-five years old and indicates she was shot twice in the head. "Fannie Sellins Autopsy Report," Labor Legacy, University of Pittsburgh, http://www.library.pitt.edu/labor_legacy/images/FannieSellens-autopsy.jpg (accessed December 18, 2012).

31. Cassedy, "Bond of Sympathy."

Bibliography

Manuscripts, Personal Papers, and Oral Histories

Coal Mining and Union Activities. Brookens Library, University of Illinois, Springfield.
Coroner's Case Files, Allegheny County. Archives of Industrial Society, University of Pittsburgh, Pittsburgh, PA.
Coroner's Inquests. 1896-98. Illinois Regional Archives Depository, University of Illinois, Springfield.
Ethnic Fraternal Organizations Oral History Project. Archives of Industrial Society, University of Pittsburgh, Pittsburgh, PA.
Fatality Records for the Homestead Works of United States Steel Company. 1909-76. Historical Society of Western Pennsylvania, Pittsburgh.
H. Samson, Inc., Records. MSS #260, Archives of the Western Pennsylvania Historical Society, Pittsburgh.
McDonald, Duncan. Papers. Abraham Lincoln Presidential Library, Springfield, IL.
Mitchell, John. Papers. 1870-1919. Microfilm. University Microfilms International, Ann Arbor, MI.
Records of the Carnegie Steel Corporation. 1853-1912. MSS #315, Historical Society of Western Pennsylvania, Pittsburgh.
Records of the Independent Order of Odd Fellows. Braddock's Field Lodge #529, Braddock, PA, ais198225, Archives Service Center, University of Pittsburgh, Pittsburgh, PA.
Report and Proceedings of the Diamond Mine Widows and Orphans Relief Committee. 1883. Wilmington Public Library, Wilmington, IL.
Saposs, David. Papers. Wisconsin State Historical Society, Madison.
Trautmann, William E., Collection. Walter P. Reuther Library, Wayne State University, Detroit.
Walker, John Hunter. Papers. 1910-55. Illinois History Collection, University of Illinois at Urbana-Champaign.
Wieck, Agnes Burns. Papers. Walter Reuther Library, Wayne State University, Detroit.

Newspapers and Trade Publications

Atlanta Constitution
Black Diamond
Carbondale (IL) Daily Free Press
Chicago Defender
Chicago Foreign Language Press Survey. Translated by Chicago Public Library Omnibus Project. Chicago: Works Project Administration, 1942. Microfilm.
Chicago Tribune
Denni Hlasatel (Chicago)
Frank Leslie's Illustrated Newspaper
Illinois Staats-Zeitung (Chicago)
Illinois State Journal (Springfield)
Illinois State Register (Springfield)
Iron Age
Los Angeles Times
Mount Olive (IL) Herald
National Labor Tribune
New York Times
Pittsburgh (PA) Gazette Times
Railway Times
Social Democrat (Terre Haute, IN)
St. Louis Daily Globe-Democrat
St. Louis Post-Dispatch
Svornost (Chicago)
United Mine Workers Journal
Wall Street Journal
Washington Post
Wilmington (IL) Advocate
Wilmington (IL) Herald

Other Sources

Abbott, Grace. "The Immigrant and Mining Communities of Illinois." In vol. 2 of *Bulletin of the Immigrants Commission*. Springfield: Illinois Printing, 1920.
———. *The Immigrant and the Community*. New York: Century, 1917.
Adams, Samuel Hopkins. "Pittsburgh's Foregone Asset, the Public Health." *Charities and the Commons* 21 (February 6, 1909): 940.
Addams, Jane. "Why the Ward Boss Rules." *Outlook*, April 1892, 879–82.
"Address of Welcome to Manufacturers." *Iron Age* (June 13, 1901): 52–53.
Adler, Jeffrey S. *First in Violence, Deepest in Dirt: Homicide in Chicago, 1875–1920*. Cambridge, MA: Harvard University Press, 2006.
Albert, Peter J., and Grace Palladino, eds. *Progress and Reaction in the Age of Reform, 1909–13*. Vol. 8 of *The Samuel Gompers Papers*. Urbana: University of Illinois Press, 2001.
Aldrich, Mark. *Death Rode the Rails: American Railroad Accidents and Safety, 1828–1965*. Baltimore, MD: Johns Hopkins University Press, 2006.

———. *Safety First: Technology, Labor, and Business in the Building of American Work Safety, 1870–1939*. Baltimore, MD: Johns Hopkins University Press, 1997.

Alexander, June Granatir. *The Immigrant Church and Community: Pittsburgh's Slovak Catholics and Lutherans, 1880–1915*. Pittsburgh, PA: University of Pittsburgh Press, 1987.

Alger, George William. *Moral Overstrain*. Boston: Houghton, Mifflin, 1906.

Almaguer, Tomás. *Racial Fault Lines: The Historical Origins of White Supremacy in California*. Berkeley: University of California Press, 1994.

Amsden, Jon, and Stephen Brier. "Coal Miners on Strike: The Transformation of Strike Demands and the Formation of a National Union." *Journal of Interdisciplinary History* 7, no. 4 (1977): 583–616.

Angle, Paul M. *Bloody Williamson: A Chapter in American Lawlessness*. New York: Alfred A. Knopf, 1952.

Ariès, Philippe. *Death in America*. Philadelphia: University of Pennsylvania Press, 1975.

———. "Forbidden Death." In *Passing: The Vision of Death in America*, edited by Charles O. Jackson, 148–52. Westport, CT: Greenwood Press, 1977.

———. *Hour of Our Death*. New York: Alfred A. Knopf, 1981.

———. *Images of Man and Death*. Cambridge, MA: Harvard University Press, 1985.

———. *Western Attitudes toward Death: From the Middle Ages to the Present*. Baltimore, MD: Johns Hopkins University Press, 1974.

Arnesen, Eric. "Specter of the Black Strikebreaker: Race, Employment, and Labor Activism in the Industrial Era." *Labor History* 44, no. 3 (2003): 319–35.

Ashbaugh, Carolyn. *Lucy Parsons: American Revolutionary*. Chicago: Charles H. Kerr, 1976.

Asher, Robert. "Business and Workers' Welfare in the Progressive Era: Workmen's Compensation Reform in Massachusetts, 1880–1911." *Business History Review* 43, no. 4 (1969): 452–75.

———. "Failure and Fulfillment: Agitation for Employers' Liability Legislation and the Origins of Workmen's Compensation in New York State, 1876–1910." *Labor History* (Spring 1983): 198–222.

Attaway, William. *Blood on the Forge*. 1941. Reprint, New York: Collier Books, 1970.

Aveling, Edward, and Eleanor Marx-Aveling. *The Working-Class Movement in America*. 2nd ed. London: Swan Sonnenschein, 1891.

Avrich, Paul. *An American Anarchist: The Life of Voltairine de Cleyre*. Princeton, NJ: Princeton University Press, 1978.

———. *The Haymarket Tragedy*. Princeton, NJ: Princeton University Press, 1984.

Bachin, Robin F. *Building the South Side: Urban Space and Civic Culture in Chicago, 1890–1919*. Chicago: University of Chicago Press, 2004.

Baker, Ray Stannard. "The Spiritual Unrest: A Vision of the New Christianity." *American Magazine*, December 1909, 176–83.

Bannister, Robert C. *Social Darwinism: Science and Myth in Anglo-American Social Thought*. Philadelphia: Temple University Press, 1979.

Baron, Ava, and Eileen Boris. "'The Body' as a Useful Category for Working-Class History." *Labor: Studies in Working-Class History of the Americas* 4, no. 2 (2007): 23–43.

Barrett, James R. *The Irish Way: Becoming American in the Multiethnic City*. New York: Penguin Press, 2012.

———. "Was the Personal Political? Reading the Autobiography of American Communism." *International Review of Social History* 53, no. 3 (2008): 395–423.

———. "Why Paddy Drank: The Social Importance of Whiskey in Pre-famine Ireland." *Journal of Popular Culture* 11, no. 1 (1977): 155–66.

———. *William Z. Foster and the Tragedy of American Radicalism*. Urbana: University of Illinois Press, 1999.

———. *Work and Community in the Jungle: Chicago's Packinghouse Workers, 1894–1922*. Urbana: University of Illinois Press, 1987.

Barrett, James R., and David R. Roediger. "Inbetween Peoples: Race, Nationality and the 'New Immigrant' Working Class." *Journal of American Ethnic History* 16 (May 1997): 3–44.

———. "The Irish and the 'Americanization' of the 'New Immigrants' in the Streets and in the Churches of the Urban United States, 1900–1930." *Journal of American Ethnic History* 24, no. 4 (2005): 3–33.

Batchen, Geoffrey. *Forget Me Not: Photography and Remembrance*. New York: Princeton Architectural Press, 2004.

"The Battle of Virden." *Locomotive Firemen's Magazine* 25, no. 5 (1898): 447–75.

Beckner, Earl R. *A History of Labor Legislation in Illinois*. Chicago: University of Chicago Press, 1929.

Bederman, Gail. *Manliness and Civilization: A Cultural History of Gender and Race in the United States, 1880–1917*. Chicago: University of Chicago Press, 1995.

Beharrell, Rev. T. G. *The New I.O.O.F. Monitor and Guide*. Indianapolis: Robert Douglass, 1898.

Beito, David T. *From Mutual Aid to the Welfare State: Fraternal Societies and Social Services, 1890–1967*. Chapel Hill: University of North Carolina Press, 2000.

Bell, Catherine. *Ritual Theory, Ritual Practice*. New York: Oxford University Press, 1992.

Bell, Thomas. *Out of This Furnace*. 1941. Reprint, Pittsburgh, PA: University of Pittsburgh Press, 1976.

Bellamy, Paul B. *A History of Workmen's Compensation, 1898–1915: From the Courtroom to the Boardroom*. New York: Garland, 1997.

The Bell Publishing Co.'s City Directory of McKeesport, Duquesne, Dravosburg, Reynoldton, Christy Park, Versailles Borough and Wilmerding, Penna., 1895. Baltimore, MD: Bell, 1895.

Bender, Thomas. "The 'Rural' Cemetery Movement: Urban Travail and the Appeal of Nature." *New England Quarterly* 47, no. 2 (1974): 196–211.

Bensel, Richard Franklin. *The Political Economy of American Industrialization, 1877–1900*. New York: Cambridge University Press, 2000.

Bergstrom, Randolph E. *Courting Danger: Injury and Law in New York City, 1870–1910*. Ithaca, NY: Cornell University Press, 1992.

Betten, Neil. *Catholic Activism and the Industrial Worker*. Gainesville: University Presses of Florida, 1976.

Beye, William, Chairman, Health Insurance Commission. *Report of the Health Insurance Commission of the State of Illinois*. Springfield: Illinois State Journal, 1919.

Blackmon, Douglas A. *Slavery by Another Name: The Re-enslavement of Black Americans from the Civil War to World War II*. New York: Anchor Books, 2009.

Blair, William A. *Cities of the Dead: Contesting the Memory of the Civil War in the South, 1865–1914*. Chapel Hill: University of North Carolina Press, 2004.

Blaney, Herbert. "The Modern Park Cemetery." In *Passing: The Vision of Death in America*, edited by Charles O. Jackson, 219–26. Westport, CT: Greenwood Press, 1977.

Blauner, Robert. "Death and Social Structure." *Psychiatry: Journal for the Study of Interpersonal Processes* 29 (November 1966): 378–94.

Blight, David W. *Race and Reunion: The Civil War in American Memory*. Cambridge, MA: Belknap Press of Harvard University Press, 2001.

Bloch, Maurice, and Jonathan Perry. "Introduction: Death and the Regeneration of Life." In *Death and the Regeneration of Life*, edited by Maurice Bloch and Jonathan Perry, 1–44. Cambridge: Cambridge University Press, 1982.

Bodnar, John. *Immigration and Industrialization: Ethnicity in an American Mill Town, 1870–1940*. Pittsburgh, PA: University of Pittsburgh Press, 1977.

———. *The Transplanted: A History of Immigrants in Urban America*. Bloomington: Indiana University Press, 1985.

———. *Workers' World: Kinship, Community, and Protest in an Industrial Society, 1900–1940*. Baltimore, MD: Johns Hopkins University Press, 1982.

Bodnar, John, Roger Simon, and Michael P. Weber. *Lives of Their Own: Blacks, Italians, and Poles in Pittsburgh, 1900–1960*. Urbana: University of Illinois Press, 1982.

Bonosky, Phillip. *Burning Valley*. 1953. Reprint, Urbana: University of Illinois Press, 1998.

Booth, Stephane Elise. "The Relationship between Radicalism and Ethnicity in Southern Illinois Coal Fields, 1870–1940." PhD diss., Illinois State University, 1983.

Bourdieu, Pierre. *Distinction: A Social Critique of the Judgment of Taste*. Cambridge, MA: Harvard University Press, 1984.

Bourke, Joanna. *Fear: A Cultural History*. Emeryville, CA: Shoemaker and Hoard, 2005.

Bowman, Leroy. "The Effects of City Civilization." In *Passing: The Vision of Death in America*, edited by Charles O. Jackson, 153–73. Westport, CT: Greenwood Press, 1977.

Boyer, Paul. *Urban Masses and Moral Order in America, 1820–1920*. Cambridge, MA: Harvard University Press, 1978.

Bradbury, Mary. *Representations of Death: A Social Psychological Perspective*. New York: Routledge, 1999.

Brandeis, Louis D. *Women in Industry*. New York: National Consumers' League, 1908.

Brands, H. W. *American Colossus: The Triumph of Capitalism, 1865–1900*. New York: Doubleday, 2010.

Bridge, James Howard. *The Inside History of the Carnegie Steel Company: A Romance of Millions*. New York: Aldine Book, 1903.

Brody, David. *Steelworkers in America: The Nonunion Era*. New York: Russell and Russell, 1960.

Brooks, John Graham. *The Social Unrest: Studies in Labor and Socialist Movements*. 1903. Reprint, New York: Macmillan, 1913.

Brophy, John. *A Miner's Life*. Madison: University of Wisconsin Press, 1964.

Brown, Dee. *The Year of the Century: 1876*. New York: Scribner, 1966.

Brown, Elspeth H. *The Corporate Eye: Photography and the Rationalization of American Commercial Culture, 1884–1929*. Baltimore, MD: Johns Hopkins University Press, 2005.

Brown, Joshua. "The Great Uprising and Pictorial Order in Gilded Age America." In *The Great Strikes of 1877*, edited by David O. Stovall, 15–54. Urbana: University of Illinois Press, 2008.

Buchanan, Joseph R. *The Story of a Labor Agitator*. New York: Outlook, 1903.

Burgoyne, Arthur G. *Homestead: A Complete History of the Struggle of July, 1892, between the Carnegie Steel Company, Limited, and the Amalgamated Association of Iron and Steel Workers*. Pittsburgh, PA: Rawsthorne Engraving and Printing, 1893.

Burton, Orville Vernon. *The Age of Lincoln*. New York: Hill and Wang, 2007.

"Buying a Man's Arm: By the Corporation Lawyer Who Made the Purchase." *American Magazine*, July 1909, 260–62.

Byington, Margaret. *Homestead: The Households of a Mill Town*. New York: Charities Publication, 1910.

By-Laws Local Union No. 605, United Mine Workers of America. Belleville, IL: Post and Zeitung, 1898.

Campbell, Helen. *Prisoners of Poverty: Women Wage-Workers, Their Trades and Their Lives*. 1887. Reprint, Boston: Little, Brown, 1900.

Canning, Kathleen. "The Body as Method? Reflections on the Place of the Body in Gender History." *Gender and History* 11, no. 3 (1999): 499–513.

Carnegie, Andrew. *Autobiography of Andrew Carnegie*. 1920. Reprint, Boston: Houghton Mifflin, 1948.

———. "Wealth." *North American Review* 391 (June 1889): 653–64.

Cashman, Sean Dennis. *America in the Gilded Age: From the Death of Lincoln to the Rise of Theodore Roosevelt*. 3rd ed. New York: New York University Press, 1993.

Cassedy, James. "A Bond of Sympathy: The Life and Tragic Death of Fannie Sellins." *Labor's Heritage* (Winter 1992): 34–47.

"The 'Casualty List' of American Industries." *Scientific American*, February 9, 1907, 126.

Catechism of the Catholic Church. New York: Catholic Book, 1994.

Centennial of Ukrainian Settlement in Pittsburgh. Pittsburgh, PA: Pittsburgh Ukrainian Festival Committee, 1982.

Chandler, Alfred D., Jr. *The Visible Hand: The Managerial Revolution in American Business*. Cambridge, MA: Harvard University Press, 1977.

Cherniak, Martin. *The Hawk's Nest Incident: America's Worst Industrial Disaster*. New Haven, CT: Yale University Press, 1986.

Chicago Commission on Race Relations. *The Negro in Chicago: A Study of Race Relations and a Race Riot*. Chicago: University of Chicago Press, 1922.

Child, Richard Washburn. "What Shall We Do with the Old?" *Everybody's Magazine*, September 1909, 355–61.

The City of Virden Proudly Celebrates Our Sesquicentennial: 150 Years as a Thriving, Growing Community. Virden, IL: n.p., 2002.

Claeys, Gregory. "The 'Survival of the Fittest' and the Origins of Social Darwinism." *Journal of the History of Ideas* 61, no. 2 (2000): 223–40.

Clawson, Mary Ann. *Constructing Brotherhood: Class, Gender, and Fraternalism*. Princeton, NJ: Princeton University Press, 1989.

"The Coal Miner." In *Statistics of Coal in Illinois, 1893*, 104–34. Springfield, IL: H. W. Rokker, 1894.

Cohen, Lizabeth. *Making a New Deal: Industrial Workers in Chicago, 1919–1939*. New York: Cambridge University Press, 1990.

Colman, Penny. *Corpses, Coffins, and Crypts: A History of Burial.* New York: Henry Holt, 1997.
Commons, John R. Introduction to *Trade Unionism and Labor Problems*, edited by John R. Commons, vii–xiv. New York: Augustus M. Kelley, 1967.
———. *Social Reform and the Church.* 1894. Reprint, Augustus M. Kelley, 1967.
"Conference of Labor and Capital." *Iron Age* (May 16, 1901): 32.
Connors, Thomas G. "The Romantic Landscape: Washington Irving, Sleepy Hollow, and the Rural Cemetery Movement." In *Mortal Remains: Death in Early America*, edited by Nancy Isenberg and Andrew Burstein, 187–203. Philadelphia: University of Pennsylvania Press, 2003.
Constitution and Laws of the United Mine Workers of America. Indianapolis: Allied Printing, 1900.
Constitution of the State of Illinois, Adopted and Ratified 1870. Springfield, IL: Weber, 1879.
Cook, Rev. Joseph. "Self-Help, State-Help, and Church-Help for Workingmen." In *Labor: Its Rights and Wrongs*, 106–14. Washington, DC: Labor Publishing, 1886.
Corbin, David Alan. *Life, Work, and Rebellion in the Coal Fields: The Southern West Virginia Miners, 1880–1922.* Urbana: University of Illinois Press, 1981.
Corn, Jacqueline. "Protective Legislation for Coal Miners, 1870–1900: Response to Safety and Health Hazards." In *Dying for Work: Workers' Safety and Health in Twentieth-Century America*, edited by David Rosner and Gerald Markowitz, 67–82. Bloomington: Indiana University Press, 1987.
Couvares, Francis G. *The Remaking of Pittsburgh: Class and Culture in an Industrializing City, 1877–1919.* Albany: State University of New York Press, 1984.
Cranston, Mary R. "A Social Clearing-House." *Harper's*, June 1906, 142–47.
Crawford, Captain Jack. *The Poet Scout: Being a Selection of Incidental and Illustrative Verses and Songs.* San Francisco: H. Keller, 1879.
Crissman, James K. *Death and Dying in Central Appalachia: Changing Attitudes and Practices.* Urbana: University of Illinois Press, 1994.
Cronon, William. *Nature's Metropolis: Chicago and the Great West.* New York: W. W. Norton, 1991.
Curl, James Stevens. *The Victorian Celebration of Death.* Phoenix Mill, UK: Sutton, 2000.
Curry, Lynne. *Modern Mothers in the Heartland: Gender, Health, and Progress in Illinois, 1900–1930.* Columbus: Ohio State University Press, 1999.
Dabakis, Melissa. *Visualizing Labor in American Sculpture: Monuments, Manliness, and the Work Ethic, 1880–1935.* New York: Cambridge University Press, 1999.
Dale, Daphne. *Our Manners and Social Customs: A Practical Guide to Deportment, Easy Manners, and Social Etiquette.* Chicago: Universal Publishing House, 1892.
Dale, Elizabeth. "'Social Equality Does Not Exist among Themselves, nor among Us': *Baylies vs. Curry* and Civil Rights in Chicago, 1888." *American Historical Review* 102, no. 2 (1997): 311–39.
Daniels, Roger. *Coming to America: A History of Immigration and Ethnicity in American Life.* 2nd ed. New York: Perennial, 2002.
David, Henry. *The History of the Haymarket Affair: A Study in American Social-Revolutionary and Labor Movements.* New York: Russell and Russell, 1936.

Davidge, Clary Sidney. "Working-Girl's Clubs." *Scribner's*, May 1894, 619–28. Reprinted in *The American 1890s: A Cultural Reader*, edited by Susan Harris Smith and Melanie Dawson, 185–93. Durham, NC: Duke University Press, 2000.

Davis, Kenneth C. *A Nation Rising: Untold Tales of Flawed Founders, Fallen Heroes, and Forgotten Fighters from America's Hidden History*. New York: Smithsonian Books, 2010.

Davis, Lyman Edwyn. "The Strike-Riot in Pennsylvania." *Independent*, September 2, 1909, 533–37.

Dawley, Alan. *Changing the World: American Progressives in War and Revolution*. Princeton, NJ: Princeton University Press, 2003.

———. *Struggles for Justice: Social Responsibility and the Liberal State*. Cambridge, MA: Harvard University Press, 1991.

Day, Marie. *Bloody Mine Riot of Virden, Illinois, 1898*. Ozark, MO: Dogwood, 1989.

"The Death Roll in Industry." *Independent*, April 13, 1905, 851.

de Cleyre, Voltairine. *The First May Day: The Haymarket Speeches, 1895–1910*. Edited by Paul Avrich. New York: Libertarian Book Club, 1980.

———. *Selected Works of Voltairine de Cleyre*. Edited by Alexander Berkman. New York: Mother Earth, 1914.

Deloria, Philip J. *Playing Indian*. New Haven, CT: Yale University Press, 1998.

Demarest, David P., ed. *The River Ran Red: Homestead, 1892*. Pittsburgh, PA: University of Pittsburgh Press, 1992.

Denning, Michael. *The Cultural Front: The Laboring of American Culture in the Twentieth Century*. New York: Verso, 1997.

Department of Mines and Minerals. *Thirty-Sixth Annual Coal Report of Illinois, 1917*. Springfield: Illinois State Journal, 1917.

———. *Thirty-Eighth Annual Coal Report of Illinois*. Springfield: Illinois State Journal, 1919.

Derickson, Alan. "The Role of the United Mine Workers in the Prevention of Work-Related Respiratory Disease, 1890–1968." In *The United Mine Workers of America: A Model of Industrial Solidarity?*, edited by John H. M. Laslett, 224–38. University Park: Pennsylvania State University Press, 1996.

———. *Workers' Health, Workers' Democracy: The Western Miners' Struggle, 1891–1925*. Ithaca, NY: Cornell University Press, 1988.

DeVault, Ileen A. *United Apart: Gender and the Rise of Craft Unionism*. Ithaca, NY: Cornell University Press, 2004.

Dickerson, Dennis C. *Out of the Crucible: Black Steelworkers in Western Pennsylvania, 1875–1980*. Albany: State University of New York Press, 1986.

DiGirolamo, Vincent. "Newsboy Funerals: Tales of Sorrow and Solidarity in Urban America." *Journal of Social History* 36 (2002): 5–30.

Diner, Hasia R. "Ethnicity and Emotions in America: Dimensions of the Unexplored." In *An Emotional History of the United States*, edited by Peter N. Stearns and Jan Lewis, 197–217. New York: New York University Press, 1998.

Directory of Homestead Borough, West Homestead Borough, Munhall Borough. Homestead, PA: Homestead Directory, 1902.

Dix, Keith. *What's a Coal Miner to Do? The Mechanization of Coal Mining*. Pittsburgh, PA: University of Pittsburgh Press, 1988.

Doten, Carroll W. "Recent Railway Accidents in the United States." *Publications of the American Statistical Association* 9, no. 69 (1905): 155–81.

Dowd, Quincy L. *Funeral Management and Costs: A World-Survey of Burial and Cremation.* Chicago: University of Chicago Press, 1921.

Dray, Philip. *There Is Power in a Union: The Epic Story of Labor in America.* New York: Doubleday, 2010.

Drudi, Dino. "A Century-Long Quest for Meaningful and Accurate Occupational Injury and Illness Statistics." *Compensation and Working Conditions* (Winter 1997): 19–27.

Dublin, Louis I. *Mortality Statistics of Insured Wage-Earners and Their Families: Experience of the Metropolitan Life Insurance Company Industrial Department, 1911 to 1916, in the United States and Canada.* New York: Metropolitan Life Insurance, 1919.

Dubofsky, Melvyn. *"Big Bill" Haywood.* New York: St. Martin's Press, 1987.

———. *We Shall Be All: A History of the Industrial Workers of the World.* Chicago: Quadrangle Books, 1969.

Dubofsky, Melvyn, and Foster Rhea Dulles. *Labor in America: A History.* 8th ed. Wheeling, IL: Harlan Davidson, 2010.

Du Bois, W. E. B. *The Philadelphia Negro: A Social Study.* 1899. Reprint, Millwood, NY: Kraus-Thomson, 1973.

———. *The Souls of Black Folk.* New York: Dover, 1994.

Duchez, Louis. "Victory at McKees Rocks." *International Socialist Review* 10, no. 4 (1909): 289–300.

Duden, Barbara. *The Woman beneath the Skin: A Doctor's Patients in Eighteenth-Century Germany.* Translated by Thomas Dunlap. Cambridge, MA: Harvard University Press, 1991.

Dyer, Thomas G. *Theodore Roosevelt and the Idea of Race.* Baton Rouge: Louisiana State University Press, 1980.

Eastman, Crystal. *Work-Accidents and the Law.* 1910. Reprint, New York: Survey Associates, 1916.

Ebel, Jonathan H. *Faith in the Fight: Religion and the American Soldier in the Great War.* Princeton, NJ: Princeton University Press, 2010.

Eckardt, A. Roy. "Death in the Judaic and Christian Traditions." In *Death in American Experience,* edited by Arien Mack, 123–48. New York: Shocken Books, 1973.

Edwards, Rebecca. *New Spirits: Americans in the Gilded Age, 1865–1905.* New York: Oxford University Press, 2006.

Edwards, Richard. *Contested Terrain: The Transformation of the Workplace in the Twentieth Century.* New York: Basic Books, 1979.

Elias, Norbert. *The Civilizing Process: The Development of Manners.* Translated by Edmund Jephcott. New York: Urizen Books, 1978.

Ely, Richard T. *The Labor Movement in America.* Rev. ed. New York: Macmillan, 1905.

Engerman, Stanley L., and Kenneth L. Sokoloff. "Technology and Industrialization, 1790–1914." In *The Cambridge Economic History of the United States,* vol. 2, *The Long Nineteenth Century,* edited by Stanley L. Engerman and Robert E. Gallman, 367–401. New York: Cambridge University Press, 2000.

English, Beth. "'I Have . . . a Lot of Work to Do': Cotton Mill Work and Women's Culture in Matoaca, Virginia, 1885–95." *Virginia Magazine of History and Biography* 114, no. 3 (2006): 357–83.

Enstad, Nan. *Ladies of Labor, Girls of Adventure: Working Women, Popular Culture, and Labor Politics at the Turn of the Twentieth Century.* New York: Columbia University Press, 1999.

Esch, Elizabeth, and David Roediger. "One Symptom of Originality: Race and the Management of Labour in the History of the United States." *Historical Materialism* 17, no. 4 (2009): 3–43.

Evans, Chris. *History of United Mine Workers of America from the Year 1890 to 1900*. Vol. 2. Indianapolis: n.p., 1918?–20.

"An Exposition of Safety Devices and Industrial Hygiene." *Scientific American,* January 26, 1907, 93.

Fairchild, Amy L. *Science at the Borders: Immigrant Medical Inspection and the Shaping of the Modern Industrial Labor Force*. Baltimore, MD: Johns Hopkins University Press, 2003.

Farrell, James J. *Inventing the American Way of Death, 1830–1920*. Philadelphia: Temple University Press, 1980.

Faunce, William A., and Robert L. Fulton. "The Sociology of Death: A Neglected Area of Research." *Social Forces* 36 (March 1958): 205–9.

Faust, Drew Gilpin. *This Republic of Suffering: Death and the American Civil War*. New York: Alfred A. Knopf, 2008.

Fay, Albert H. *Coal Mine Fatalities in the United States, 1870–1914*. Washington, DC: Government Printing Office, 1916.

Feifel, Herman, ed. *The Meaning of Death*. New York: McGraw-Hill, 1959.

Feldman, Herman. *Racial Factors in American Industry*. New York: Harper and Brothers, 1931.

Feurer, Rosemary, ed. *Remember Virden, 1898*. Chicago: Illinois Humanities Council, 1998.

Filene, Peter G. "An Obituary for 'the Progressive Movement.'" *American Quarterly* 22, no. 1 (1970): 20–34.

Fink, Leon. "Looking Backward: Reflections on Workers' Culture and Certain Dilemmas within Labor History." In *In Search of the Working Class: Essays in American Labor History and Political Culture*, 175–200. Urbana: University of Illinois Press, 1994.

———. *Workingmen's Democracy: The Knights of Labor and American Politics*. Urbana: University of Illinois Press, 1985.

Fischback, Price V. "The Miners Work Environment: Safety and Company Towns in the Early 1900s." In *The United Mine Workers of America: A Model of Industrial Solidarity?*, edited by John H. M. Laslett, 201–23. University Park: Pennsylvania State University Press, 1996.

Fitch, John A. "The Closed Shop." *Survey,* November 8, 1919, 91.

———. "The Labor Policies of Unrestricted Capital." *Survey,* April 6, 1912, 17.

———. "Old Age at 40." *American Magazine,* March 1911, 655–64.

———. *The Steel Workers*. 1910. Reprint, Pittsburgh, PA: University of Pittsburgh Press, 1989.

Flanagan, Maureen. *America Reformed: Progressives and Progressivisms, 1890s–1920s*. New York: Oxford University Press, 2007.

Flynn, Elizabeth Gurley. *The Rebel Girl: An Autobiography*. New York: International, 1973.

Foner, Eric. *Free Soil, Free Labor, Free Men: The Ideology of the Republican Party before the Civil War*. New York: Oxford University Press, 1970.

Foner, Nancy, and George M. Frederickson, eds. *Not Just Black and White: Historical and Contemporary Perspectives on Immigration, Race, and Ethnicity in the United States*. New York: Russell Sage Foundation, 2004.

Foner, Philip. *History of the Labor Movement in the United States*. Vol. 3, *The Policies and Practices of the American Federation of Labor, 1900–1909*. New York: International, 1964.
———. *History of the Labor Movement in the United States*. Vol. 4, *The Industrial Workers of the World, 1905–1917*. New York. International Publishers, 1965.
———. *Organized Labor and the Black Worker, 1619–1973*. New York: Praeger, 1974.
Foster, William Z. *The Great Steel Strike*. 1920. Reprint, New York: Arno Press, 1969.
Foucault, Michel. *The History of Sexuality*. Translated by Robert Hurley. New York: Vintage Books, 1990.
Fox, Maier B. *United We Stand: The United Mine Workers of America, 1890–1990*. Washington, DC: United Mine Workers of America, 1990.
Francis, Owen. "The Saga of Joe Magarac: Steelman." *Scribner's Magazine*, November 1931, 505–11.
French, Stanley. "The Cemetery as Cultural Institution: The Establishment of Mount Auburn and the 'Rural Cemetery Movement.'" In *Death in America*, edited by David E. Stannard, 69–91. Philadelphia: University of Pennsylvania Press, 1974.
Funchion, Michael F. "Irish Chicago: Church, Homeland, Politics, and Class—the Shaping of an Ethnic Group, 1870–1900." In *Ethnic Chicago: A Multicultural Portrait*, edited by Melvin G. Holli and Peter d' A. Jones, 57–92. Grand Rapids, MI: William B. Eerdmans, 1995.
Garland, Hamlin. "Homestead and Its Perilous Trades: Impressions of a Visit." *McClure's Magazine*, June 1894, 3–20.
———. *Prairie Radical: Writings from the 1890s*. Edited by Donald Pizer. Urbana: University of Illinois Press, 2010.
Gebhart, John C. *The Reasons for Present-Day Funeral Costs: A Summary of Facts Developed by the Advisory Committee on Burial Survey in the Course of an Impartial Study of the Burial Industry*. New York: Metropolitan Life Insurance, 1926.
Geertz, Clifford. *The Interpretation of Cultures*. New York: Basic Books, 1973.
Genovese, Eugene. *Roll, Jordan, Roll: The World the Slaves Made*. New York: Pantheon Books, 1974.
George, Henry. *Progress and Poverty*. Garden City, NY: Doubleday, Page, 1879.
George, John E. "The Coal Miners' Strike of 1897." *Quarterly Journal of Economics* 12, no. 2 (1898): 186–208.
———. "The Settlement in the Coal-Mining Industry." *Quarterly Journal of Economics* 12, no. 4 (1898): 447–60.
Gilbert, James. *Perfect Cities: Chicago's Utopias of 1893*. Chicago: University of Chicago Press, 1991.
Gilley, Jennifer, and Stephen Burnett. "Deconstructing and Reconstructing Pittsburgh's Man of Steel: Reading Joe Magarac against the Context of the 20th-Century Steel Industry." *Journal of American Folklore* 111, no. 442 (1998): 392–408.
Gillman, Howard. *The Constitution Besieged: The Rise and Demise of "Lochner" Era Police Powers Jurisprudence*. Durham, NC: Duke University Press, 1993.
Gilmore, Glenda Elizabeth. *Who Were the Progressives?* Boston: Bedford/St. Martin's, 2002.
Ginger, Ray. *Age of Excess: The United States from 1877 to 1914*. New York: Macmillan, 1965.
Glickman, Lawrence. *A Living Wage: American Workers and the Making of Consumer Society*. Ithaca, NY: Cornell University Press, 1997.

Goldberg, Joseph P., and William T. Moye. *The First Hundred Years of the Bureau of Labor Statistics*. Washington, DC: Government Printing Office, 1985.

Goldman, Emma. *Living My Life, in Two Volumes*. Vol. 1. Garden City, NY: Garden City, 1931.

Goldmark, Josephine. *Fatigue and Efficiency: A Study in Industry*. New York: Survey Associates, 1912.

Golin, Steve. *The Fragile Bridge: Paterson Silk Strike, 1913*. Philadelphia: Temple University Press, 1988.

Gompers, Samuel. "Address to the Annual Meeting of the National Civic Federation (1916)." In *Milestone Documents of American Leaders*, edited by Paul Finkelman, 2:853–54. Dallas: Schlager Group, 2009.

———. "Employers' Liability Law and the Courts." *American Federationist* 14, no. 5 (1907): 330–32.

———. "What Does Labor Want?" Paper presented at the International Labor Congress, Chicago, September 1893.

Goodrich, Carter. *The Miner's Freedom: A Study of the Working Life in a Changing Industry*. Boston: Marshall Jones, 1925.

Goody, Jack. *Death, Property, and the Ancestors: A Study of the Mortuary Customs of the Lodagaa of West Africa*. Stanford, CA: Stanford University Press, 1962.

———. "Death and the Interpretation of Culture: A Bibliographic Overview." *American Quarterly* 26 (December 1974): 448–55.

Gordon, David M., Richard Edwards, and Michael Reich. *Segmented Work, Divided Workers: The Historical Transformation of Labor in the United States*. New York: Cambridge University Press, 1982.

Gordon, Linda. *The Great Arizona Orphan Abduction*. Cambridge, MA: Harvard University Press, 1999.

———. *Pitied but Not Entitled: Single Mothers and the History of Welfare, 1890–1935*. New York: Free Press, 1994.

Gordon, Robert W. "Law as a Vocation: Holmes and the Lawyer's Path." In *The Path of the Law and Its Influence: The Legacy of Oliver Wendell Holmes, Jr.*, edited by Steven J. Burton, 7–32. New York: Cambridge University Press, 2000.

Gorer, Geoffrey. *Death, Grief, and Mourning in Contemporary Britain*. London: Cresset Press, 1965.

———. "The Pornography of Death." *Encounter* 5 (October 1955): 49–52.

Gorn, Elliott J. *Mother Jones: The Most Dangerous Women in America*. New York: Hill and Wang, 2001.

Gottlieb, Amy Zahl. "British Coal Miners: A Demographic Study of Braidwood and Streator, Illinois." *Journal of the Illinois State Historical Society* 72, no. 3 (1979): 179–92.

———. "The Influence of British Trade Unionists on the Regulation of the Mining Industry in Illinois, 1872." *Labor History* 19, no. 3 (1978): 397–415.

Gottlieb, Peter. *Making Their Own Way: Southern Blacks' Migration to Pittsburgh, 1916–30*. Urbana: University of Illinois Press, 1987.

Graebner, William. *Coal-Mining Safety in the Progressive Period: The Political Economy of Reform*. Lexington: University Press of Kentucky, 1976.

Grainger, Roger. "Let Death Be Death: Lessons from the Irish Wake." *Mortality* 3, no. 2 (1998): 129–41.

Grant, Madison. *The Passing of the Great Race; or, The Racial Basis of European History.* New York: Charles Scribner's Sons, 1916.
Green, Archie. *Only a Miner: Studies in Recorded Coal-Mining Songs.* Urbana: University of Illinois Press, 1972.
———. *Wobblies, Pile Butts, and Other Heroes: Laborlore Explorations.* Urbana: University of Illinois Press, 1993.
Green, James. *Death in the Haymarket: A Story of Chicago, the First Labor Movement and the Bombing That Divide Gilded Age America.* New York: Anchor Books, 2006.
Greene, Julie. *Pure and Simple Politics: The American Federation of Labor and Political Activism, 1881–1917.* New York: Cambridge University Press, 1998.
Greenwald, Richard A. *The Triangle Fire, the Protocols of Peace, and Industrial Democracy in Progressive Era New York.* Philadelphia: Temple University Press, 2005.
Grier, Katherine C. "The Decline of the Memory Palace: The Parlor after 1890." In *American Home Life, 1880–1930: A Social History of Spaces and Services*, edited by Jessica H. Foy and Thomas J. Schlereth, 49–74. Knoxville: University of Tennessee Press, 1992.
Grimes, Ronald L. *Deeply into the Bone: Re-inventing Rites of Passage.* Berkeley: University of California Press, 2000.
Grosh, Rev. A. B. *The Odd Fellows Manual.* New York: Clark and Maynard, 1874.
Grossman, James R. "African-American Migration to Chicago." In *Ethnic Chicago: A Multicultural Portrait,* edited by Melvin G. Holli and Peter d' A. Jones, 303–40. Grand Rapids, MI: William Eerdmans, 1995.
———. *Land of Hope: Chicago, Black Southerners, and the Great Migration.* Chicago: University of Chicago Press, 1989.
Guglielmo, Thomas. *White on Arrival: Italians, Race, Color, and Power in Chicago, 1890–1945.* New York: Oxford University Press, 2003.
Gupta, Akhil, and James Ferguson. "Beyond 'Culture': Space, Identity, and the Politics of Difference." In *Culture, Power, Place: Explorations in Critical Anthropology*, edited by Akhil Gupta and James Ferguson, 33–51. Durham, NC: Duke University Press, 1997.
Gutman, Herbert. "Labor in the Land of Lincoln: Coal Miners on the Prairie." In *Power and Culture: Essays on the American Working Class*, edited by Ira Berlin, 117–212. New York: Pantheon Books, 1987.
———. "The Labor Policies of the Large Corporation in the Gilded Age: The Case of the Standard Oil Company." In *Power and Culture: Essays on the American Working Class*, edited by Ira Berlin, 213–54. New York: Pantheon Books, 1987.
———. "Protestantism and the American Labor Movement: The Christian Spirit in the Gilded Age." *American Historical Review* 72 (October 1966): 74–101.
———. *Work, Culture, and Society in Industrializing America.* New York: Vintage Books, 1977.
Halttunen, Karen. *Confidence Men and Painted Women: A Study of Middle Class Culture in America, 1830–1870.* New Haven, CT: Yale University Press, 1982.
Hamilton, Alice. *Exploring the Dangerous Trades.* Boston: Little, Brown, 1943.
Hapgood, Hutchins. *The Spirit of Labor.* Edited by James R. Barrett. 1907. Reprint, Urbana: University of Illinois Press, 2004.
Hapke, Laura. "Phillip Bonosky's *Burning Valley.*" *Solidarity.* http://www.solidarity-us.org/node/1964 (accessed May 21, 2013).
Hard, William. "The Law of the Killed and Wounded." *Everybody's Magazine*, September 1908, 361–71.

———. "Making Steel and Killing Men." *Everybody's Magazine*, November 1907, 579–99.
Haring, H. A. "Three Classes of Labor to Avoid: Prejudices and Habits Displayed by Men in Certain Occupations." *Industrial Management* 62, no. 6 (1921): 370–73.
Harper, Samuel A. *The Law of Workmen's Compensation in Illinois: The Illinois Workmen's Compensation Act of 1913 with Discussion and Annotations, Tables and Forms.* Chicago: Callaghan, 1914.
Harris, Neil. "The Cemetery Beautiful." In *Passing: The Vision of Death in America*, edited by Charles O. Jackson, 103–11. Westport, CT: Greenwood Press, 1977.
Harvey, David. *The Condition of Postmodernity: An Enquiry into the Origins of Cultural Change.* Cambridge, MA: Blackwell, 1990.
———. *Consciousness and the Urban Experience: Studies in the History and Theory of Capitalist Urbanization.* Baltimore, MD: Johns Hopkins University Press, 1985.
———. *Social Justice and the City.* Baltimore, MD: Johns Hopkins University Press, 1973.
Hawkins, Mike. *Social Darwinism in European and American Thought, 1860–1945: Nature as Model and Nature as Threat.* New York: Cambridge University Press, 1997.
Hayden, Dolores. *The Power of Place: Urban Landscapes as Public History.* Cambridge, MA: MIT Press, 1995.
Hayhurst, E. R. "Health of Illinois Coal Miners." In *Report of the Health Insurance Commission of the State of Illinois*, 376–402. Springfield: Illinois State Journal, 1919.
Haywood, Big Bill. *Bill Haywood's Book: The Autobiography of William D. Haywood.* New York: International, 1929.
Henrik, Burton J. *The Life of Andrew Carnegie.* 2 vols. Garden City, NY: Doubleday, Doran, 1932.
"The Heroes of the Locomotive." *Locomotive Engineers' Monthly Journal* 1, no. 4 (1867): 1–3.
Hertz, Robert. *Death and the Right Hand.* 1906. English translation, Glencoe, IL: Free Press, 1960.
Hicken, Victor. "The Virden and Pana Mine Wars of 1898." *Journal of the Illinois State Historical Society* 52, no. 2 (1959): 263–78.
Hicks, John D. *The Populist Revolt: A History of the Farmers' Alliance and the People's Party.* Minneapolis: University of Minnesota Press, 1931.
Higbie, Frank T. *Indispensable Outcasts: Hobo Workers and Community in the American Midwest, 1880–1930.* Urbana: University of Illinois Press, 2003.
Higham, John. *Strangers in the Land: Patterns of American Nativism, 1860–1925.* New Brunswick, NJ: Rutgers University Press, 1955.
Hijiya, James A. "American Gravestones and Attitudes toward Death: A Brief History." *Proceedings of the American Philosophical Society* 127, no. 5 (1983): 339–63.
Hill, Herbert. "Myth-Making as Labor History: Herbert Gutman and the United Mine Workers of America." *International Journal of Politics, Culture and Society* 2, no. 2 (1988): 132–200.
Hill, Rebecca Nell. "Men, Mobs, and Law: Defense Campaigns and U.S. Radical History." PhD diss., University of Minnesota, 2000.
Hillerman, Barbara Dodd. "Chrysallis of Gloom: Nineteenth Century American Mourning Costume." In *A Time to Mourn: Expressions of Grief in Nineteenth Century America*, edited by Martha V. Pike and Janice Gray Armstrong, 91–106. Stony Brook, NY: Museums at Stony Brook, 1980.

Hillquit, Morris. *Socialism and the National Civic Federation*. New York: n.p., 1911.
Hirsch, Arnold R. *Making the Second Ghetto: Race and Housing in Chicago, 1940–1960*. 1983. Reprint, Chicago: University of Chicago Press, 1998.
Historical Society of Oak Park and River Forest. *Nature's Choicest Spot: A Guide to Forest Home and German Waldheim Cemeteries*. Oak Park, IL: Historical Society of Oak Park and River Forest, 1998.
Hobsbawm, Eric. "Introduction: Inventing Traditions." In *The Invention of Tradition*, edited by Eric Hobsbawm and Terence Ranger, 1–14. New York: Cambridge University Press, 1983.
———. *Workers: Worlds of Labor*. New York: Pantheon Books, 1984.
Hockey, Jenny. "Changing Death Rituals." In *Grief, Mourning and Death Ritual*, edited by Jenny Hockey and Jeanne Katz, 185–211. Philadelphia: Open University Press, 2001.
———. "Women in Grief: Cultural Representation and Social Practice." In *Death, Gender and Ethnicity*, edited by Jenny Hockey and Neil Small David Field, 89–107. New York: Routledge, 1997.
Hoffman, Beatrix. *The Wages of Sickness: The Politics of Health Insurance in Progressive America*. Chapel Hill: University of North Carolina Press, 2001.
Hoffman, Frederick L. "Fatal Accidents in Coal Mining." *Bulletin of the Bureau of Labor*, no. 90 (1910): 437–674.
———. "Industrial Accidents." *Bulletin of the Bureau of Labor* 27, no. 78 (1908): 417–65.
———. "Industrial Accidents in the United States and Their Relative Frequency in Different Occupations." Address presented at the Detroit Conference of Accident Underwriters, Milwaukee, 1914.
———. "Pauper Burials and the Interment of the Dead in Large Cities." Address presented at the National Conference of Social Work, Atlantic City, NJ, June 4, 1919.
Hofstadter, Richard. *Social Darwinism in American Thought*. 1944. Reprint, Boston: Beacon Press, 1992.
Hoganson, Kristin L. *Fighting for American Manhood: How Gender Politics Provoked the Spanish-American and Philippine-American Wars*. New Haven, CT: Yale University Press, 1998.
Hogg, J. Bernard. "The Homestead Strike of 1892." PhD diss., University of Chicago, 1943.
Holt, James. "Trade Unionism in the British and U.S. Steel Industries, 1880–1914." *Labor History* 18, no. 1 (1977): 5–31.
Holt, Marilyn Irvin. *The Orphan Trains*. Lincoln: University of Nebraska Press, 1992.
Homestead: The Story of a Steel Town, 1860–1945. Pittsburgh: Historical Society of Western Pennsylvania, 1988.
Horton, Frederick W. *Coal-Mine Accidents in the United States, 1896–1912, with Monthly Statistics for 1912*. Washington, DC: Government Printing Office, 1913.
———. *Coal-Mine Accidents in the United States and Foreign Countries*. Washington, DC: Government Printing Office, 1913.
Hours of Work as Related to Output and Health of Workers: Silk Manufacturing. Boston: National Industrial Conference Board, 1919.
Howells, W. D. "A Sennight of the Centennial." *Atlantic Monthly*, July 1876, 96.
Hucke, Matt, and Ursula Bielski. *Graveyards of Chicago*. Chicago: Lake Claremont Press, 1999.

Hughes, Langston, and Arna Bontemps, eds. *The Book of Negro Folklore*. New York: Dodd, Mead, 1958.

Hume, Janice. *Obituaries in American Culture*. Jackson: University Press of Mississippi, 2000.

Hunter, Louis C. *A History of Industrial Power in the United States, 1780–1930*. Vol. 2, *Steam Power*. Charlottesville: University Press of Virginia, 1985.

Illinois Bureau of Labor Statistics. *Coal in Illinois, 1893*. Springfield, IL: H. W. Rokker, 1894.

———. *Coal in Illinois, 1894: Containing the Eleventh Annual Reports of the State Inspectors of Mines*. Edited by George A. Schilling. Springfield, IL: Ed. F. Hartman, 1895.

———. *Coal in Illinois, 1898: Containing the Fifteenth Annual Report of the State Inspector of Mines*. Springfield, IL: Phillips Brothers, 1899.

———. *Eighteenth Annual Coal Report, 1899*. Springfield, IL: Phillips Brothers, 1899.

———. *Fourth Biennial Report of the Bureau of Labor Statistics of Illinois*. Springfield, IL: H. W. Rokker, 1886.

———. *Statistics of Coal in Illinois, 1887*. Springfield, IL: H. W. Rokker, 1887.

———. *Statistics of Coal in Illinois, 1889*. Springfield, IL: Springfield Printing, 1890.

———. *Statistics of Coal in Illinois, 1891*. Springfield, IL: H. W. Rokker, 1891.

———. *Statistics of Coal Production in Illinois, 1883: A Supplemental Report of the State Bureau of Labor Statistics*. Springfield, IL: H. W. Rokker, 1883.

———. *Third Biennial Report of the Bureau of Labor Statistics of Illinois*. Springfield, IL: H. W. Rokker, 1884.

———. *Thirteenth Biennial Report of the Bureau of Labor Statistics of the State of Illinois, 1904*. Springfield, IL: Phillips Brothers, 1907.

———. *Twenty-Fourth Annual Coal Report, 1905*. Springfield: Illinois State Journal, 1906.

Ingham, John N. "A Strike in the Progressive Era: McKees Rocks, 1909." *Pennsylvania Magazine of History and Biography* 90, no. 3 (1966): 353–77.

Isenberg, Nancy, and Andrew Burstein, eds. *Mortal Remains: Death in Early America*. Philadelphia: University of Pennsylvania Press, 2003.

Jackson, Charles O. "Death in American Life." In *Passing: The Vision of Death in America*, edited by Charles O. Jackson, 229–43. Westport, CT: Greenwood Press, 1977.

Jackson, Kenneth T., and Camilo José Vergara. *Silent Cities: The Evolution of the American Cemetery*. New York: Princeton Architectural Press, 1989.

Jacobson, Matthew Frye. *Barbarian Virtues: The United States Encounters Foreign Peoples at Home and Abroad, 1876–1917*. New York: Hill and Wang, 2000.

———. *Whiteness of a Different Color: European Immigrants and the Alchemy of Race*. Cambridge, MA: Harvard University Press, 1998.

Jacoby, Sanford M. *Employing Bureaucracy: Managers, Unions and the Transformation of Work in the 20th Century*. Mahwah, NJ: Lawrence Erlbaum Associates, 2004.

James, William. "What Makes a Life Significant." In *Talks to Teachers on Psychology: And to Students on Some of Life's Ideals*, 265–301. New York: Hill and Wang, 1899.

Jensen, Richard. *The Winning of the Midwest: Social and Political Conflict, 1888–1896*. Chicago: University of Chicago Press, 1971.

Johnson, Russell L. *Warriors to Workers: The Civil War and the Formation of Urban-Industrial Society in a Northern City*. New York: Fordham University Press, 2003.

Jones, Dot. "Serfdom and Slavery: Women's Work in Wales, 1890–1930." In *Class, Community and the Labour Movement: Wales and Canada, 1850–1930*, edited by Deian

R. Hopkin and Gregory S. Kealey, 86–100. St. John's, Newfoundland: Committee on Canadian Labour History, 1989.

Jones, Esyllt. "Politicizing the Laboring Body: Working Families, Death, and Burial in Winnipeg's Influenza Epidemic, 1918–1919." *Labor: Studies in Working-Class History of the Americas* 3, no. 3 (2006): 57–75.

Jones, Mary Harris. *The Autobiography of Mother Jones*. 1925. Reprint, Chicago: Charles H. Kerr, 1990.

Journal of the House of Representatives of the Thirty-Third General Assembly. Springfield, IL: H. W. Rokker, 1883.

Journal of the Senate of the Thirty-Third General Assembly of the State of Illinois. Springfield, IL: H. W. Rokker, 1883.

Justi, Herman. "Common Sense and the Labor Problem." In *Miner's Prospectus*. Reprinted in *The Labor Problem in the United States: An Independent Contribution towards Its Solution*. New York: Atheneum, 1878.

Kalisch, Philip A. "Death Down Below: Coal Mine Disasters in Three Illinois Counties, 1904–1962." *Journal of the Illinois State Historical Society* 65, no. 1 (1972): 5–21.

Kanigel, Robert. *The One Best Way: Frederick Winslow Taylor and the Enigma of Efficiency*. New York: Viking, 1997.

Karsten, Peter. *Heart versus Head: Judge-Made Law in Nineteenth-Century America*. Chapel Hill: University of North Carolina Press, 1997.

Kasson, John F. *Civilizing the Machine: Technology and Republican Values in America, 1776–1900*. New York: Grossman, 1976.

———. *Houdini, Tarzan, and the Perfect Man: The White Male Body and the Challenge of Modernity in America*. New York: Hill and Wang, 2001.

Kaster, Gregory L. "Labour's True Man: Organised Workingmen and the Language of Manliness in the USA, 1827–1877." *Gender and History* 13, no. 1 (2001): 24–64.

Katzman, David M., and William M. Tuttle Jr., eds. *Plain Folk: The Life Stories of Undistinguished Americans*. Urbana: University of Illinois Press, 1982.

Kauffman, Christopher J. *Faith and Fraternalism: The History of the Knights of Columbus, 1882–1982*. New York: Harper and Row, 1982.

Kaufman, Jason. *For the Common Good? American Civic Life and the Golden Age of Fraternity*. New York: Oxford University Press, 2002.

Kaufman, Stuart B., and Peter J. Albert, eds. *The American Federation of Labor and the Rise of Progressivism, 1902–6*. Vol. 6 of *The Samuel Gompers Papers*. Urbana: University of Illinois Press, 1997.

———. *The American Federation of Labor under Siege, 1906–9*. Vol. 7 of *The Samuel Gompers Papers*. Urbana: University of Illinois Press, 1999.

Kearl, Michael. "Death as a Measure of Life: A Research Note on the Kastenbaum-Spilka Strategy of Obituary Analysis." *Omega* 1, no. 17 (1986–87): 68–78.

Keiser, John H. "Black Strikebreakers and Racism in Illinois, 1865–1900." *Journal of the Illinois State Historical Society* 65, no. 3 (1972): 313–26.

———. *Building for the Centuries: Illinois, 1865 to 1898*. Urbana: University of Illinois Press, 1977.

———. "The Union Miners Cemetery at Mt. Olive, Illinois: A Spirit-Thread of Labor History." *Journal of the Illinois State Historical Society* 62, no. 3 (1969): 229–66.

Kellehear, Allan. *A Social History of Dying*. New York: Cambridge University Press, 2007.

Kelley, Florence. *Modern Industry in Relation to the Family, Health, Education, Morality*. New York: Longmans, Green, 1914.

Kellogg, Paul. "Community and Workshop." In *Wage-Earning Pittsburgh*, edited by Paul U. Kellogg, 3–32. New York: Survey Associates, 1914.

———. "The McKee's Rocks Strike." *Survey*, August 7, 1909, 656–65.

Kennedy, David M. *Over Here: The First World War and American Society*. New York: Oxford University Press, 1986.

Kens, Paul. *"Lochner v. New York": Economic Regulation on Trial*. Lawrence: University Press of Kansas, 1998.

Kephart, William M. "Status after Death." *American Sociological Review* 15, no. 5 (1950): 635–43.

Kertzer, David I. *Ritual, Politics, and Power*. New Haven, CT: Yale University Press, 1988.

Kessler-Harris, Alice. *In Pursuit of Equity: Women, Men, and the Quest for Economic Citizenship in 20th-Century America*. New York: Oxford University Press, 2001.

———. *Out to Work: A History of Wage-Earning Women in the United States*. 20th anniversary ed. New York: Oxford University Press, 2003.

———. "Treating the Male as 'Other': Redefining the Parameters of Labor History." *Labor History* 34 (1993): 190–204.

Kimmel, Michael S. *Manhood in America: A Cultural History*. 2nd ed. New York: Oxford University Press, 2006.

———. "Two Political Cultures in the Progressive Era: The National Consumers' League and the American Association for Labor Legislation." In *U.S. History as Women's History: New Feminist Essays*, edited by Alice Kessler-Harris, Linda K. Kerber, and Kathryn Kish Sklar, 36–62. Chapel Hill: University of North Carolina Press, 1995.

Kleinberg, S. J. "Death and the Working Class." *Journal of Popular Culture* 11 (Summer 1977): 193–209.

———. *The Shadow of the Mills: Working-Class Families in Pittsburgh, 1870–1907*. Pittsburgh, PA: University of Pittsburgh Press, 1989.

———. *Widows and Orphans First: The Family Economy and Social Welfare Policy, 1880–1939*. Urbana: University of Illinois Press, 2006.

Knobel, Dale T. *Paddy and the Republic: Ethnicity and Nationality in Antebellum America*. Middletown, CT: Wesleyan University Press, 1986.

Kolko, Gabriel. *The Triumph of Conservatism: A Reinterpretation of American History, 1900–1916*. New York: Free Press, 1963.

Kornbluh, Joyce L., ed. *Rebel Voices: An I.W.W. Anthology*. Ann Arbor: University of Michigan Press, 1964.

Korson, George. *Coal Dust on the Fiddle: Songs and Stories of the Bituminous Industry*. Philadelphia: University of Pennsylvania Press, 1943.

Koslofsky, Craig M. *The Reformation of the Dead: Death and Ritual in Early Modern Germany, 1450–1700*. New York: St. Martin's Press, 2000.

Koukol, Alois B. "A Slav's a Man for A' That." In *Wage-Earning Pittsburgh*, edited by Paul U. Kellogg, 61–77. New York: Survey Associates, 1914.

Krass, Peter. *Carnegie*. Hoboken, NJ: John Wiley and Sons, 2002.

Krause, Paul. *The Battle for Homestead, 1880–1892: Politics, Culture, and Steel.* Pittsburgh, PA: University of Pittsburgh Press, 1992.

The Labor Problem in the United States: An Independent Contribution towards Its Solution. New York: Atheneum, 1878.

Laderman, Gary. *Rest in Peace: A Cultural History of Death and the Funeral Home in Twentieth-Century America.* New York: Oxford University Press, 2003.

———. *The Sacred Remains: American Attitudes toward Death, 1799–1883.* New Haven, CT: Yale University Press, 1996.

Lang, Lucy Robins. *Tomorrow Is Beautiful.* New York: Macmillan, 1948.

Lankton, Larry. *Cradle to Grave: Life, Work, and Death at the Lake Superior Copper Mines.* New York: Oxford University Press, 1991.

Lantz, Herman R. *People of Coal Town.* New York: Columbia University Press, 1958.

Laqueur, Thomas. "Bodies, Death, and Pauper Funerals." *Representations*, no. 1 (February 1983): 109–30.

Laslett, John H. M. *Colliers across the Sea: A Comparative Study of Class Formation in Scotland and the American Midwest, 1830–1924.* Urbana: University of Illinois Press, 2000.

Laurie, Bruce. *Artisans into Workers: Labor in Nineteenth-Century America.* 1989. Reprint, Urbana: University of Illinois Press, 1997.

Lause, Mark. *Young America: Land, Labor, and the Republican Community.* Urbana: University of Illinois Press, 2005.

Laws of the State of Illinois Enacted by the Thirty-Third General Assembly. Springfield, IL: H. W. Rokker, 1883.

Leavitt, Judith Walzer. *The Healthiest City: Milwaukee and the Politics of Health Reform.* Princeton, NJ: Princeton University Press, 1982.

Lee, Erika. *At America's Gates: Chinese Immigration during the Exclusion Era, 1882–1943.* Chapel Hill: University of North Carolina Press, 2003.

Leichliter, C. H. "The War at Zeigler." *Everyday Magazine*, February 1905, 300–306.

Leonard, Cynthia. "Union Miners Cemetery." *Illinois State Genealogical Society Quarterly* 16, no. 2 (1984): 84–85.

Levine, Susan. *Labor's True Woman: Carpet Weavers, Industrialization, and Labor Reform in the Gilded Age.* Philadelphia: Temple University Press, 1984.

Lewis, Lloyd, and Henry Justin Smith. *Chicago: The History of Its Reputation.* Chicago: Harcourt, Brace, 1929.

Lewis, Ronald L. *Black Coal Miners in America: Race, Class, and Community Conflict, 1780–1980.* Lexington: University Press of Kentucky, 1987.

Licht, Walter. *Industrializing America: The Nineteenth Century.* Baltimore, MD: Johns Hopkins University Press, 1995.

———. "Studying Work: Personnel Policies in Philadelphia Firms, 1850–1950." In *Masters to Managers: Historical and Comparative Perspectives on American Employers*, edited by Sanford Jacoby, 43–73. New York: Columbia University Press, 1987.

———. *Working for the Railroad: The Organization of Work in the Nineteenth Century.* Princeton, NJ: Princeton University Press, 1983.

Linden-Ward, Blanche. *Silent City on a Hill: Landscapes of Memory and Boston's Mount Auburn Cemetery.* Columbus: Ohio State University Press, 1989.

Link, Arthur S., ed. *The Papers of Woodrow Wilson*. Princeton, NJ: Princeton University Press, 1983.
Link, Arthur S., and Richard L. McCormick. *Progressivism*. Arlington Heights, IL: Harlan Davidson, 1983.
Linkh, Richard M. *American Catholicism and European Immigrants, 1900–1924*. New York: Center for Migration Studies, 1975.
Lipsitz, George. *Rainbow at Midnight: Labor and Culture in the 1940s*. Urbana: University of Illinois Press, 1994.
Lloyd, Henry Demarest. *Wealth against Commonwealth*. New York: Harper and Brothers, 1894.
Lodge, Henry Cabot. "The Restriction of Immigration." *North American Review* 152, no. 410 (1891): 27–36.
Long, Priscilla. *Where the Sun Never Shines: A History of America's Bloody Coal Industry*. New York: Paragon House, 1989.
Lukas, J. Anthony. *Big Trouble: A Murder in a Small Western Town Sets Off the Struggle for the Soul of America*. New York: Simon and Schuster, 1997.
Luker, Ralph E. *The Social Gospel in Black and White: American Racial Reform, 1885–1912*. Chapel Hill: University of North Carolina Press, 1991.
MacLaury, Judson. "Government Regulation of Workers' Safety and Health, 1877–1917." United States Department of Labor. http://www.dol.gov/oasam/programs/history/mono-regsafeintrotoc.htm (accessed July 14, 2010).
MacLeod, Malcolm. "A Death at Deer Lake: Catalyst of a Forgotten Newfoundland Strike." *Labour/Le Travail* 16 (1985): 179–92.
Mancini, Matthew J. *One Dies, Get Another: Convict Leasing in the American South, 1866–1928*. Columbia: University of South Carolina Press, 1996.
Mark, Clarence H. "The Industrial Scrap Heap." *American Federationist* 14, no. 2 (1907): 89–91.
Markwell, David. "A Turning Point: The Lasting Impact of the 1898 Virden Riot." *Journal of the Illinois State Historical Society* 99, nos. 3–4 (2006): 211–27.
Matsunami, Kodo. *International Handbook of Funeral Customs*. Westport, CT: Greenwood Press, 1998.
McCartin, Joseph A. *Labor's Great War: The Struggle for Industrial Democracy and the Origins of Modern American Labor Relations, 1912–1921*. Chapel Hill: University of North Carolina Press, 1997.
McDannell, Colleen. "Parlor Piety: The Home as Sacred Space in Protestant America." In *American Home Life, 1880–1930: A Social History of Spaces and Services*, edited by Jessica H. Foy and Thomas J. Schlereth, 162–89. Knoxville: University of Tennessee Press, 1992.
McGerr, Michael E. *A Fierce Discontent: The Rise and Fall of the Progressive Movement in America, 1870–1920*. New York: Free Press, 2003.
McGreevy, John T. *Parish Boundaries: The Catholic Encounter with Race in the Twentieth-Century Urban North*. Chicago: University of Chicago Press, 1996.
McKinley, Blaine. "'A Religion of the New Time': Anarchist Memorials to the Haymarket Martyrs, 1888–1917." *Labor History* 28 (Summer 1987): 386–400.
McLean, George N. *The Rise and Fall of Anarchy in America*. Chicago: R. G. Badoux, 1888.

McLeod, Hugh. *Piety and Poverty: Working-Class Religion in Berlin, London and New York, 1870–1914*. New York: Holmes and Meier, 1996.
McMath, Robert C., Jr. *American Populism: A Social History*. New York: Hill and Wang, 1992.
McNeill, George E. "Coal Miners." In *The Labor Movement: The Problem of To-Day*, edited by George E. McNeill, 241–67. Boston: A. M. Bridgman, 1886.
———, ed. *The Labor Movement: The Problem of Today*. New York: A. M. Bridgman, 1886.
———. "The Philosophy of the Labor Movement." Paper presented at the International Labor Congress, Chicago, September 1893.
———. *A Study of Accidents and Accident Insurance*. Boston: Insurance Topics, 1900.
Meigs, Mark. *Optimism at Armageddon: Voices of American Participants in the First World War*. New York: New York University Press, 1997.
Mellor, Philip A. "Death in High Modernity: The Contemporary Presence and Absence of Death." In *The Sociology of Death: Theory, Culture, Practice*, edited by David Clark, 11–30. Cambridge, MA: Blackwell, 1993.
Meltzer, Milton. *Bread—and Roses: The Struggle of American Labor, 1865–1915*. New York: Alfred A. Knopf, 1967.
Merithew, Caroline Waldron. "'We Were Not Ladies': Gender, Class, and a Women's Auxiliary Battle for Mining Unionism." *Journal of Women's History* 18, no. 2 (2006): 63–94.
Merithew, Caroline Waldron, and James R. Barrett. "'We Are Brothers in the Face of Starvation': Forging an Interethnic Working Class Movement in the 1894 Bituminous Coal Strike." *Mid-America* 83, no. 2 (2001): 121–54.
Messer-Kruse, Timothy. *The Trial of the Haymarket Anarchists: Terrorism and Justice in the Gilded Age*. New York: Palgrave Macmillan, 2011.
Miller, Donald L. *City of the Century: The Epic of Chicago and the Making of America*. New York: Simon and Schuster, 1996.
Miller, Stuart Creighton. *The Unwelcome Immigrant: The American Image of the Chinese, 1785–1882*. Berkeley: University of California Press, 1969.
Mink, Gwendolyn. *Old Labor and New Immigrants in American Political Development: Union, Party, and State, 1875–1920*. Ithaca, NY: Cornell University Press, 1986.
Minutes of the Sixteenth Annual Convention of the United Mine Workers of America. Indianapolis: Cheltenham Press, 1905.
Mitford, Jessica. *The American Way of Death*. New York: Simon and Schuster, 1963.
"Modern Improvements and the Workingmen." *Iron Age* (August 11, 1892): 244.
Montgomery, David. *Citizen Worker: The Experience of Workers in the United States with Democracy and the Free Market during the Nineteenth Century*. New York: Cambridge University Press, 1993.
———. *The Fall of the House of Labor: The Workplace, the State, and American Labor Activism, 1865–1925*. New York: Cambridge University Press, 1987.
———. "Nationalism, American Patriotism, and Class Consciousness among Immigrant Workers in the United States in the Epoch of World War I." In *Struggle a Hard Battle: Essays on Working-Class Immigrants*, edited by Dirk Hoerder, 327–51. DeKalb: Northern Illinois University Press, 1986.
———. "Strikes in Nineteenth Century America." *Social Science History* 4, no. 1 (1980): 81–104.

———. *Workers' Control in America: Studies in the History of Work, Technology, and Labor Struggles*. New York: Cambridge University Press, 1979.
Moseley, James G. *A Cultural History of Religion in America*. Westport, CT: Greenwood Press, 1981.
Mudge, S. R. "Visit to Albany, N.Y." *Locomotive Engineers' Monthly Journal* 1, no. 4 (1867): 21–22.
Murphy, Kevin P. *Political Manhood: Red Bloods, Mollycoddles, and the Politics of Progressive Era Reform*. New York: Columbia University Press, 2008.
Murray, Robert K. *Red Scare: A Study in National Hysteria, 1919–1920*. Minneapolis: University of Minnesota Press, 1955.
Nasaw, David. *Andrew Carnegie*. New York: Penguin Press, 2006.
Nelson, Bruce C. "Revival and Upheaval: Religion, Irreligion, and Chicago's Working Class in 1886." *Journal of Social History* 25, no. 2 (1991): 233–53.
Nelson, Dana D. *National Manhood: Capitalist Citizenship and the Imagined Fraternity of White Men*. Durham, NC: Duke University Press, 1998.
Nelson, Daniel. *Managers and Workers: Origins of the New Factory System in the United States, 1880–1920*. Madison: University of Wisconsin Press, 1975.
Nelson, Scott Reynolds. *Steel Drivin' Man: John Henry, the Untold Story of an American Legend*. New York: Oxford University Press, 2006.
Neuberger, Julia. *Dying Well: A Guide to Enabling a Good Death*. 2nd ed. San Francisco: Radcliffe, 2004.
Ngai, Mae M. *Impossible Subjects: Illegal Aliens and the Making of Modern America*. Princeton, NJ: Princeton University Press, 2004.
Nutmeg. "The Drivers of the Iron Horse." *Locomotive Engineers' Monthly Journal* 1, no. 4 (1867): 5–6.
Oberdeck, Kathryn J. *The Evangelist and the Impresario: Religion, Entertainment, and Cultural Politics in America, 1884–1914*. Baltimore, MD: Johns Hopkins University Press, 1999.
"Obituary." *Locomotive Engineers' Monthly Journal* 1, no. 3 (1867): 23–24.
Oblinger, Carl D. *Divided Kingdom: Work, Community, and the Mining Wars in the Central Illinois Coal Fields during the Great Depression*. Springfield: Illinois State Historical Society, 1991.
O'Connor, Edwin. *The Last Hurrah*. Boston: Little, Brown, 1956.
O'Connor, Stephen. *Orphan Trains: The Story of Charles Loring Brace and the Children He Saved and Failed*. New York: Houghton Mifflin, 2001.
Odencrantz, Louise C. *Italian Women in Industry*. New York: Russell Sage Foundation, 1919.
O'Donnell, Edward. "Women as Bread Winners: The Error of the Age." *American Federationist* 4 (1897): 186–87.
"On Being 75: A Look Back." Special supp., *U.S. Steel News* 41, no. 2 (1976).
"One Cause of Steam Boiler Accidents." *Locomotive Engineers' Monthly Journal* 1, no. 3 (1867): 11–12.
Orleck, Annelise. *Common Sense and a Little Fire: Women and Working-Class Politics in the United States, 1900–1965*. Chapel Hill: University of North Carolina Press, 1995.
Orsi, Robert Anthony. *The Madonna of 115th Street: Faith and Community in Italian Harlem, 1880–1950*. New Haven, CT: Yale University Press, 1985.

Ortiz, Paul. *Emancipation Betrayed: The Hidden History of Black Organizing and White Violence in Florida from Reconstruction to the Bloody Election of 1920*. Berkeley: University of California Press, 2005.

O'Súilleabháin, Seán. *Irish Wake Amusements*. Cork: Mercier Press, 1967.

"Other Labor Controversies." *Independent*, August 25, 1904, 414.

Ozanne, Robert. *A Century of Labor-Management Relations at McCormick and International Harvester*. Madison: University of Wisconsin Press, 1967.

Page, Brian D. "Local Matters: Race, Place, and Community Politics after the Civil War." PhD diss., Ohio State University, 2009.

Patterson, I. R. "From Div. No. 72." *Locomotive Engineers' Monthly Journal* 1, no. 5 (1867): 6–7.

Pattison, William D. "The Cemeteries of Chicago: A Phase of Land Utilization." *Annals of the Association of American Geographers* 45, no. 3 (1955): 245–57.

———. "Land for the Dead of Chicago." Master's thesis, University of Chicago, 1952.

Peck, Gunther. "Manly Gambles: The Politics of Risk on the Comstock Lode, 1860–1880." *Journal of Social History* 26, no. 4 (1993): 701–23.

Peiss, Kathy. *Cheap Amusements: Working Women and Leisure in Turn-of-the-Century New York*. Philadelphia: Temple University Press, 1986.

Pessano, Antonio C. "The Organization of Manufacturers: A Necessity to Obtain the Best Results from Organized Labor." *Iron Age* 67 (March 14, 1901): 21–25.

Phelan, Craig. *Divided Loyalties: The Public and Private Life of Labor Leader John Mitchell*. Albany: State University of New York Press, 1994.

Piehler, G. Kurt. "The War Dead and the Gold Star: American Commemoration of the First World War." In *Commemorations: The Politics of National Identity*, edited by John R. Gillis, 168–85. Princeton, NJ: Princeton University Press, 1994.

"Piety in the Coal-Pits." *Christian Recorder* (Philadelphia), September 28, 1872.

Pittenger, Mark. "A World of Difference: Constructing the 'Underclass' in Progressive America." *American Quarterly* 49, no. 1 (1997): 26–65.

Pitti, Stephen J. *The Devil in Silicon Valley: Northern California, Race, and Mexican Americans*. Princeton, NJ: Princeton University Press, 2003.

Pittsburgh and Allegheny Directory. Pittsburgh, PA: R. L. Polk and R. L. Dudley, 1900.

Pleck, Elizabeth. *Celebrating the Family: Ethnicity, Consumer Culture, and Family Rituals*. Cambridge, MA: Harvard University Press, 2000.

———. *Domestic Tyranny: The Making of American Social Policy against Family Violence from Colonial Times to the Present*. 1987. Reprint, Urbana: University of Illinois Press, 2004.

———. "A Mother's Wages: Income Earning among Married Italian and Black Women, 1896–1911." In *The American Family in Social Historical Perspective*, edited by Michael Gordon, 490–510. 2nd ed. New York: St. Martin's Press, 1978.

Plumbe, George E., ed. *The Daily News Almanac and Political Register for 1898*. Chicago: Chicago Daily News, 1898.

Porter, Glenn. "Industrialization and the Rise of Big Business." In *The Gilded Age: Essays on the Origins of Modern America*, edited by Charles W. Calhoun, 1–18. Wilmington, DE: SR Books, 1996.

Proceedings of the Joint Executive Board Meeting of the Coal Operators' Association of the Fifth and Ninth Districts of Illinois and the United Mine Workers of America District No. 12, January 11, 12, 13, 14 and 15, 1921. St. Louis: n.p., 1921.

Proceedings of the Joint Executive Board Meeting of the Coal Operators' Association of the Fifth and Ninth Districts of Illinois and the United Mine Workers of America District No. 12, February 8, 9, 15 and 16, 1921. St. Louis: n.p., 1921.

Proceedings of the Twentieth Annual Convention of the National Lodge, A. A. of I. and S. W. Held in Cleveland, Ohio, May 21–June 1. Pittsburgh, PA: n.p., 1895.

"Progressive 'Labor' Decision." *Chautauquan* 66 (April 1912): 148.

Puckle, Bertram S. *Funeral Customs: Their Origin and Development*. London: T. Werner Laurie, 1926.

Rabinbach, Anson. *The Human Motor: Energy, Fatigue, and the Origins of Modernity*. Berkeley: University of California Press, 1990.

Rabinowitz, Howard N. *Race Relations in the Urban South, 1865–1890*. New York: Oxford University Press, 1978.

Rakes, Paul H. "Acceptable Casualties: Power, Culture, and History in the West Virginia Coalfields, 1900–1945." PhD diss., West Virginia University, 2002.

Ramirez, Bruno. *When Workers Fight: The Politics of Industrial Relations in the Progressive Era, 1898–1916*. Westport, CT: Greenwood Press, 1978.

Rauschenbusch, Walter. "The Ideals of Social Reformers." *American Journal of Sociology* 2, no. 2 (1896): 202–19.

———. "The Stake of the Church in the Social Movement." *American Journal of Sociology* 3, no. 1 (1897): 18–30.

Reed, Christopher Robert. *Black Chicago's First Century*. Vol. 1, *1833–1900*. Columbia: University of Missouri Press, 2005.

Report of the Industrial Commission on the Relations and Conditions of Capital and Labor Employed in the Mining Industry. Washington, DC: Government Printing Office, 1901.

Report of the Joint Special Committee to Investigate Chinese Immigration. Washington, DC: Government Printing Office, 1877. Reprint, New York: Arno Press, 1978.

Report on Conditions of Employment in the Iron and Steel Industry in the United States. Vol. 3, *Working Conditions and the Relations of Employers and Employees*. Washington, DC: Government Printing Office, 1913.

Report on Conditions of Employment in the Iron and Steel Industry in the United States. Vol. 4, *Accidents and Accident Prevention*. Washington, DC: Government Printing Office, 1913.

Reports of the Industrial Commission on Immigration. Washington, DC: Government Printing Office, 1901.

Rice, Stephen P. *Minding the Machine: Languages of Class in Early Industrial America*. Berkeley: University of California Press, 2004.

Richardson, Ruth. *Death, Dissection, and the Destitute*. 2nd ed. 1987. Reprint, Chicago: University of Chicago Press, 2000.

"The Risks and Diseases of Toil." *Independent* 55 (January 15, 1903): 154–55.

Roberts, Peter. "Immigrant Wage-Earners." In *Wage-Earning Pittsburgh*, edited by Paul U. Kellogg, 33–60. New York: Survey Associates, 1914.

Robinson, Jesse S. *The Amalgamated Association of Iron, Steel and Tin Workers*. Baltimore, MD: Johns Hopkins University Press, 1920.

Rodgers, Daniel T. *Atlantic Crossings: Social Politics in a Progressive Age*. Cambridge, MA: Harvard University Press, 1998.

———. "In Search of Progressivism." *Reviews in American History* 10, no. 4 (1982): 113–32.

———. "Republicanism: The Career of a Concept." *Journal of American History* 79, no. 1 (1992): 11–38.

Roediger, David R. "And Die in Dixie: Funerals, Death, and Heaven in the Slave Community, 1700–1865." *Massachusetts Review* 22 (1981): 163–83.

———. *How Race Survived History: From Settlement and Slavery to the Obama Phenomenon*. New York: Verso, 2008.

———. *The Wages of Whiteness: Race and the Making of the American Working Class*. Rev. ed. New York: Verso, 1999.

———. *Working toward Whiteness: How America's Immigrants Became White; The Strange Journey from Ellis Island to the Suburbs*. New York: Basic Books, 2005.

Roediger, David R., and Philip S. Foner. *Our Own Time: A History of American Labor and the Working Day*. Westport, CT: Greenwood Press, 1989.

Roediger, David R., and Franklin Rosemont, eds. *The Haymarket Scrapbook*. Chicago: Charles H. Kerr, 1986.

Roethlisberger, F. J., and W. J. Dickson. *Management and the Worker: Technical vs. Social Organization in an Industrial Plant*. Cambridge, MA: Harvard University Press, 1934.

Rogers, Donald Wayne. *Making Capitalism Safe: Work Safety and Health Regulation in America, 1880–1940*. Urbana: University of Illinois Press, 2009.

Roosevelt, Theodore. "Sarah Knisley's Arm." Pts. 1 and 2. *Collier's*, January 25, 1913, 8–9, 22–23; February 1, 1913, 8–9.

———. "Value of an Athletic Training." *Harper's Weekly*, December 23, 1893, 1236.

Rose, Sarah F. "'Crippled' Hands: Disability in Labor and Working-Class History." *Labor: Studies in Working Class History of the Americas* 2, no. 1 (2005): 27–54.

Rose, Sonya O. "Class Formation and the Quintessential Worker." In *Reworking Class*, edited by John R. Hall, 133–68. Ithaca, NY: Cornell University Press, 1997.

Rosenzweig, Roy. *Eight Hours for What We Will: Workers and Leisure in an Industrial City, 1870–1920*. Cambridge: Cambridge University Press, 1983.

Rosner, David, and Gerald Markowitz, eds. *Dying for Work: Workers' Safety and Health in Twentieth-Century America*. Bloomington: Indiana University Press, 1989.

Ross, E. A. *Old World in the New: The Significance of Past and Present Immigration to the American People*. New York: Century, 1914.

Rössel, Jörg. "Industrial Structure, Union Strategy, and Strike Activity in American Bituminous Coal Mining, 1881–1894." *Social Science History* 26, no. 1 (2002): 1–32.

Rotundo, E. Anthony. *American Manhood: Transformations in Masculinity from the Revolution to the Modern Era*. New York: Basic Books, 1993.

Roy, Andrew. *A History of the Coal Miners of the United States*. Columbus, OH: J. L. Trauger, 1903.

Rutherford, H. Richard. *The Death of Christian: The Order of Christian Funerals*. Collegeville, MN: Liturgical Press, 1990.

Ryan, Mary P. *Civic Wars: Democracy and Public Life in the American City during the Nineteenth Century*. Berkeley: University of California Press, 1997.

"Safety and Security." *Outlook*, September 15, 1906, 99.

"A Safety Devices Exhibition." *Outlook*, February 16, 1907, 344.

"The Safety of American Mines." *Colliery Guardian* 95 (January 24, 1908): 174.

Salvatore, Nick. *Eugene V. Debs: Citizen and Socialist*. Urbana: University of Illinois Press, 1982.

Sandburg, Carl. *Chicago Poems*. New York: Henry Holt, 1916.

———. *The Chicago Race Riots: July 1919*. 1919. Reprint, New York: Harcourt, Brace, and World, 1969.

———. "The Sayings of Henry Stephens." In *Carl Sandburg: Selected Poems*, edited by George Hendrick and Willene Hendrick, 167. San Diego: Harcourt, Brace, 1996.

Sangster, Margaret E. *Good Manners for All Occasions: A Practical Manual*. New York: Christian Herald, 1904.

Sartorius von Waltershausen, August. *The Workers' Movement in the United States, 1879–1885*. Translated by Harry Drost. Edited by David and Marcel van der Linden Montgomery. 1886. Reprint, New York: Cambridge University Press, 1998.

Saxton, Alexander. *The Indispensable Enemy: Labor and the Anti-Chinese Movement in California*. Berkeley: University of California Press, 1971.

———. *The Rise and Fall of the White Republic: Class Politics and Mass Culture in Nineteenth-Century America*. 1990. Reprint, New York: Verso, 2003.

Schaack, Michael J. *Anarchy and Anarchists: A History of the Red Terror and the Social Revolution in America*. Chicago: F. J. Schulte, 1889.

Schama, Simon. *The American History: A Future*. New York: Ecco, 2009.

Schantz, Mark S. *Awaiting the Heavenly Country: The Civil War and America's Culture of Death*. Ithaca, NY: Cornell University Press, 2008.

Schlereth, Thomas J. *Victorian America: Transformations in Everyday Life, 1876–1915*. New York: HarperCollins, 1991.

Schmidt, James D. *Industrial Violence and the Legal Origins of Child Labor*. New York: Cambridge University Press, 2010.

Schmitt, Peter J. "Grave Matters: American Cemeteries in Transition." *Journal of Urban History* 3, no. 18 (1992): 338–45.

Schneirov, Richard. *Labor and Urban Politics: Class Conflict and the Origins of Modern Liberalism in Chicago, 1864–97*. Urbana: University of Illinois Press, 1998.

Schrag, Peter. *Not Fit for Our Society: Nativism and Immigration*. Berkeley: University of California Press, 2010.

Sclair, Ellen. "Ethnic Cemeteries: Underground Rites." In *Ethnic Chicago: A Multicultural Portrait*, edited by Melvin G. Holli and Peter d' A. Jones, 618–39. Grand Rapids, MI: William B. Eerdmans, 1995.

Scott, Joan W. "Experience." In *Feminists Theorize the Political*, edited by Judith Butler and Joan Wallach Scott, 22–40. New York: Routledge, 1992.

Seale, Clive. *Constructing Death: The Sociology of Dying and Bereavement*. New York: Cambridge University Press, 1998.

Seeman, Erik R. *Death in the New World: Cross-cultural Encounters, 1492–1800*. Philadelphia: University of Pennsylvania Press, 2010.

Sellers, Christopher C. *Hazards of the Job: From Industrial Disease to Environmental Science*. Chapel Hill: University of North Carolina Press, 1997.

Serrin, William. *Homestead: The Glory and Tragedy of an American Steel Town*. New York: Times Books, 1992.

Sewell, William. *Work and Revolution in France: The Language of Labor from the Old Regime to 1848*. New York: Cambridge University Press, 1980.

Shah, Nayan. *Contagious Divides: Epidemics and Race in San Francisco's Chinatown*. Berkeley: University of California Press, 2001.

Shapiro, Karin A. *A New South Rebellion: The Battle against Convict Labor in the Tennessee Coalfields, 1871–1896*. Chapel Hill: University of North Carolina Press, 1998.

Shovers, Brian. "The Perils of Working in the Butte Underground: Industrial Fatalities in the Copper Mines, 1880–1920." *Montana* (Spring 1987): 26–39.

Simon, Andreas. *Chicago: The Garden City*. Chicago: Franz Gindele, 1893.

Sinclair, Upton. *The Jungle*. Edited by James R. Barrett. 1906. Reprint, Urbana: University of Illinois Press, 1988.

Sixteenth Annual Report of the Commissioner of Labor, 1901: Strikes and Lockouts. Washington, DC: Government Printing Office, 1901.

Sklar, Kathryn Kish. *Florence Kelley and the Nation's Work*. New Haven, CT: Yale University Press, 1995.

Skocpol, Theda. *Protecting Soldiers and Mothers: The Political Origins of Social Policy in the United States*. Cambridge, MA: Belknap Press of Harvard University Press, 1992.

Slavishak, Edward. *Bodies of Work: Civic Display and Labor in Industrial Pittsburgh*. Durham, NC: Duke University Press, 2008.

Sloane, David Charles. *The Last Great Necessity: Cemeteries in American History*. Baltimore, MD: Johns Hopkins University Press, 1991.

Slotkin, Richard. *The Fatal Environment: The Myth of the Frontier in the Age of Industrialization, 1800–1890*. Norman: University of Oklahoma Press, 1985.

———. *Lost Battalions: The Great War and the Crisis of American Nationality*. New York: Henry Holt, 2005.

———. *Regeneration through Violence: The Mythology of the American Frontier, 1600–1860*. Middletown, CT: Wesleyan University Press, 1973.

Smith, Barbara Ellen. *Digging Our Own Graves: Coal Miners and the Struggle over Black Lung Disease*. Philadelphia: Temple University Press, 1987.

Smith, Rufus D. "Some Phases of the McKee's Rocks Strike." *Survey*, October 2, 1909, 38–46.

Smith, Suzanne E. *To Serve the Living: Funeral Directors and the African American Way of Death*. Cambridge, MA: Harvard University Press, 2010.

"The Social Gospel." *Biblical World* 40, no. 3 (1912): 147–51.

Spear, Allan H. *Black Chicago: The Making of a Negro Ghetto, 1890–1920*. Chicago: University of Chicago Press, 1967.

Spencer, C. A. "Black Benevolent Societies and the Development of Black Insurance Companies in Nineteenth Century Alabama." *Phylon* 46, no. 3 (1985): 251–61.

Spickard, Paul. *Almost All Aliens: Immigration, Race, and Colonialism in American History and Identity*. New York: Routledge, 2007.

Spinney, Robert G. *City of Big Shoulders: A History of Chicago*. DeKalb: Northern Illinois University Press, 2000.

Stanley, Amy Dru. *From Bondage to Contract: Wage Labor, Marriage, and the Market in the Age of Slave Emancipation*. New York: Cambridge University Press, 1998.

Stannard, David E. *The Puritan Way of Death: A Study in Religion, Culture, and Social Change*. New York: Oxford University Press, 1977.

State Mining Board. *Coal in Illinois, 1911*. Springfield: Illinois State Journal, 1912.

———. *Thirteenth Annual Coal Report of Illinois, 1911*. Springfield: Illinois State Journal, 1912.

Stead, William T. *If Christ Came to Chicago! A Plea for the Union of All Who Love in the Service of All Who Suffer.* London: Review of Reviews, 1894.

Stearns, Carol Z., and Peter N. Stearns. *Anger: The Struggle for Emotional Control in America's History.* Chicago: University of Chicago Press, 1986.

Steffens, Lincoln. "Chicago: Half Free and Fighting On." *McClure's Magazine,* October 1903, 563–77.

Stein, Leon. *The Triangle Fire.* Ithaca, NY: Cornell University Press, 2001.

Stein, Leon, and Philip Taft, eds. *Workers Speak: Self-Portraits.* New York: Arno Press, 1971.

Stiles, T. J. *The First Tycoon: The Epic Life of Cornelius Vanderbilt.* New York: Vintage Books, 2010.

Stockton, Richard, and 100 Coal Miners. *Underground in Illinois: How Coal Miners Live, Work, and Struggle for Unity.* Chicago: National Research League, n.d.

Stone, Katherine. "The Origins of Job Structures in the Steel Industry." *Review of Radical Political Economics* 6, no. 2 (1974): 61–97.

Storrs, Landon R. Y. *Civilizing Capitalism: The National Consumers' League, Women's Activism, and Labor Standards in the New Deal Era.* Chapel Hill: University of North Carolina Press, 2000.

Stout, Steve. "Tragedy in November: The Cherry Mine Disaster." *Journal of the Illinois State Historical Society* 72, no. 1 (1979): 57–70.

Stowell, Myron. *"Fort Frick"; or, The Siege of Homestead: A History of the Famous Struggle between the Amalgamated Association of Iron and Steel Workers and the Carnegie Steel Company (Limited) of Pittsburg [sic], PA.* Pittsburg, PA: Pittsburg Printing, 1893.

Stromquist, Shelton. *Reinventing "the People": The Progressive Movement, the Class Problem, and the Origins of Modern Liberalism.* Urbana: University of Illinois Press, 2006.

Strong, Josiah. "Address of Rev. Dr. Josiah Strong." *American Missionary* 49, no. 12 (1895): 423–24.

———. "Our Industrial Juggernaut." *North American Review* 183 (November 16, 1906): 1030–36.

———. "Social Life and Christian Ministry." *Outlook,* July 16, 1904, 652–58.

Stuckey, Sterling. *Slave Culture: Nationalist Theory and Foundations of Black America.* New York: Oxford University Press, 1987.

Sub-District No. 6. *Constitution of Sub-District No. 6 (Belleville) of District No. 12, United Mine Workers of America.* N.p.: 1905.

Suffern, Arthur E. *The Coal Miners' Struggle for Industrial Status: A Study of the Evolution of Organized Relations and Industrial Principles in the Coal Industry.* New York: Macmillan, 1926.

Suisher, Peter. "From Div. No. 24." *Locomotive Engineers' Monthly Journal* 1, no. 4 (1867): 6–8.

Sumner, William Graham. *What Social Classes Owe to Each Other.* New York: Harper and Brothers, 1884.

Sutherland, Daniel E. *The Expansion of Everyday Life, 1860–1876.* Fayetteville: University of Arkansas Press, 2000.

Taillon, Paul Michel. "'What We Want Is Good, Sober Men': Masculinity, Respectability, and Temperance in the Railroad Brotherhoods, c. 1870–1910." *Journal of Social History* 36, no. 2 (2002): 319–38.

Takaki, Ronald. *A Different Mirror: A History of Multicultural America*. Rev. ed. New York: Back Bay Books, 2008.

Taylor, F. W. *The Principles of Scientific Management*. New York: Harper and Brothers, 1911.

Taylor, Graham. *Pioneering on Social Fronts*. 1931. Reprint, New York: Arno Press, 1972.

Taylor, Lou. *Mourning Dress: A Costume and Social History*. Boston: George Allen and Unwin, 1983.

Temin, Peter. "Manufacturing." In *American Economic Growth: An Economist's History of the United States,* edited by Lance E. Davis et al., 418–67. New York: Harper and Row, 1972.

Tentler, Leslie Woodcock. *Seasons of Grace: A History of the Catholic Archdiocese of Detroit*. Detroit: Wayne State University Press, 1990.

"Terrible Accident in a Mine." *Christian Recorder* (Philadelphia), April 18, 1868.

Tharp, Brent Warren. "'Preserving Their Form and Features': The Role of Coffins in the American Understanding of Death, 1607–1870." PhD diss., College of William and Mary, 1996.

"They Don't Suit the 'Intellectuals.'" *American Federationist* 20 (February 1913): 128–32.

Thomas, W. I. "Eugenics: The Science of Breeding Men." *American Magazine*, June 1909, 190–97.

Thompson, E. P. *The Making of the English Working Class*. New York: Vintage Books, 1963.

Thompson, Neil. "Masculinity and Loss." In *Death, Gender and Ethnicity*, edited by Jenny Hockey and Neil Small David Field, 76–88. New York: Routledge, 1997.

Thurston, Herbert. "Christian Burial." In *The Catholic Encyclopedia: An International Work of Reference on the Constitution, Doctrine, Discipline, and History of the Catholic Church*, 3. New York: Robert Appleton, 1908. http://www.newadvent.org/cathen/03071a.htm (accessed October 22, 2012).

Tingley, Donald. *The Structuring of a State: The History of Illinois, 1899–1928*. Urbana: University of Illinois Press, 1980.

Trachtenberg, Alan. *The Incorporation of America: Culture and Society in the Gilded Age*. New York: Hill and Wang, 1982.

Trice, Thomas Reed. "The 'Body Politic': Russian Funerals and the Politics of Representation, 1841–1921." PhD diss., University of Illinois at Urbana-Champaign, 1998.

———. "Rites of Protest: Populist Funerals in Imperial St. Petersburg, 1876–1878." *Slavic Review* 60, no. 1 (2001): 50–74.

Turbin, Carole. *Working Women of Collar City: Gender, Class, and Community in Troy, New York, 1864–86*. Urbana: University of Illinois Press, 1992.

Turner, Victor. *The Ritual Process, Structure and Anti-Structure*. Chicago: Aldine, 1969.

Tussey, Jean Y., ed. *Eugene V. Debs Speaks*. New York: Pathfinder Press, 1970.

Tuttle, William M., Jr. *Race Riot: Chicago in the Red Summer of 1919*. 1970. Reprint, Urbana: University of Illinois Press, 1996.

United Mine Workers of America. *Constitution of the Twelfth District (Illinois) of the United Mine Workers of America*. Joliet, IL: Joliet Republican Printing, 1900.

———. *Constitution of the Twelfth District of the United Mine Workers of America*. Joliet, IL: Joliet Republican Printing, 1902.

———. *Constitution of the Twelfth District of the United Mine Workers of America*. Joliet, IL: Allied Printers, 1916.

———. *Minutes of the Twelfth Annual Convention, 1901*. Indianapolis: Hollenbeck Press, 1901.

———. *Official Report of the Tenth Annual Convention of District 12, United Mine Workers of America and Joint Convention of Miners and Operators*. Springfield, IL: Joliet Republican Printing, 1899.

Urofsky, Melvin I. "State Courts and Protective Legislation during the Progressive Era: A Reevaluation." *Journal of American History* 72, no. 1 (1985): 63–91.

U.S. Bureau of the Census. *Religious Bodies, 1916*. Washington, DC: Government Printing Office, 1920.

U.S. Commission on Industrial Relations. *Industrial Relations: Final Report and Testimony*. Washington, DC: Government Printing Office, 1916.

U.S. Department of Labor, Bureau of Labor Statistics. *Accidents and Accident Prevention in Machine Building*. By Lucian W. Chaney and Hugh S. Hanna. Vol. 216. Washington, DC: Government Printing Office, 1917.

———. *Causes of Death by Occupation: Occupational Mortality Experience of the Metropolitan Life Insurance Company, Industrial Department, 1911–1913*. By Louis I. Dublin. Washington, DC: Government Printing Office, 1917.

———. *Industrial Accident Statistics*. Vol. 157. Washington, DC: Government Printing Office, 1915.

———. *Preventable Death in Cotton Manufacturing Industry*. By Arthur Reed Perry. Washington, DC: Government Printing Office, 1919.

U.S. House of Representatives. *Peonage in Western Pennsylvania: Hearings Before the Committee on Labor of the House of Representatives*. 62nd Cong. Washington, DC: Government Printing Office, 1911.

U.S. Immigration Commission. *Abstracts of Reports of the Immigration Commission*. Vol. 1. Washington, DC: Government Printing Office, 1911.

———. *Dictionary of Races and Peoples*. S. Doc. 662. 61st Cong., 3rd sess. Washington, DC: Government Printing Office, 1911.

———. *Immigrants in Industries*. Pt. 1, *Bituminous Coal Mining*. Washington, DC: Government Printing Office, 1911.

U.S. Senate, Committee on Education and Labor. *Report of the Committee of the Senate upon the Relations between Labor and Capital*. 4 vols. 1885. Reprint, New York: Arno Press, 1976.

Van Valkenburg, Jon. *The Knights of Pythias Complete Manual and Textbook*. Canton: OH: Memento, 1887.

Vapnek, Lara. *Breadwinners: Working Women and Economic Independence, 1865–1920*. Urbana: University of Illinois Press, 2009.

Verdery, Katherine. *The Political Lives of Dead Bodies: Reburial and Postsocialist Change*. New York: Columbia University Press, 1999.

Vojan, J. E. S. *The Semi-centennial Jubilee of the Bohemian National Cemetery Association in Chicago, Illinois*. Chicago: Bohemian National Cemetery Association, 1927.

Von Drehle, Dave. *Triangle: The Fire That Changed America*. New York: Atlantic Monthly Press, 2003.

Vorse, Mary Heaton. *Men and Steel*. New York: Boni and Liveright, 1920.

Waldron, Caroline Anne. "'The Great Spirit of Solidarity': The Illinois Valley Mining Communities and the Formation of Interethnic Consciousness, 1889–1917." PhD diss., University of Illinois, 2000.

Walker, Charles Rumford. *Steel: The Diary of a Furnace Worker*. Boston: Atlantic Monthly Press, 1922.
Walker, Francis A. "Immigration and Degradation." *Forum* 11 (1891): 634–44.
———. *Political Economy*. New York: Henry Holt, 1888.
———. "Restriction of Immigration." *Atlantic Monthly*, June 1896, 822–29.
Wall, Joseph Frazier. *Andrew Carnegie*. New York: Oxford University Press, 1970.
Wallace, Anthony F. C. *St. Clair: A Nineteenth-Century Coal Town's Experience with a Disaster-Prone Industry*. New York: Alfred A. Knopf, 1987.
Ware, Norman. *The Labor Movement in the United States, 1860–1895: A Study in Democracy*. Gloucester, MA: P. Smith, 1959.
Warne, Frank Julian. *The Coal-Mine Workers: A Study in Labor Organization*. New York: Longmans, Green, 1905.
———. "The Effect of Unionism upon the Mine Worker." *Annals of the American Academy of Political and Social Science* 21 (January 1903): 20–35.
———. *The Immigrant Invasion*. New York: Dodd, Mead, 1913.
———. *The Slav Invasion and the Mine Workers*. Philadelphia: Lippincott, 1904.
Warner, W. Lloyd. *The Living and the Dead: A Study of Symbolic Life of Americans*. New Haven, CT: Yale University Press, 1959.
Watchorn, Robert. "The Cost of Coal in Human Life." *Outlook*, May 22, 1909, 171–83.
Webb, Sydney, and Beatrice Webb. *Industrial Democracy*. 1897. Reprint, London: Longmans, Green, 1914.
Weber, Adna F. "Employers' Liability and Accident Insurance." *Political Science Quarterly* 17, no. 2 (1902): 256–83.
Weinberg, Carl. "'Hotter than San Juan Hill': The Battle of Virden, the UMWA and the Challenge of Solidarity." In *Remember Virden, 1898*, edited by Rosemary Feuer, 5–8. Chicago: Illinois Humanities Council, 1998.
———. *Labor, Loyalty, and Rebellion: Southwestern Illinois Coal Miners and World War I*. Carbondale: Southern Illinois University Press, 2005.
Weinstein, James. *The Corporate Ideal in the Liberal State, 1900–1918*. Boston: Beacon Press, 1968.
Weir, Robert E. *Beyond Labor's Veil: The Culture of the Knights of Labor*. University Park: Pennsylvania State University Press, 1995.
Weitz, Eric D. "Class Formation and Labor Protest in Mining Communities of Southern Illinois and the Ruhr, 1890–1925." *Labor History* 27, no. 1 (1985–86): 85–105.
Welke, Barbara Young. *Recasting American Liberty: Gender, Race, Law, and the Railroad Revolution, 1865–1920*. Cambridge: Cambridge University Press, 2001.
Wells, David A. "The Economic Disturbances since 1873." *Popular Science Monthly*, September 1887, 577–97.
Wells, Ida B. *Crusade for Justice: The Autobiography of Ida B. Wells*. Edited by Alfreda M. Duster. Chicago: University of Chicago Press, 1970.
Wells, Robert V. *Facing the "King of Terrors": Death and Society in an American Community, 1750–1990*. New York: Cambridge University Press, 2000.
Whatley, Warren C. "African American Strikebreaking from the Civil War to the New Deal." *Social Science History* 17, no. 4 (1993): 525–58.
White, G. Edward. *Justice Oliver Wendell Holmes: Law and the Inner Self*. New York: Oxford University Press, 1993.

White, Richard. *Railroaded: The Transcontinentals and the Making of Modern America.* New York: W. W. Norton, 2011.

White, Ronald C., Jr., and C. Howard Hopkins. *The Social Gospel: Religion and Reform in Changing America.* Philadelphia: Temple University Press, 1976.

Wiebe, Robert H. *Businessmen and Reform: A Study of the Progressive Movement.* Cambridge, MA: Harvard University Press, 1962.

——. *The Search for Order, 1877–1920.* New York: Hill and Wang, 1967.

Wieck, Edward A. *The American Miners' Association: A Record of the Origin of Coal Miners' Unions in the United States.* New York: Russell Sage Foundation, 1940.

Wilentz, Sean. *Chants Democratic: New York City and the Rise of the American Working Class, 1789–1850.* New York: Oxford University Press, 1984.

——. *The Rise of American Democracy: Jefferson to Lincoln.* New York: W. W. Norton, 2005.

Williams-Searle, John. "Cold Charity: Manhood, Brotherhood, and the Transformation of Disability, 1870–1900." In *The New Disability History: American Perspectives,* edited by Paul K. Longman and Lauri Umansky, 157–86. New York: New York University Press, 2001.

——. "Courting Risk: Disability, Masculinity, and Liability on Iowa's Railroads, 1868–1900." *Annals of Iowa* 58 (Winter 1999): 27–77.

——. "Risk, Disability, and Citizenship: U.S. Railroaders and the Federal Employers' Liability Act." *Disability Studies Quarterly* 28, no. 3 (2008). http://dsq-sds.org/article/view/113 (accessed May 16, 2013).

Wilson, William B. *Report of William B. Wilson, National Secretary-Treasurer United Mine Workers of America, Year Ending December 31, 1902.* Indianapolis: Hollenbeck Press, 1903.

Windel, Ann Steinbrecher. "John Wentworth, His Contribution to Chicago." *Papers in Illinois History and Transactions for the Year 1937* (1938): 1–17.

Windmuller, Louis. "Graveyards as a Menace to the Commonweal." *North American Review* 167, no. 501 (1898): 211–22.

Wing, Frank E. "Thirty-Five Years of Typhoid: The Fever's Economic Cost to Pittsburgh and the Long Fight for Pure Water." *Charities and the Commons* 21 (February 6, 1909): 923–39.

Wing, M. T. C. "The Flag at McKee's Rocks." *Survey,* October 2, 1909, 45–46.

Witt, John Fabian. *The Accidental Republic: Crippled Workingmen, Destitute Widows, and the Remaking of American Law.* Cambridge, MA: Harvard University Press, 2004.

Woloch, Nancy. *"Muller v. Oregon": A Brief History with Documents.* Boston: Bedford/St. Martin's, 1996.

Wood, Gregory. "'Beyond the Age of Earning': Masculinity, Work, and Age Discrimination in the Automobile Industry, 1916–1939." *Labor* 3, no. 2 (2006): 91–120.

——. "The Problem of the Old Man: Manhood, Class, and Retirement in the United States, 1910s–1950s." PhD diss., University of Pittsburgh, 2006.

Woodburn, James. "Social Dimensions of Death in Four African Hunting and Gathering Societies." In *Death and the Regeneration of Life,* edited by Maurice Bloch and Jonathan Perry, 187–210. Cambridge: Cambridge University Press, 1982.

Woods, Katharine Pearson. "Accidents in Factories and Elsewhere." *Publications of the American Statistical Association* 4, no. 32 (1895): 303–21.

Worcester, Wood F., and Daisy Worthington Worcester. *Family Budgets of Typical Cotton-Mill Workers*. Washington, DC: Government Printing Office, 1911.
Wright, Carroll D. "The Amalgamated of Iron and Steel Workers." *Quarterly Journal of Economics* 7, no. 4 (1893): 400–432.
———. "The Factory System as an Element of Civilization." *Journal of Social Science* 16 (1882): 101–26.
———. *The Working Girls of Boston*. 1889. Reprint, New York: Arno Press, 1969.
Wright, R. R., Jr. "One Hundred Negro Steel Workers." In *Wage-Earning Pittsburgh*, edited by Paul U. Kellogg, 97–110. New York: Survey Associates, 1914.
Wright, Roberta Hughes, and Wilbur B. Hughes III. *Lay Down Body: Living History in African American Cemeteries*. Detroit: Visible Ink Press, 1996.
Wyman, Mark. *Round-Trip to America: The Immigrants Return to Europe, 1880–1930*. Ithaca, NY: Cornell University Press, 1993.
Wynn, David Robert. "Trade Unions and the 'New' Immigration: A Study of the United Mine Workers of America, 1890–1920." PhD diss., London School of Economics, 1976.
Yalom, Marilyn. *The American Resting Place: Four Hundred Years of History through Our Cemeteries and Burial Grounds*. Boston: Houghton Mifflin, 2008.
Yans-McLaughlin, Virginia. *Family and Community: Italian Immigrants in Buffalo, 1880–1930*. Ithaca, NY: Cornell University Press, 1977.
Zeidel, Robert F. *Immigrants, Progressives, and Exclusion Politics: The Dillingham Commission, 1900–1927*. DeKalb: Northern Illinois University Press, 2004.
Zelizer, Viviana A. "Human Values and the Market: The Case of Life Insurance and Death in 19th Century America." *American Journal of Sociology* 84, no. 3 (1978): 591–610.
Zion Cemetery Project. "Zion Cemetery History." http://www.zioncommunityproject.org/history.php (accessed November 24, 2014).
Zolberg, Aristide R. *A Nation by Design: Immigration Policy in the Fashioning of America*. New York: Russell Sage Foundation, 2006.
Zunz, Olivier. *Making America Corporate, 1870–1920*. Chicago: University of Chicago Press, 1990.

Index

AAISW, 98, 100–106, 108–9
accident crisis, 8–9, 11; immigration and, 23–24, 27; race and, 27–30; relationships of production as a cause, 14–15; social Darwinism and, 19; solutions to, 31–39
accidents, 144, 145, 146; in coal mines, 79–82, 84, 86; in iron and steel mills, 113–120, 130. *See also* mine disasters
Adamson Act, 146
Addams, Jane, 48, 147
AFL. *See* American Federation of Labor (AFL)
African Americans: cemeteries created by, 94; community building, 124, 126; as convict laborers, 29; fraternal organizations of, 94, 122–23, 124, 126; as migrants, 99; as miners, 88, 90, 93–94; in proletarian fiction, 29–30; segregation of, 57–60, 150–51; as steelworkers, 111, 123
alcohol, 18, 40, 71, 131
Alger, George William, 21–22
Alger, Horatio, 51
Altgeld, John Peter, 49, 65
Amalgamated Association of Iron and Steel Workers (AAISW), 98, 100–106, 108–9
American Association for Labor Legislation (AALL), 32
American Federation of Labor (AFL): attitudes of, toward immigrant workers, 129; and liability reform, 31–32, 38; and women workers, 22–23; and working conditions, 34, 146

American Institute of Social Service (AISS), 31, 32–33
American Miners' Association (AMA), 84
anarchists, 61–66
Ars moriendi, 71, 142, 143. *See also* good death
artisans, 10, 13, 15, 21
assimilation, 56, 124

Beman, Solon, 51
Bilyeu, Frank, 91
Black, William Perkins, 62
Bloody Sunday, 134–135
body, the: as category of analysis, 8–9; commodification of, 15; as object of discipline, 40; representations of, 19–21, 27, 69, 100; as vulnerable, 31, 33, 38
Bohemian National Cemetery, 44, 47, 53–57
Bonsack, James, 12
Brandeis, Louis, 35–36
Brandeis Brief, 35–36
breadwinner. *See* male breadwinner ideology

Calvary Cemetery, 53
Campbell, Helen, 16
carelessness, 81–82
Carnegie, Andrew, 19, 100–101, 107
Carnegie Steel Company, 100–101, 105, 106, 107–8, 109
Catholic faith, 53, 90, 106, 123–24, 125. *See also* Roman Catholic Church

cemeteries, 5, 42–67; historical evolution of, 44–47; as landscape of class, 42, 47–52; Protestant, 53, 75; and racial discrimination, 57–60, 67; as real estate, 44, 49, 51; Roman Catholic, 52, 53, 54, 67, 75, 103, 135. *See also* rural cemeteries
Chicago-Virden Coal Company, 88–89, 91, 92, 93
Chinese Exclusion Act, 25
Chinese immigrants, 24–26
Christianity, 62, 65, 72, 144–45
citizenship, 23, 24, 26–27, 56, 68, 85, 150, 152
Civil Rights Act (Illinois), 59–60
Civil Rights Act of 1872 (U.S.), 24
Civil War: casualties of, 8, 31, 143, 151; as challenge to a good death, 71, 143; as turning point in burial practices, 3, 154; veterans of, 55
Clayton Act, 146
Columbian Exposition, 50, 65, 66
Commons, John R., 32, 38–39
contract, freedom of, 15, 21, 33–36
Cook County Cemetery, 48, 49, 52
Croatian Fraternal Union, 121, 122
cultures of industrialization, 11, 41, 42, 54–55, 91, 120–21, 143. *See also* industrialization
Currlin, Ablert, 63

dead work, 80
deathways, 68, 108, 142
Debs, Eugene V., 22, 20, 50, 95, 136, 148, 149
de Cleyre, Voltairine, 63, 66
Decoration Day, 56–57, 104
Delaney, William W., 107
democracy, industrial, 99, 152, 153
disability, 33
discipline, 12, 15, 18, 28, 99, 107, 111, 154; resistance to, 39–40
disease, 25, 46, 67, 99, 120–21, 142, 150
division of labor, 12, 16, 76, 99, 127–28

Eastman, Crystal, 37–38, 98, 114–16, 117, 119
embalming, 4
Engel, George, 61, 66
Eugenics Record Office, 27
ethnicity: and cemeteries, 52–57, 61, 67; and fraternal organizations, 121–23, 126; and funerals, 103, 104–105; and occupational stratification, 116–17, 118; and spatial segregation, 127
Exposition of Safety Devices and Industrial Hygiene, 33

factory system, 12–13, 17–18
Fielden, Samuel, 65
First Catholic Slovak Union, 121, 122
Fischer, Adolph, 61
Fitch, John, 109, 113, 117
foremen, 30, 111–12; attitudes of, toward immigrants, 116; emergence of, 14–15; power of, 22, 117, 118, 130, 154; role of, in workplace hierarchy, 98, 99
Forest Home Cemetery, 44, 59–60
Foster, William Z., 66, 153
Franklin, Benjamin, 23
fraternal organizations: burial benefits of, 83, 122; and establishment of cemeteries, 54, 59, 61, 94; and mutual aid, 121–23, 126–27; as part of immigrant life, 58, 124; rituals of, 86, 87, 97, 103–104, 121, 124–26, 137
freethinkers, 53–54, 55
Frick, Henry Clay, 100, 105
funerals: after the battle at Homestead, 103–106; in coal mine communities, 72, 72, 79, 91–92, 95; expenses of, 117, 130; of the Haymarket defendants, 61–63; during McKees Rocks strike, 131–33, 134–35; of members of fraternal organizations, 121, 124–26; of slaves, 94; as social commentary, 43, 81, 83, 123, 139, 142, 144–46; union participation in, 85, 86–87, 91–92, 97, 153; of the Victorian era, 3, 144, 154

Galilean Fisherman Lodge, 122
Garland, Hamlin, 112
Gary, Elbert H., 32
Gaskill, John, 59–60
Geary Act, 25
Getty, Henry Harrison, 49, 51, 52, 67
Gilded Age, 4
Gitterle, Joseph, 91, 94, 95
Goldman, Emma, 63, 66
Goldmark, Josephine, 35–36
Gompers, Samuel, 39, 141, 146, 147–48
good death, 71, 121, 142–43. *See also under* wages
Graceland Cemetery, 44, 47, 49–52, 66
Grand Army of the Republic, 56
Grant, Madison, 27, 29
Great Migration, 58
Green, Edward D., 59
Guthrie, Woody, 97

Hard, William, 32, 33, 37, 114, 118

Index

Harmon, William, 91
Harris, Thomas, 58
Harrison, Carter, 49, 56, 61
Hayes, Rutherford B., 25
Haymarket Affair, 40, 43, 61–63, 65–66, 67, 143
Haywood, Big Bill, 7, 148
Henry, John, 1–2, 5, 6
Hill, Joe, 155
Hoffstot, Frank N., 127–28, 130, 131, 133
Home Club of Steelton, Pa., 122
Homestead strike, 40, 98–99, 100–108, 113, 128, 137, 139
Horvath, Steve, 131–132, 133, 134
Howells, William Dean, 17, 154
"hunky," 30, 116, 129, 133, 138

Illinois Miners' Benevolent Association, 84, 85
immigrants: as accident prone, 37; attitudes toward, 82–83; as percentage of workforce, 83. *See also* "hunky"
immigration, 43, 52, 82, 110–12, 135; attitudes about, 23–30, 82–83; and fears of radicalism, 65–66; restriction of, 55, 133
Immigration Act of 1902, 25
Immigration Restriction League, 26
Independent Order of Foresters, 83
Independent Order of Odd Fellows (IOOF), 63, 86, 103, 104, 122, 124–26
industrial democracy, 99, 152, 153
industrialization, 1, 9–19, 50, 98–99; emotional impact of, 96; immigrants and, 29, 57, 111–12; and organization of work, 68–69, 110–13; and unsafe workplaces, 21; workers' responses to, 39–41, 137, 141–46, 150. *See also* cultures of industrialization
Industrial Workers of the World (IWW), 7, 146–47, 149, 155; and McKees Rocks strike, 133, 136, 137, 138
insurance, 37, 59, 83, 121, 127
International Working People's Association, 39
IOOF. *See* Independent Order of Odd Fellows (IOOF)
Irish immigrants, 24, 26, 28, 29, 53, 82, 118
IWW. *See* Industrial Workers of the World (IWW)

James, William, 20
Jim Crow, 29, 57–58, 90, 151
Jones, Mary Harris "Mother," 62, 66, 95, 155

Kaemmerer, Ernst, 91, 94, 95
Kearney, Denis, 24
Kelley, Florence, 32, 34–35, 147
Knights of Labor, 40, 84, 85, 89, 154
Knights of Pythias, 103–104

labor, division of, 12, 16, 76, 99, 127–28
Lang, Lucy Robins, 65
Laughlin, Harry, 27
law: liability, 21–22, 31–32, 37, 81, 82, 117; protective, 31, 33–36; shorter-hours, 23, 35–36
Lincoln, Abraham, 10, 61, 65, 91
Lincoln Cemetery, 59
Lingg, Louis, 61
Lodge, Henry Cabot, 26–27
Ludlow massacre, 40, 145, 146

machines: dehumanizing impact of, 15, 16, 113; replacing workers, 110; and transformation of work, 12–13, 112, 130; virtues of, 17–18, 39
Magarac, Joe, 138–39
male breadwinner ideology, 23, 31, 93, 118, 122, 125
manhood, 20, 22, 40, 82, 92–93, 112, 150. *See also* masculinity
martyrs: Haymarket, 62–66; McKees Rocks, 131; Virden, 91, 92, 94–96
masculinity, 1, 21, 22, 23, 30, 41. *See also* manhood
McCormick, Cyrus, 49
McCormick, Cyrus, Jr., 13
McKees Rocks strike, 127–38
McLean, George, 64
McNeill, George E., 40
memorial services: after battle at Virden, 91, 94–95; at Diamond, 72–73; Haymarket, 63–65; lack of, 1; at McKees Rocks, 131–32; politics of, 43, 97, 142, 144–45; in steel communities, 108, 124–26; UMWA and, 86
mine disasters: Avondale, Pa., 69, 78, 96; Cherry, Ill., 38, 69, 79, 96, 145; Coulterville, Ill., 69–70, 77, 78; Diamond, Ill., 69, 70–77, 78, 84; Monongah, W.Va., 38, 145
Mitchell, John, 82, 89, 91, 95
monuments, 42–43, 46, 47, 51, 153; in Bohemian National Cemetery, 55–57; for coal miners, 86, 94–95, 145; for the Haymarket martyrs, 64–66; of the wealthy, 2, 3, 49–50, 51
Morse, Samuel, 24

Mount Auburn Cemetery, 46–47
Mount Glenwood Cemetery, 59
Mount Greenwood Cemetery, 58
Mount Hope Cemetery, 58
Mount Olive Cemetery, 94
Mt. Olive, Ill., 86, 91, 94–95
Muller v. Oregon (1908), 35–36

National Civic Federation, 18, 147
National Consumers' League (NCL), 32, 34–36
National Federation of Miners, 84–85
National Origins Quota Act of 1924, 27
National Slovak Society, 121, 122
National Woman's Party, 23
nativism, 24
Neebe, Oscar, 65

Oak Hill Cemetery, 59
O'Donnell, Edward, 23
O'Donnell, Hugh, 106
"Only a Miner," 68, 96–97
orphans, 72, 107, 118, 122

Pana Coal Company, 88
Pana riot, 93–94
Panic of 1907, 127
Parsons, Albert, 61, 63, 66
Parsons, Lucy, 63–64, 65, 66, 95
paternalism, 23, 93, 105, 126, 146
Paterson Silk Strike, 145–46
patriarchy, 10
Pattison, Robert E., 106
pauper's burial, 48–49, 83, 86, 123. *See also* potter's field
Pearl Bergoff Agency, 133, 137
People v. Hall, 24
People v. Williams (1907), 34
Pinkertons, 100, 101–102, 103, 104, 105, 107, 128
Pittsburgh Survey, 32, 33, 37, 98, 109
potter's field, 48–49, 51, 52, 66–67, 83
Pressed Steel Car Company, 127–28, 129–30, 133–37, 138
Progressive Era, 4, 20, 27, 32
Pullman, George, 49, 50–51, 52, 67
Pullman strike, 40, 50

racism, scientific, 29, 30, 99
railroads: casualties caused by, 8, 69, 115; and economic growth, 9, 17; labor practices of, 16, 27–28; workers on, 22, 24

Railroad strikes of 1877, 17, 18–19, 40
Ratchford, Michael, 87, 91
reformers, 42, 114, 118; and immigration, 26; and liability laws, 37–38; and living conditions, 120–21; and the power of the state, 38–39, 41, 146; and women's work, 22–23, 33–36; and working conditions, 31–36
resolutions in memoriam, 85, 91, 92
risk, 30, 69, 78, 81, 96, 116; celebration of, 22–23, 41; ignorance of, 68
Ritchie v. People of Illinois (1895), 34
rituals of death: of coal miners, 68, 79, 81, 85–87, 90–92, 97; disruption of, 71–72, 76; of fraternal organizations, 124–27; importance of, for the living, 3; industrialization's impact on, 42–43; of the middle class, 3; politics of, 103, 132, 135, 137, 139–40, 152, 154–55; of the Victorian Era, 3–4, 47; and women's roles, 76; working people's, 2–3, 5–6, 43, 142–46
Roman Catholic Church, 105, 123, 130; and conflict over burial, 53–54, 57; Irish influence in, 53. *See also* Catholic faith
Roosevelt, Theodore, 20, 26, 148
Ross, E. A., 29, 30
rural cemeteries, 46–47

Safety First, 32
safety laws, 32, 117, 145; for coal mining, 77–78, 82, 84–85
Sandburg, Carl, 48, 50, 51
Schilling, George, 51, 65
Schwab, Michael, 65
scientific racism, 29, 30, 99
Security Benefit Association, 83
Sellins, Fannie, 153
Simon, Andreas, 52
skill: and dangerous work, 29, 81, 116; erosion of, 13–15, 40, 110–12; impact of, on funerals, 103, 104; and power, 13, 98, 100–102, 110–12; and prejudice, 99; as source of fragmentation, 107, 108, 127, 129, 137–38; and wages, 119; women and, 34. *See also* artisans
Slovak Evangelical Union, 122
Smith, E. W., 91, 94, 95
Smith, Jane Norman, 23
social Darwinism, 19, 32, 40
Social Gospel, 31
Sons of Zion, 94
Spanish-American War, 88–89, 90
Spies, August, 61, 65, 66

Stanford, Leland, 28
St. Adalbert Cemetery, 53, 56
St. Boniface Cemetery, 53
St. Casimir Cemetery, 53
Stowe, Lyman Beecher, 82–83
strikebreakers, 60, 88–89, 93, 96, 101, 106, 128–38
strikes, 28, 60, 84, 87, 96, 143, 145–46, 152. *See also specific strikes*
Strong, Josiah, 31–33
Sullivan, Louis, 49
Supreme Court: Illinois, 34, 59, 60; U.S., 36, 60

Taylor, Frederick W., 14, 20–21
Taylor, Graham, 64
Trautmann, William, 133
Triangle Shirtwaist Factory Fire, 38, 145

UMWA. *See* United Mine Workers of America (UMWA)
undertakers, 4, 43, 48, 73, 90, 103, 121
Union Miners Cemetery, 94–95
Union Miners Day, 95
Union Republic Club, 122
United Mine Workers of America (UMWA), 82, 85–91, 93–97, 108, 145, 148, 153
United Mine Workers Journal, 91, 92
U.S. Commission on Industrial Relations, 38–39
U.S. Steel, 32, 108, 109, 138

Vanderbilt, Cornelius, 2, 5, 76
Victorian era, 3–4, 16, 47, 119, 144, 154
Virden strike, 88–93

wages, 44, 50, 81, 85, 97, 109, 141; and the factory system, 17–18; and good death, 103, 104; impact of industrialization on, 111–12; impact of race and ethnicity on, 28, 129; loss of, 33, 37, 122; perceived threats to, 23, 24, 26; as strike demands, 87, 128, 137, 152
Waldheim Cemetery, 44, 47, 61–66, 67, 95
Walker, Charles Rumford, 112–13
Walker, Francis Amasa, 30
Walsh, Frank, 38–39
Warne, Frank Julian, 30
Watchorn, Robert, 82
Weinert, Albert, 65
Welch, Edward, 91
Wells-Barnett, Ida B., 59
Wentworth, "Long" John, 51–52, 67
Western Federation of Miners, 7
widows, 21, 72–75, 151; employment of, 37, 118–19; at funerals, 103, 105; paternalism toward, 83, 85, 93, 125–26, 145; strike activity of, 102
Wilson, Woodrow, 147, 148–49, 150, 153
Wise, C. A., 129, 136, 137
Woman's Peace Party, 147
women workers, 118–19; Brandeis brief on, 35–36; opposition to, 22–23; wages of, 119
working conditions: in coal mines, 69, 79–81, 96; and immigrants, 24, 27, 28, 30; in iron and steel mills, 98, 112–16, 121, 130; perceived as manly, 20–21, 22, 23; and race, 29; as targets for reform, 31, 37, 78–81
Workingmen's Party, 24
workmen's compensation, 20, 38, 117, 146
World War I, 100, 145–52
Wright, Carroll D., 12, 17–18,
Wunders Cemetery, 49, 52

Zdrubek, Frank, 53–54
Zion Cemetery, 94

MICHAEL K. ROSENOW is an assistant professor at the University of Central Arkansas.

The Working Class in American History

Worker City, Company Town: Iron and Cotton-Worker Protest
    in Troy and Cohoes, New York, 1855–84   *Daniel J. Walkowitz*
Life, Work, and Rebellion in the Coal Fields: The Southern West Virginia
    Miners, 1880–1922   *David Alan Corbin*
Women and American Socialism, 1870–1920   *Mari Jo Buhle*
Lives of Their Own: Blacks, Italians, and Poles in Pittsburgh, 1900–1960
    John Bodnar, Roger Simon, and Michael P. Weber
Working-Class America: Essays on Labor, Community, and American Society
    Edited by Michael H. Frisch and Daniel J. Walkowitz
Eugene V. Debs: Citizen and Socialist   *Nick Salvatore*
American Labor and Immigration History, 1877–1920s:
    Recent European Research   *Edited by Dirk Hoerder*
Workingmen's Democracy: The Knights of Labor and American Politics   *Leon Fink*
The Electrical Workers: A History of Labor at General Electric
    and Westinghouse, 1923–60   *Ronald W. Schatz*
The Mechanics of Baltimore: Workers and Politics in the Age of Revolution,
    1763–1812   *Charles G. Steffen*
The Practice of Solidarity: American Hat Finishers in the Nineteenth Century
    David Bensman
The Labor History Reader   *Edited by Daniel J. Leab*
Solidarity and Fragmentation: Working People and Class Consciousness
    in Detroit, 1875–1900   *Richard Oestreicher*
Counter Cultures: Saleswomen, Managers, and Customers in American
    Department Stores, 1890–1940   *Susan Porter Benson*
The New England Working Class and the New Labor History
    Edited by Herbert G. Gutman and Donald H. Bell
Labor Leaders in America   *Edited by Melvyn Dubofsky and Warren Van Tine*
Barons of Labor: The San Francisco Building Trades and Union Power
    in the Progressive Era   *Michael Kazin*
Gender at Work: The Dynamics of Job Segregation by Sex during World War II
    Ruth Milkman
Once a Cigar Maker: Men, Women, and Work Culture in American
    Cigar Factories, 1900–1919   *Patricia A. Cooper*
A Generation of Boomers: The Pattern of Railroad Labor Conflict
    in Nineteenth-Century America   *Shelton Stromquist*
Work and Community in the Jungle: Chicago's Packinghouse Workers,
    1894–1922   *James R. Barrett*
Workers, Managers, and Welfare Capitalism: The Shoeworkers and Tanners
    of Endicott Johnson, 1890–1950   *Gerald Zahavi*
Men, Women, and Work: Class, Gender, and Protest in the New England
    Shoe Industry, 1780–1910   *Mary Blewett*
Workers on the Waterfront: Seamen, Longshoremen, and Unionism
    in the 1930s   *Bruce Nelson*

German Workers in Chicago: A Documentary History of Working-Class Culture
    from 1850 to World War I   *Edited by Hartmut Keil and John B. Jentz*
On the Line: Essays in the History of Auto Work   *Edited by Nelson Lichtenstein
    and Stephen Meyer III*
Labor's Flaming Youth: Telephone Operators and Worker Militancy,
    1878–1923   *Stephen H. Norwood*
Another Civil War: Labor, Capital, and the State in the Anthracite Regions
    of Pennsylvania, 1840–68   *Grace Palladino*
Coal, Class, and Color: Blacks in Southern West Virginia, 1915–32
    Joe William Trotter Jr.
For Democracy, Workers, and God: Labor Song-Poems and Labor Protest,
    1865–95   *Clark D. Halker*
Dishing It Out: Waitresses and Their Unions in the Twentieth Century
    Dorothy Sue Cobble
The Spirit of 1848: German Immigrants, Labor Conflict, and the Coming
    of the Civil War   *Bruce Levine*
Working Women of Collar City: Gender, Class, and Community
    in Troy, New York, 1864–86   *Carole Turbin*
Southern Labor and Black Civil Rights: Organizing Memphis Workers
    Michael K. Honey
Radicals of the Worst Sort: Laboring Women in Lawrence, Massachusetts,
    1860–1912   *Ardis Cameron*
Producers, Proletarians, and Politicians: Workers and Party Politics in Evansville
    and New Albany, Indiana, 1850–87   *Lawrence M. Lipin*
The New Left and Labor in the 1960s   *Peter B. Levy*
The Making of Western Labor Radicalism: Denver's Organized Workers,
    1878–1905   *David Brundage*
In Search of the Working Class: Essays in American Labor History
    and Political Culture   *Leon Fink*
Lawyers against Labor: From Individual Rights to Corporate Liberalism
    Daniel R. Ernst
"We Are All Leaders": The Alternative Unionism of the Early 1930s
    Edited by Staughton Lynd
The Female Economy: The Millinery and Dressmaking Trades, 1860–1930
    Wendy Gamber
"Negro and White, Unite and Fight!": A Social History of Industrial Unionism
    in Meatpacking, 1930–90   *Roger Horowitz*
Power at Odds: The 1922 National Railroad Shopmen's Strike   *Colin J. Davis*
The Common Ground of Womanhood: Class, Gender, and Working Girls' Clubs,
    1884–1928   *Priscilla Murolo*
Marching Together: Women of the Brotherhood of Sleeping Car Porters
    Melinda Chateauvert
Down on the Killing Floor: Black and White Workers in Chicago's
    Packinghouses, 1904–54   *Rick Halpern*

Labor and Urban Politics: Class Conflict and the Origins of Modern Liberalism
   in Chicago, 1864–97   *Richard Schneirov*
All That Glitters: Class, Conflict, and Community in Cripple Creek
   Elizabeth Jameson
Waterfront Workers: New Perspectives on Race and Class   *Edited by Calvin Winslow*
Labor Histories: Class, Politics, and the Working-Class Experience
   Edited by Eric Arnesen, Julie Greene, and Bruce Laurie
The Pullman Strike and the Crisis of the 1890s: Essays on Labor and Politics
   Edited by Richard Schneirov, Shelton Stromquist, and Nick Salvatore
AlabamaNorth: African-American Migrants, Community, and Working-Class
   Activism in Cleveland, 1914–45   *Kimberley L. Phillips*
Imagining Internationalism in American and British Labor, 1939–49   *Victor Silverman*
William Z. Foster and the Tragedy of American Radicalism   *James R. Barrett*
Colliers across the Sea: A Comparative Study of Class Formation in Scotland
   and the American Midwest, 1830–1924   *John H. M. Laslett*
"Rights, Not Roses": Unions and the Rise of Working-Class Feminism,
   1945–80   *Dennis A. Deslippe*
Testing the New Deal: The General Textile Strike of 1934 in the American South
   Janet Irons
Hard Work: The Making of Labor History   *Melvyn Dubofsky*
Southern Workers and the Search for Community: Spartanburg County,
   South Carolina   *G. C. Waldrep III*
We Shall Be All: A History of the Industrial Workers of the World
   (abridged edition)   *Melvyn Dubofsky, ed. Joseph A. McCartin*
Race, Class, and Power in the Alabama Coalfields, 1908–21   *Brian Kelly*
Duquesne and the Rise of Steel Unionism   *James D. Rose*
Anaconda: Labor, Community, and Culture in Montana's Smelter City   *Laurie Mercier*
Bridgeport's Socialist New Deal, 1915–36   *Cecelia Bucki*
Indispensable Outcasts: Hobo Workers and Community in the American Midwest,
   1880–1930   *Frank Tobias Higbie*
After the Strike: A Century of Labor Struggle at Pullman   *Susan Eleanor Hirsch*
Corruption and Reform in the Teamsters Union   *David Witwer*
Waterfront Revolts: New York and London Dockworkers, 1946–61   *Colin J. Davis*
Black Workers' Struggle for Equality in Birmingham   *Horace Huntley
   and David Montgomery*
The Tribe of Black Ulysses: African American Men in the Industrial South
   William P. Jones
City of Clerks: Office and Sales Workers in Philadelphia, 1870–1920
   Jerome P. Bjelopera
Reinventing "The People": The Progressive Movement, the Class Problem,
   and the Origins of Modern Liberalism   *Shelton Stromquist*
Radical Unionism in the Midwest, 1900–1950   *Rosemary Feurer*
Gendering Labor History   *Alice Kessler-Harris*
James P. Cannon and the Origins of the American Revolutionary Left,
   1890–1928   *Bryan D. Palmer*

Glass Towns: Industry, Labor, and Political Economy in Appalachia, 1890–1930s
  Ken Fones-Wolf
Workers and the Wild: Conservation, Consumerism, and Labor in Oregon,
  1910–30   *Lawrence M. Lipin*
Wobblies on the Waterfront: Interracial Unionism in Progressive-Era
  Philadelphia   *Peter Cole*
Red Chicago: American Communism at Its Grassroots, 1928–35   *Randi Storch*
Labor's Cold War: Local Politics in a Global Context   *Edited by Shelton Stromquist*
Bessie Abramowitz Hillman and the Making of the Amalgamated Clothing Workers
  of America   *Karen Pastorello*
The Great Strikes of 1877   *Edited by David O. Stowell*
Union-Free America: Workers and Antiunion Culture   *Lawrence Richards*
Race against Liberalism: Black Workers and the UAW in Detroit
  David M. Lewis-Colman
Teachers and Reform: Chicago Public Education, 1929–70   *John F. Lyons*
Upheaval in the Quiet Zone: 1199/SEIU and the Politics of Healthcare Unionism
  Leon Fink and Brian Greenberg
Shadow of the Racketeer: Scandal in Organized Labor   *David Witwer*
Sweet Tyranny: Migrant Labor, Industrial Agriculture, and Imperial Politics
  Kathleen Mapes
Staley: The Fight for a New American Labor Movement   *Steven K. Ashby*
  and C. J. Hawking
On the Ground: Labor Struggles in the American Airline Industry   *Liesl Miller Orenic*
NAFTA and Labor in North America   *Norman Caulfield*
Making Capitalism Safe: Work Safety and Health Regulation in America,
  1880–1940   *Donald W. Rogers*
Good, Reliable, White Men: Railroad Brotherhoods, 1877–1917   *Paul Michel Taillon*
Spirit of Rebellion: Labor and Religion in the New Cotton South   *Jarod Roll*
The Labor Question in America: Economic Democracy in the Gilded Age
  Rosanne Currarino
Banded Together: Economic Democratization in the Brass Valley   *Jeremy Brecher*
The Gospel of the Working Class: Labor's Southern Prophets in New Deal
  America   *Erik Gellman and Jarod Roll*
Guest Workers and Resistance to U.S. Corporate Despotism   *Immanuel Ness*
Gleanings of Freedom: Free and Slave Labor along the Mason-Dixon Line,
  1790–1860   *Max Grivno*
Chicago in the Age of Capital: Class, Politics, and Democracy during the Civil War
  and Reconstruction   *John B. Jentz and Richard Schneirov*
Child Care in Black and White: Working Parents and the History
  of Orphanages   *Jessie B. Ramey*
The Haymarket Conspiracy: Transatlantic Anarchist Networks   *Timothy Messer-Kruse*
Detroit's Cold War: The Origins of Postwar Conservatism   *Colleen Doody*
A Renegade Union: Interracial Organizing and Labor Radicalism   *Lisa Phillips*
Palomino: Clinton Jencks and Mexican-American Unionism in the American
  Southwest   *James J. Lorence*

Latin American Migrations to the U.S. Heartland: Changing Cultural Landscapes in Middle America   *Edited by Linda Allegro and Andrew Grant Wood*
Man of Fire: Selected Writings   *Ernesto Galarza, ed. Armando Ibarra and Rodolfo D. Torres*
A Contest of Ideas: Capital, Politics, and Labor   *Nelson Lichtenstein*
Making the World Safe for Workers: Labor, the Left, and Wilsonian Internationalism   *Elizabeth McKillen*
The Rise of the Chicago Police Department: Class and Conflict, 1850–1894   *Sam Mitrani*
Workers in Hard Times: A Long View of Economic Crises   *Edited by Leon Fink, Joseph A. McCartin, and Joan Sangster*
Redeeming Time: Protestantism and Chicago's Eight-Hour Movement, 1866–1912   *William A. Mirola*
Struggle for the Soul of the Postwar South: White Evangelical Protestants and Operation Dixie   *Elizabeth Fones-Wolf and Ken Fones-Wolf*
Free Labor: The Civil War and the Making of an American Working Class   *Mark A. Lause*
Death and Dying in the Working Class, 1865–1920   *Michael K. Rosenow*